BLACK BOOKS GALORE!

Guide to More Great African American Children's Books

Other Black Books Galore! Titles

The Black Books Galore! Guide to Great African American Children's Books

The Black Books Galore! Guide to Great African American Children's Books about Girls

The Black Books Galore! Guide to Great African American Children's Books about Boys

BLACK BOOKS GALORE!

Guide to More Great African American Children's Books

DONNA RAND

TONI TRENT PARKER

John Wiley & Sons, Inc.
New York • Chichester • Weinheim • Brisbane • Singapore • Toronto

To my dear husband, Barry. Thanks for your love and support.

D. R.

To my mother, Viola Scales Trent, and the memory of my father, William J. Trent jr. With all my love, and much appreciation.

T. T. P.

Copyright © 2001 by Donna Rand and Toni Trent Parker. All rights reserved
Published by John Wiley & Sons, Inc.
Published simultaneously in Canada

Design and production by Navta Associates, Inc.

Permissions and credits begin on page 244.

ISBN 0-471-37525-X

Printed in the United States of America
10 9 8 7 6 5 4 3 2 1

Contents

Foreword

by Evelyn K. Moore

President and CEO, National Black Child Development Institute (NBCDI)

The *Black Books Galore! Guide to More Great African American Children's Books* is the fourth in a series of guides designed to help parents, teachers, and other interested adults identify good books for and about African American children. These books will educate, entertain, and enrich young readers, and pave the way to a lifetime of learning. Additionally, for the black child, reading these books will reinforce his or her cultural identity.

Black children need not read only black books, but black books should definitely be a part of their library to encourage the development of their positive racial identity and cultural knowledge. It is validating for African American children to read books written from the black perspective about black people. A well-written book, with images and situations that a child can relate to, can be vital in promoting a child's self-esteem.

Begin sharing these positive, racially affirming books with your young children today. Just as reading to toddlers and preschoolers lays the foundation for their language development and early reading skills, reading black children's books to them helps establish their early, positive self-image. And, of course, the benefits only accrue as you continue to share these books with your children as they grow.

In the endeavor to expose your children to the wonderful world of reading through African American children's books, be selective about the books you choose. Ensure that the books you present to your children offer entertaining stories, enriching messages, and educationally sound lessons featuring positive images of black people and life to motivate and uplift them, like those recommended in the comprehensive series of Black Books Galore! guides to books about African American children.

Acknowledgments

We WOULD LIKE to acknowledge and thank several special friends and associates who believed in and supported us from the beginning.

First and foremost, we would like to thank our friend Sheila Foster for her original vision of Black Books Galore! We know she is proud that the legacy she began is continuing.

We have been extremely blessed with a number of wonderful friends who encouraged us and who have been especially supportive. Thank you, Kim and Sy Green, and Diana Parker for your generous hospitality during our early book promotions.

A project of this scope requires many checks and balances, so we heartily acknowledge and thank Lucille Goodwin for her charitable administrative support.

We would like to thank Kent Amos for his invaluable assistance in helping us network with Evelyn Moore, and Ms. Moore for her thoughtful preparation of this book's foreword.

There were several special friends and relatives to whom we extend our sincere thanks for small favors that meant so much. Thank you, Kay and Wendell Holloway, Judy Scales-Trent, Dr. Marjorie Parker, Reverend Blair Moffett, James and Betty Ebron, Earl Graves, Valerie Wilson, and Frank Borges.

We were genuinely pleased to work with Marcia Samuels, our managing editor, on this book. Her professional counsel and support were priceless. And, of course, we extend our heartfelt thanks and gratitude to Carole Hall, our friend and editor-in-chief at John Wiley & Sons, Inc., who started us on this road by encouraging us to write our first book and who served as the catalyst and mentor on this project.

Introduction

THE TWO YEARS since we published the *Black Books Galore! Guide to Great African American Children's Books* have been a tremendous period of validation and reinforcement. Within weeks of publication, our book was nominated for the 1999 NAACP Image Award for Children's Literature, and several magazines—among them *Emerge, Black Enterprise,* and *BET Weekend*—wrote extremely positive reviews about the guide. We also received scores of notes and letters congratulating us on, and thanking us for, our book.

When we first conceived the idea of writing a guide dedicated to books for and about African American children we knew that it would be an important resource. Our years of experience producing African American children's book festivals introduced us to hundreds of enthusiastic parents and teachers who told us, over and over again, that access to these books is critical but often difficult. As far as we knew, there was nothing else on the market to direct parents, educators, and librarians to a comprehensive list of positive, self-affirming books for black children; and we still haven't seen anything as complete. The response to our first guide was so positive, and the demand for more information so great, that we knew we had to go further.

So, we have compiled a second annotated guide, this one containing four hundred and fifty additional books for the children in your life. Together, these two guides offer access to credible information on almost one thousand books for and about African American children. While the selection of African American children's books is extremely small in relation to the total number of children's books published every year—less than 2 percent—there are still many wonderful books for and about African American children that many parents and educators have yet to find.

In our first book, *Black Books Galore! Guide to Great African American Children's Books,* we recommended five hundred titles that were carefully selected to represent a broad cross-section of subjects and styles, written and illustrated by a wonderfully diverse group of authors and illustrators. Our selections included everything from concept, picture, and story books for babies to third graders to a cache of nonfiction, chapter books, poetry books, and novels for older children. This second guide offers a completely different selection of titles that are guaranteed to educate, entertain, and enrich every child.

As in our first guide, we have included many books in each of the following categories:

History, Heritage, and Biography Books. An impressive number of African American history, heritage, and biography selections are included in this guide to help children fill in the significant gaps in the African American story, and to gain a broader perspective of the roles and contributions of past and present generations of African American people who helped build our country.

Art, Poetry, and Music Books. Much of our African American culture is reflected in our art, music, and poetry. The cultural expressions that we have identified in this guide capture the best works of many of the most renowned and talented African Americans in the arts. Many of the works reflect the historical and emotional soul of African Americans.

Folktales, Fairy Tales, and Legends. We have included dozens of African American, African, and Caribbean folktales, fairy tales, and legends that reflect the values, fantasies, and belief systems of many centuries of black people. These books are important to ensure that we remain connected to our roots, and that our cultural legacy is passed on to the next generation.

African and Caribbean Books. There is an ample selection of books about African and Caribbean characters and subjects, since those cultures are naturally embraced in the African American experience.

Additionally, in this second volume we have identified several books that feature African American characters as a part of our greater society. There are several books about black children playing and interacting with nonblack children, such as *You're Not My Best Friend Anymore* [344], *Beach Babble* [6], and *Courtney's Birthday Party* [157], and books about black children befriending nonblack adults, such as *Miz Berlin Walks* [252] and *Elijah's Angel* [167]. Additionally, we have included more books about bi-racial children and families, like *Two Mrs. Gibsons* [330], *Hope* [193], and *You Be Me, I'll Be You* [115]. These stories offer a balanced view of life for the young children who live in this multicultural nation.

In our first volume we purposely selected books that were still in print. Therefore, while there were a number of classic titles, many others were newer publications. The goal was to provide a list of books that were readily available through booksellers, as well as in local and school libraries. In this volume, we offer a wider selection of books, such as classics like *Turtle Knows Your Name* [328] and *To Hell with Dying* [445], that may no longer be available from booksellers, but are still favorite library selections, as well as newly published titles.

The most important feature of these selections is that they all center on black children, black families, or black people. Reading these books demonstrates that people of color are worthy of publication and is validating and encouraging to young readers as they build their identities.

Daryl Wells, the illustrator of *Two Mrs. Gibsons* [330], underscored our point in her biographical sketch featured in the book *Just Like Me: Stories and Self-Portraits by Fourteen Artists*. She said, "When I was growing up, I didn't understand why the crayon labeled 'flesh' in my crayon box wasn't the color of my skin. As a way of proving that my color was also beautiful and real, I went through all my favorite storybooks and colored in the characters with the brown crayons. In this way I was able to relate to them as if they were really part of my world."

A Parent's Point of View

We began our journey into the world of African American children's books in 1992 as parents seeking books for and about our own African American children. Since we are neither professional educators nor librarians, we have remained true to our original role. Therefore, every book in this guide is recommended by us as parents.

As always, we have applied three principles to our selections. First, we chose books that are age appropriate. The story lines and concepts are written and developed for children in each age group. You, of course, are the final judge regarding your children's maturity and reading levels. Second, we have carefully selected books that do not stereotype black, female, or male characters. The whole point of this guide is to help African American children see themselves realistically and positively. Third, we recommend only those books that we would give to our own children.

There are several books in this guide that contain nonstandard English, in either black or Caribbean dialect. There is a school of thought that suggests that these books are culturally and literarily significant and that the language, when used in the context of the character, place, and time, is appropriate. Others believe that reading nonstandard English is counterproductive to a child's language development. Rather than making that decision for you, we have clearly identified books that contain significant passages of *nonstandard English* or *Caribbean dialect* for your consideration.

This guide, paired with our first, provides the most comprehensive list of African American children's books available. It is our hope that you will use this information to introduce black children—in fact, all children—to the breadth and depth of this genre of wonderful books.

How Good Books Help Children Grow

by James P. Comer, M.D.

GOOD BOOKS provide opportunities for parents to help children develop reading and language skills, a positive racial identity, and self-esteem, as well as the skills needed in many social situations. And when introduced to books early, children often develop a passion for reading and learning. When this is the case, young people can use books to help promote their own learning and development, with less and less pressure from parents and teachers.

I hasten to point out, however, that neither school readiness nor good self-esteem or racial-group esteem rests primarily on a child's ability to read. Good child rearing lays the foundation for *all* these developments. Reading builds on and strengthens the foundation and helps to promote overall growth. Knowledge about development, then, can help you support it, as well as help you select or guide young people to useful reading materials.

What Children Need from Birth to Four

In the first three years children are little learning machines, bundles of energy seeking expression and trying to find out about themselves, including their racial and gender identity, and their immediate world—parents, families, friends, neighborhood, and so on. They are trying to bring their bodies, feelings, and behaviors in line with what is expected by the people who are important to them.

Good care—protection, love, guidance, and skill building—gives young children an inner core of good feelings about themselves. The child's performance in the neighborhood, with kin and friend, or in the family social network deepens the core of good feelings. This is the initial "stuff" of self-confidence and self-esteem.

What Children Need from Five to Eight

Between five and eight years of age, children should develop a passion for reading and learning, and they master the kind of behavior that is needed in school. They want to work—read, make things, do things. They also very much want to be like the adults around them—big people doing big-people things. This enables parents to encourage them to grow in positive ways. And good performance in school creates and deepens a sense of confidence and self-esteem. Also, racial and gender awareness grow, but a positive "take" must be promoted during this period; otherwise the negative message of the larger society can have a troublesome impact.

A positive sense of racial identity begins with answering the questions about race that children have in a calm and confident way, and by teaching them that racial antagonisms expressed by other people are the shortcomings of those people, not their own. It is important to help them learn how to handle these matters in ways that don't require them to spend a huge amount of energy on somebody else's problem, and to learn how to handle such antagonisms in a way that won't make matters worse.

What Children Need from Eight to Twelve and Up

Somewhere between eight and twelve years of age children begin to place themselves in the scheme of things. They begin to understand that they are part of a particular family and group with certain possibilities and limits and that they are different from certain other people and groups. Their behaviors, hopes, and aspirations begin to be shaped by their self-placement. Their confidence in school and ability to get along with others also influences these placements.

During this period children move strongly beyond membership only in a family to membership in groups in school. The relationships between parent and child need not be the kind of teenage rebellion that is often described. But the relationship must be changed in a way that enables young people to take more responsibility for their own lives. Parents must become less intrusive but remain as guides and supporters. This will allow young people to feel belonging both in the family and in the groups beyond the family.

Books about African culture and history and the American experience of blacks are helpful with the identity issue for young people who are having a good overall developmental experience. But books about African American history should show how the experiences of blacks and other groups were different. Information alone may not be helpful. For example, if books discuss African American inventors only in isolation, it's possible to conclude that by comparison, blacks invented very little. But if the great obstacles to achievement are understood, the achievement of African American inventors becomes remarkable. It is for this reason that I am particularly interested in biographies that show what blacks must overcome to achieve.

Many books will not make the necessary explanations, but books provide a general knowledge base and stimulate questions. The questions raised and the discussions that follow permit parents to help young people gain deep understanding. They also permit parents to have conversations with their children that are about something other than what the children are or are not doing that they should or shouldn't be doing. This creates an opportunity for close and more positive relationships.

It is worthwhile, then, for parents to give some thought to what is going on with young people developmentally, selecting and eventually suggesting books that will help them deal with all aspects of their growth. And don't stop there: keep reading and keep talking.

(Excerpted from *Black Books Galore! Guide to Great African American Children's Books*)

How to Use This Guide

THE MAIN ENTRIES in this guide have been organized into three parts, which list books appropriate for the following reading levels:

- Babies and preschoolers
- Early readers (kindergarten to grade three)
- Middle readers (grades four to eight)

The titles in each chapter are arranged alphabetically. The entries are numbered sequentially from 1 to 450, for easy cross-referencing. Throughout the book, numbers appearing in brackets, such as [257], refer to entry numbers, not page numbers. Book titles that appeared in the original *Black Books Galore! Guide to Great African American Children's Books* appear with bracketed numbers, such as [v1-231], referring to the Volume One entry number.

Each numbered entry includes the title, subtitle, author, and illustrator; the publisher of the hardcover and softcover editions; the original publication date of the book; and a brief synopsis of the book. We have also noted significant awards and listed any sequel, prequel, companion, or series titles for your reference.

Books that contain nonstandard language are identified by one or more of the following phrases: "Nonstandard English," "Caribbean Dialect," or "Use of N Word" (in cases where the derogatory racial slur is used).

"The Creators" and Other Special Features

Pictures of book covers and text excerpts from many of the books are placed throughout to better impart the flavor of the books. Additionally, twenty-five talented authors and illustrators are spotlighted in "The Creators" boxes to give you insight into their creative motivations. In the main entries, the names of these featured artists are followed by a star (☆) and the page number on which their box appears. Here is a complete list of the creators:

Sandra Belton	Walter Dean Myers
Gavin Curtis	Jerdine Nolen
Ruby Dee and Ossie Davis	Denise Lewis Patrick
Diane Dillion and Leo Dillon	Harriette Gillem Robinet
Sharon M. Draper	Irene Smalls
Karen English	Eleanora Tate
George Ford Jr.	Glennette Tilley Turner
Elizabeth Fitzgerald Howard	Cornelius Van Wright and Ying-Hwa Hu
E. B. Lewis	Mildred Pitts Walter
Cedric Lucas	Carole Boston Weatherford
Sharon Bell Mathis	Sharon Dennis Wyeth

"The Season for Reading" Calendar is a special section designed to lead parents to books of seasonal interest. Appendix A lists several books that may be of general interest. Appendix B is an updated list of books that have received Coretta Scott King, Reading Rainbow, Newbery, and Caldecott awards. Appendix C directs you to several Internet sites of general interest. Finally there are four indexes to help you find what you want—or to browse: an index of titles, including the entries and all other books mentioned within the entries, an index of authors, an index of illustrators, and an index of topics.

How to Get Your Hands on the Books in This Guide

The books in this guide should be available through your school or public library, or at a bookstore. Libraries may be able to accommodate your special requests. If they do not have a book you want in their own system, they may be able to borrow it through an interlibrary loan arrangement.

If a book is still in print, you should be able to order it through your local bookseller. To find or order your selection, you should have the title and the author's name. There are a number of African American specialty bookstores throughout the country whose staffs may be very knowledgeable about these and other books and who may be able to supply these titles for you easily.

And of course, you can always contact us, Black Books Galore!, at 65 High Ridge Rd, #407, Stamford, CT 06905 (telephone: 203-359-6925; fax: 203-359-3226; Web site: www.blackbooksgalore.com) to order your selection of African American children's books. Please enclose a self-addressed, stamped, business-size envelope if you would like a response to an inquiry.

"The Season for Reading" Calendar

We have created *a list of theme-oriented selections that are appropriate for the many seasons and holidays of the year. Of course, sharing these books with your young readers at special times will launch you and your child into a full year of educational, entertaining, and enriching books for all seasons.*

JANUARY

Winter

It's cold outside, but young readers will enjoy these heartwarming stories about the season.

The Black Snowman [v1-133]
Do Like Kyla [v1-27]
From My Window [37]
The Longest Wait [239]
Snow on Snow on Snow [v1-97]
The Snowy Day [v1-98]

Martin Luther King Day

Celebrate the life and legacy of this African American icon and American hero.

Happy Birthday, Dr. King! [v1-192]
Happy Birthday, Martin Luther King [v1-191]
Just Like Martin [v1-368]
Let Freedom Ring: A Ballad of Martin Luther King, Jr. [235]
Meet Martin Luther King, Jr.: A Man of Peace with a Dream for All People [247]
My Dream of Martin Luther King [v1-234]

FEBRUARY

Black History Month

Every month is Black History Month. In this special season, help young readers focus on African American history and heritage through these selections.

Amistad Rising: A Story of Freedom [119]
Bound for America: The Forced Migration of Africans to the New World [365]

Explore Black History with Wee Pals [169]
Through Loona's Door: A Tammy and Owen Adventure with Carter G. Woodson [v1-413]
Through My Eyes [442]

Valentine's Day

Give young readers something from the heart—a book about the holiday of love.

Don't Be My Valentine: A Classroom Mystery [163]
Hopscotch Love: A Family Treasury of Love Poems [390]
Secret Valentine [94]
Super-Fine Valentine [317]

MARCH

Women's History Month

Women have done it all! Read about many of the African American women who have left their marks on America.

The Bus Ride [143]
Dinner at Aunt Connie's House [v1-160]
Osceola: Memories of a Sharecropper's Daughter [421]
Madam C.J. Walker: Entrepreneur [413]
Susie King Taylor: Destined to Be Free [v1-408]

APRIL

Easter

Spring has arrived, marked by Easter, a favorite childhood holiday. Share books about the season of renewal.

Easter Parade [166]
Miz Fannie Mae's Fine New Easter Hat [253]

Baseball

It is time for America's favorite pastime. Read stories about the game and some of the legendary African Americans who played it.

The Bat Boy and His Violin [128]
Fair Ball!: 14 Great Stars from Baseball's Negro Leagues [378]
First in the Field: Baseball Hero Jackie Robinson [379]
Leagues Apart: The Men and Times of the Negro Baseball Leagues [232]
Teammates [v1-288]

Children's Poetry Week

Broaden young readers' literary education by introducing them to expressive books of poetry written just for them.

A Dime a Dozen [372]
Isn't My Name Magical?: Sister and Brother Poems [210]
Jump Back, Honey: The Poems of Paul Laurence Dunbar [398]
Make a Joyful Sound: Poems for Children by African-American Poets [v1-225]
The Palm of My Heart: Poetry by African American Children [v1-392]

MAY

Mother's Day

We celebrate our mothers on a single day in May, but they deserve our love and admiration every day of the year.

In My Momma's Kitchen [206]
Flowers for Mommy [v1-33]
Gettin' Through Thursday [177]
Ma Dear's Apron [v1-222]
Read for Me, Mama [289]

JUNE

Father's Day

We love fathers, too! And there are a number of exemplary books that celebrate and pay tribute to these special men in our lives.

Always My Dad [118]

Daddy Calls Me Man [24]

In Daddy's Arms I Am Tall: African Americans Celebrating Fathers [205]

Kevin and His Dad [226]

Octopus Hugs [85]

Juneteenth

Expose young readers to the significance of this traditional holiday from African American history.

Freedom's Gifts: A Juneteenth Story [v1-181]

Juneteenth Jamboree [v1-213]

JULY

Summer

It's the season for vacations, camp, going to the beach, and other warm-weather activities. Make sure that your young readers are still going to bed with a good book every night.

Gregory Cool [v1-189]

Knoxville, Tennessee [v1-65]

Lemonade Sun: And Other Summer Poems [233]

One Hot Summer Day [v1-87]

Summer Wheels [312]

Independence Day

Observe our country's birthday with books about the creation of our nation and the annual celebrations.

Celebration! [147]
Come All You Brave Soldiers: Blacks in the Revolutionary War [369]
Phoebe the Spy [423]

AUGUST

Family Reunions

Many extended families come together during this season to celebrate their heritage.

Bigmama's [132]
Tanya's Reunion [320]
Trina's Family Reunion [327]
We Had a Picnic This Sunday Past [335]

SEPTEMBER

Back to School

Put young readers in the right frame of mind for their return to school with books about other young students.

Jamaica and the Substitute Teacher [58]
Madoulina: A Girl Who Wanted to Go to School [241]
My Mom Is My Show-and-Tell [262]
Running the Road to ABC [v1-271]
Virgie Goes to School with Us Boys [334]

Grandparents' Month

Read about the cherished elders, our grandparents, who are so important in our lives.

Granddaddy's Gift [184]
Grandma's Hands [186]
Keepers [224]
No Mirrors in My Nana's House [84]
Sophie [104]

OCTOBER

Halloween

Get in the spirit of this scary, ghostly holiday with stories to thrill and chill young readers.

Celie and the Harvest Fiddler [v1-143]
Halloween Monster [v1-45]
Jenny Reen and the Jack Muh Lantern [v1-207]
Jezebel's Spooky Spot [216]
Vampire Bugs: Stories Conjured from the Past [446]

NOVEMBER

National Children's Book Week

Select any favorite book or focus on many of the wonderful African American children's books that have endured the test of time to become classics.

Amazing Grace [v1-121]
Aunt Flossie's Hats (and Crab Cakes Later) [v1-123]
The Boy and the Ghost [139]
Drylongso [375]
Tar Beach [v1-287]

Thanksgiving

It's time to give thanks for family, friends, homes, and other blessings. Give young readers books that help them focus on the gifts in their lives.

Because You're Lucky [129]
Boundless Grace [138]
I Love My Family [v1-52]
I Love My Hair! [200]
Money Troubles [255]

DECEMBER

Christmas

Books should be on every child's Christmas list, especially some of these seasonal favorites.

An Angel Just Like Me [122]
The Bells of Christmas [130]
Carol of the Brown King: Nativity Poems [16]
Christmas for 10 [22]
Christmas in the Big House, Christmas in the Quarters [v1-328]

Kwanzaa

More and more African American families are celebrating this reflective holiday. Present young readers with books to help them understand the significance and rituals of Kwanzaa.

The Children's Book of Kwanzaa: A Guide to Celebrating the Holiday [368]
K Is for Kwanzaa: A Kwanzaa Alphabet Book [223]
Kwanzaa: A Family Affair [404]
Kwanzaa: Africa Lives in a New World Festival [405]
Seven Days of Kwanzaa: A Holiday Step Book [95]

Books for
Babies and Preschoolers

THE MINDS OF TODDLERS and preschoolers are just waiting to be filled with ideas, information, and impressions to help them operate in the world. There is no other period in their lives when they will learn as much in such a brief span of time. So this is the ideal period to introduce them to books that will set the stage for later learning. We have selected a number of books that offer basic preschool skills. *Afro-Bets Book of Shapes* [I], *C Is for City* [13], *Christmas for 10* [22], and others teach shapes, counting, reciting the alphabet, phonics, and other pre-reading skills.

Read these books to your child as often as possible. Children at this age learn through repetition and actually enjoy the familiarity of a favorite story. The books need to be colorful and attractive to appeal to the young eye. Often books that are written in rhyme make a lasting impression on young minds.

Reading should be a fun activity that young children enjoy. So we have included dozens of books for this age group that are guaranteed to capture young imaginations and bring them back for more, more, and more! Favorite fairy tales like *Hansel and Gretel* [47] and *Little Red Riding Hood* [67] are told with contemporary twists and bright

illustrations. Young readers can also escape into brilliant fantasies like *Kofi and the Butterflies* [65] and *Swinging on a Rainbow* [106], or giggle to the nonsense in books like *Maebelle's Suitcase* [68], *Bear on a Bike* [7], and *Julius* [64].

Make sure that your toddlers and preschoolers get plenty of exposure to selections that are just for fun. They can learn in these early years that a book is an excellent alternative to video entertainment.

As he or she grows, a young child needs to be nurtured as a whole person. As parents we can feed the spirit as well as the mind, with beautiful books like *Give Me Grace: A Child's Daybook of Prayers* [42] to help build spirituality. We can offer books like *Happy to Be Nappy* [48], *Cherish Me* [20], and *No Mirrors in My Nana's House* [84] to help develop positive self-images and racial identities. And we can expose children to the arts even at this early age, through books like *Dance* [25] or *Carol of the Brown King: Nativity Poems* [16].

The key is to offer your young children a wide variety of books that expose them to new concepts and ideas that may help them discover what they have within and learn more about the world outside of themselves.

Afro-Bets Books of Shapes [1]

Written by Margery W. Brown
Illustrated by Culverson Blair

Softcover: Just Us
Published 1991

Langston and the rest of the Afro-Bets kids introduce young readers to the six basic shapes: circles, squares, rectangles, triangles, diamonds, and hearts. The rhyming text identifies and describes each shape and then relates the shape to everyday objects that preschoolers will recognize. Companion books are *Afro-Bets ABC Book, Afro-Bets Book of Colors,* and *Afro-Bets 123 Book* [v1-4].

Baby Animals [2]

Written by Margaret Wise Brown
Illustrated by Susan Jeffers

Hardcover: Random House
Published 1989

This lovely bedtime story, out of print since 1941, has been republished featuring a young African American farm girl. As all of the farm animals awaken, so does the young child. As the baby animals eat their midday meals, so does the young child. Finally, as the baby animals settle down to sleep for the night, so does the young child. This sweet story with captivating illustrations will become a bedtime or anytime favorite.

Baby Dance [3]

BB

Written by Ann Taylor
Illustrated by Marjorie Van Heerden

Board Book: HarperFestival, HarperCollins
Published 1999

A simple rhyme sung by a playful daddy as he dances with his baby girl will become a favorite for your little one. The daddy and child in this delightful book are portrayed as a loving pair.

A Baby Just Like Me [4]

Written and illustrated by Susan Winter

Hardcover: Dorling Kindersley
Published 1994

Curly-haired Susan considers sending her baby sister back to wherever she came from. She had expected her new sister to play with her, but all the baby does is lie there. Besides, Mommy gives the new baby all her attention, leaving Susan out. Once Mommy tunes in to Susan's feelings, she reassures her of her love and that the baby will soon grow up to be just like Susan.

Ballerina Girl [5]

Written by Kirsten Hall
Illustrated by Michael Koelsch

Softcover: Children's Press
Published 1994

A little girl proudly shows off her pink tutu, and her ballet spins and turns. This book is designed for new readers, featuring thirty-four well chosen words that are repeated throughout the story in an engaging rhyme to help reinforce word recognition and comprehension.

Beach Babble [6]

Written and illustrated by Kimberly Knutson

Hardcover: Marshall Cavendash
Published 1998

Three young children—two girls and a boy—enjoy a fun-filled day at the beach. They play every game imaginable in the sand and the waves with hermit crabs, sea shells, and each other, until the day is done. But there is always tomorrow!

Bear on a Bike [7]

Easy Bla

Written by Stella Blackstone
Illustrated by Debbie Harter

Hardcover: Barefoot Beginners
Published 1998

This book has all of the elements to make it popular with young toddlers. The text is lyrical, with a catchy repeated phrase, and the illustrations are bright and whimsical. The story follows the escapades of a young boy and a bear who takes him on fantastic adventures to a castle, a forest, a beach, an island, and more.

Big Friend, Little Friend [8]

Written by Eloise Greenfield
Illustrated by Jan Spivey Gilchrist

Board Book: Black Butterfly
Published 1991

A little boy enjoys the friendship and companionship of both an older child and a younger one. He is cared for by his older friend and in turn nurtures the younger one. The colorful illustrations show the children teaching and helping one another. Other books in this series include *Daddy and I* [v1-24], *I Make Music* [52], and *My Doll, Keshia* [78].

Bringing the Rain to Kapiti Plain [9]

Written by Verna Aardema   ***Reading Rainbow* Feature Book**
Illustrated by Beatriz Vidal

Hardcover and softcover: Dial
Published 1981

This story is about a young African herdsman, Ki-pat, who shot an arrow into a cloud to bring rain down onto the drought-stricken plains. The text was adapted to the cadence of the familiar "House that Jack Built," and shares its cumulative refrain, which builds from verse to verse. Young children love both rhymes and rhythms, which are paired nicely in this delightful poem.

Brown Like Me [10]

Written and illustrated by Noelle Lamperti

Hardcover: New Victoria
Published 1999

Noelle, a young African American girl adopted by a white family, is sometimes "lonesome for brown." As a way of validating her own color, Noelle makes a game of finding other things that are brown like herself. In a series of special-effect photographs and childlike drawings, Noelle shares her joy of brown boots, brown leaves, a brown rug, and her own bright brown eyes, curly brown hair, and smooth brown skin.

Busy Bea [11]

Written and illustrated by Nancy Poydar

Hardcover: Margaret K. McElderry, Maxwell Macmillan
Published 1994

Little Bea is always so busy doing something or other that she absentmindedly loses her things. One day she loses her raincoat, another her lunch box, and then her jacket. Her mother often declares that Bea would lose her nose if it were not attached to her face. When Bea loses the special sweater that her grandma made for her, she knows that she must find it. She searches frantically, until a kind teacher directs her to the school's Lost and Found, where she rediscovers all of her lost belongings.

Busy Toes [12]

Written by C.W. Bowie
Illustrated by Fred Willingham

Hardcover: Whispering Coyote
Published 1998

Sweet, innocent children of all colors, infants to pre-adolescents, wiggle, wave, taste, and tickle their toes in this well illustrated poetic book about the "little piggies" at the ends of their feet.

C Is for City [13]

Written by Nikki Grimes
Illustrated by Pat Cummings

Hardcover: Lothrop, Lee & Shepard
Published 1995

Dazzling illustrations bring the city scenes in this alphabet book to life. Young readers will enjoy the alphabetic rhyme that calls for them to find a page full of objects named in the poem. Each page is dedicated to a letter. S, for example, contains a stickball, a strawberry snow cone, a skyscraper soaring straight, a street sweeper, and a skateboard. Then, once they have found the obvious objects, they can search further for a sandal, a seashell, a star, a stone, a stop sign, and more hidden in the intensely colorful scenes.

The Calypso Alphabet [14]

Written by John Agard
Illustrated by Jennifer Bent

Hardcover: Henry Holt
Published 1989

Young readers will learn the alphabet, Caribbean style, with words and sights from island life. Some of the more unusual representations are K for kaiso, "a song with a sweet-sweet jump-up beat" and M for Mooma, another name for Mommy. There are other new terms, so a helpful glossary is found in the back.

Caribbean Dream [15]

Written and illustrated by Rachel Isadora

Hardcover: G.P. Putnam's Sons, Putnam & Grossett
Published 1998

A thoughtful poem is illustrated with equally thoughtful watercolor illustrations of young children standing, playing, swimming, running, and dancing at their Caribbean island home. Large print, simple words, and a rhythmic verse makes this an excellent easy-to-read selection for beginning readers.

Carol of the Brown King: Nativity Poems [16]

Written by Langston Hughes
Illustrated by Ashley Bryan

J/811/Hug

Hardcover: Atheneum, Simon & Schuster
Published 1998

Ashley Bryan is well known for his illustrations of African American spirituals and poetry. In this book, his expressive, colorful paintings are paired with
six nativity poems by Langston Hughes. The black faces that illustrate each
short poem will have special meaning for African American children anxious
to know that their people were part of the Christmas story.

Case of the Missing Cookies [17]

Written by Denise Lewis Patrick ☆ 133
Illustrated by Stacey Schuett

Softcover: Aladdin, Simon & Schuster
Published 1996

James and Vanessa, of the *Gullah Gullah Island* television series, are hot on
the trail of a cookie bandit. The two young sleuths follow the evidence (a trail
of cookie crumbs) through the living room, the backyard, the garden, the
beach, and finally to the playground, where they find the culprit, Binyah
Binyah Pollywog. Other books in the series include *Families, Phooey!; Happy
Birthday, Daddy* [v1-46]; *Rain, Rain, Go Away;* and *Shaina's Garden* [97].

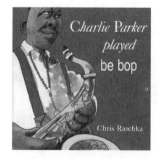

Charlie Parker Played Be Bop [18]

Written and illustrated
by Chris Raschka

Easy Ras

Reading Rainbow Review Book

Hardcover: Orchard
Published 1992

Have fun with this book of auditory delights about the music that comes out
of Charlie Parker's saxophone. When read with the right intonations, the
jazz sounds, "Be Bop, Fisk Fisk, Lollipop, Boomba, Boomba," and more will
delight young readers. After a while they are bound to read or even sing
along.

THE CREATORS

Sandra Belton

AUTHOR

"All of my books have given me the wonderful opportunity to tell some of the stories my friends and I hungered to read when we were growing up—stories about the kids we were. In their own way, these books, no matter who the particular characters are, can share some parts about the way we looked and talked, the places we could (but sometimes couldn't) go to, the things we thought about, the communities we lived in, and the heroes and adults who surrounded and helped shape our lives."

OUR FAVORITES

Ernestine & Amanda [vl-339]

Ernestine & Amanda: Mysteries on Monroe Street [377]

From Miss Ida's Porch [vl-347]

May'naise Sandwiches & Sunshine Tea [vl-229]

Charlie's House [19]

Written by Reviva Schermbrucker
Illustrated by Niki Daly

Hardcover: Viking Penguin
Published 1991

A young South African boy, Charlie, builds a model house for his family from mud, sticks, and cardboard scraps, imagining that it is the house of his dreams. In his imagination, the rooms are big and include a living room, a bedroom for his mother and granny, and even a room for himself. Charlie's dream is shattered by the reality that he lives in a shanty made of leaky scrap-metal siding.

Cherish Me [20]

Written by Joyce Carol Thomas
Illustrated by Nneka Bennett

Hardcover: HarperFestival, HarperCollins
Published 1998

A bright toddler is the subject of a short, self-affirming poem. An older reader would correctly interpret the poem as an acknowledgment of black beauty, but the youngest readers will simply enjoy the pictures of the playful young girl and the soft cadence of the words. Most touching is the line, "I am beautiful by design."

Chidi Only Likes Blue: An African Book of Colors [21]

Written and photographed by Ifeoma Onyefulu

Hardcover: Cobblehill
Published 1997

Nneka's little brother, Chidi, loves the color blue because it is the only color he knows, so Nneka decides to teach him the names of other colors. Using objects in their African village, Nneka shows Chidi examples of red, found in the special *igwe* (cap) worn by the village chiefs; yellow, in the *gari* (cassava grain) that they eat; and black, in the *uli* (seed paint) that they use to paint the village homes. Young readers will learn their colors as well as something about Africa through the photographs of the village and people. There are five companion books: *A Is for Africa* [v1-1], *Emeka's Gift: An*

African Counting Story [v1-29], *Grandfather's Work: A Traditional Healer in Nigeria* [44], *Ogbo: Sharing Life in an African Village* [v1-247], and *A Triangle for Adaora: An African Book of Shapes.*

Christmas for 10 [22]

Easy Fal

Written and illustrated by Cathryn Falwell

Hardcover: Clarion, Houghton Mifflin
Published 1998

A loving family comes together to prepare for Christmas, counting each activity from one star to top the tree to ten hands stringing popcorn chains. Their joy is so complete that they recount from one to ten again, this time including five baskets to pack and nine silver bells to ring. This cheerful Christmas book is the companion to *Feast for 10* [v1-31].

The Colors of Us [23]

Written and illustrated by Karen Katz

Hardcover: Henry Holt
Published 1999

Seven-year-old Lena, preparing to paint a picture of herself, asks her mother how to mix brown paint. Lena's mother takes her on a walk and points out that people come in many shades of brown: the brown of cinnamon, the brown of French toast, the light yellow-brown of peanut butter, honey brown, chocolate brown, and more. The enlightened young girl goes home and paints pictures of her friends in their many glorious shades of brown.

Daddy Calls Me Man [24]

Easy Joh

Written by Angela Johnson
Illustrated by Rhonda Mitchell

Hardcover: Orchard
Published 1997

A very young boy is colorfully portrayed in vibrant illustrations of four poems written from his unique perspective. The most heartwarming selection, "Baby Sister," reflects his pride in his new sibling and the love that is shared by the entire family.

Dance [25]

Written by Bill T. Jones and Susan Kuklin
Photographs by Susan Kuklin

Hardcover: Hyperion
Published 1998

Renowned dancer and choreographer Bill T. Jones is pictured in a great many dance poses demonstrating the expressiveness of the human body. This book has few words, but the color photographs of the talented artist speak volumes.

The Dance of the Rain Gods [26]

Written and illustrated by Julee Dickerson Thompson

Softcover: Africa World
Published 1994

When a small child is frightened by a loud thunderstorm, her mother tells her a comforting story to explain the loud noises and violent flashes of light. The story, told in poetic verse, describes how the Afro-American gods—Niar, Duolc, D'niw, Rednuht, Gninthgil, and Liah—put on a dramatic show for the earth, a show that we see as a storm. (Hint: the names of the Afro-American gods are simply the elements of the storm spelled backwards.) The dramatic Afro-centric illustrations combine airbrush, laser prints, and watercolors.

Daniel's Dog [27]

Written by Jo Ellen Bogart
Illustrated by Janet Wilson

Softcover: Blue Ribbon, Scholastic
Published 1990

Daniel is very understanding when his mother must spend less time with him and more with his new baby sister. It appears that Daniel is mature enough to play alone, until his mother learns that Daniel is playing with an imaginary dog—a ghost dog named Lucy. Daniel's belief in his special pet extends even further when he introduces his best friend, Norman, to another ghost dog.

Dexter Gets Dressed! [28]

Written and illustrated by Ken Wilson-Max

Hardcover: Kingfisher
Published 1998

Young readers can help Dexter get dressed in this interactive book. Large type and colorful illustrations reveal Dexter in various states of dress, and in felt clothes that require a certain level of dexterity to manipulate the buttons, zipper, and laces.

Digby [29]

Written by Barbara Shook Hazen
Illustrated by Barbara Phillips-Duke

Softcover: HarperTrophy, HarperCollins
Published 1997

A young boy is eager to play with his dog, Digby, but Digby can't run and play anymore. The boy's sister explains that Digby is getting old and isn't as energetic as he once was. But Digby is still a good and loyal friend, and still very capable of giving lots of love. Colorfully illustrated, this book, one of the I Can Read series, offers an excellent lesson for young pet owners.

Elizabeti's Doll [30]

Written by Stephanie Stuve-Bodeen
Illustrated by Christy Hale

Hardcover: Lee & Low
Published 1998

When her mother has a new baby boy, Elizabeti, a young Tanzanian girl, wants to have a baby of her own to care for. So she adopts a doll, of sorts. Elizabeti's doll is a rock. Nonetheless, she holds it, feeds it, bathes it, and cares for it in the same nurturing way she sees her mother care for her baby brother. One evening, Elizabeti's doll disappears. She frantically searches for it, and then discovers that someone has mistaken it for a cooking stone. Elizabeti reclaims her rock doll and resumes her loving care. *Mama Elizabeti* is the sequel to this storybook.

Everett Anderson's Friend [31]

Written by Lucille Clifton   Coretta Scott King Honor: Author
Illustrated by Ann Grifalconi

Hardcover: Henry Holt
Published 1976

"*A girl named Maria who wins at ball is fun to play with after all.*"

Young Everett looks forward to meeting his new neighbors. He hopes that they have boys so he can have some new playmates, but is immediately deflated when he discovers that the family has only girls. Everett has no expectation that Maria and her sisters can play ball or shoot marbles until she proves otherwise. Poetic text is the hallmark of this series, which also includes *Everett Anderson's Christmas Coming, Everett Anderson's Goodbye* [v1-167], *Everett Anderson's 1-2-3, Everett Anderson's Nine Month Long* [32], *Everett Anderson's Year* [33], and *Some of the Days of Everett Anderson* [102].

Everett Anderson's Nine Month Long [32]

Written by Lucille Clifton
Illustrated by Ann Grifalconi

Hardcover: Henry Holt
Published 1978

Young Everett is ambivalent about his mother's new marriage and the "almost" dad in his life. As the newlyweds plan for a new baby, they offer Everett assurances that he is still loved and cherished by his mother and accepted by his new stepfather. Their perceptive approach and Everett's tender reactions are offered in verse, as are other sensitive topics in the series, including *Everett Anderson's Christmas Coming, Everett Anderson's Goodbye* [v1-167], *Everett Anderson's 1-2-3, Everett Anderson's Friend* [31], *Everett Anderson's Year* [33], and *Some of the Days of Everett Anderson* [102].

Everett Anderson's Year [33]

Written by Lucille Clifton
Illustrated by Ann Grifalconi

Hardcover: Henry Holt
Published 1974

Seven-year-old Everett Anderson shares his reflections of each month of the year in twelve verses. Everett's unique perspective, as the only child of a single mother, are sometimes serious, sometimes emotional, and sometimes humorous. In September, Everett recites that he knows where Africa is, can count to ten, and went to school every day the previous year, so he wonders why he has to go again. This series also includes *Everett Anderson's Christmas Coming, Everett Anderson's 1-2-3, Everett Anderson's Friend* [31], *Everett Anderson's Goodbye* [v1-167], *Everett Anderson's Nine Month Long* [32], and *Some of the Days of Everett Anderson* [102].

Fingers, Nose, and Toes [34]

Written by Patricia Hinds
Photographs by John Pinderhughes

Board Book: Essence, Golden Books
Published 1997

Toddlers learn the parts of their bodies and their functions in this bright board book. A series of delightful children are photographed wiggling their toes, running on strong legs, and smelling sweet flowers. The palm-size, sculpted-edge book is just right for little hands to grasp. Three other books in the Shaped Little Nugget Book series are *My First Words* [79], *My Five Senses* [80], and *Ring! Bang! Boom!* [91]

Flip-Flops [35]

Written and illustrated by Nancy Cote

Hardcover: Albert Whitman
Published 1998

Meggie and her mother are going to the beach on a summer day, but Meggie can't find her other flip-flop, so she goes with only one. Meggie finds several creative uses for the single sandal. At different times during the day, the lone flip-flop serves as a fan, a sand shovel, a clam digger, and finally a note pad, when she writes the name and number of a new friend on it. The illustrations in the beach story are playful and engaging.

Flower Garden [36]   Easy Bun

Written by Eve Bunting
Illustrated by Kathryn Hewitt

Hardcover: Harcourt Brace
Published 1994

Flower Garden

A little girl and her daddy lovingly shop for flowers—pansies, daisies, daffodils, and tulips—and plant them in a window box as a surprise birthday present for her mommy. The details of this project are simply told in verse, accompanied by lush, lifelike illustrations.

Gavin Curtis

AUTHOR

"Ultimately, my objective in telling stories that resonate with my own childhood experiences is to validate the lives of children who today might feel marginalized by the absence of their authentic images in literature and pop culture. Just because an event occurs on 145th Street and Amsterdam Avenue does not make it any less significant to its participants than the happenings on Main Street, USA."

OUR FAVORITE

The Bat Boy and His Violin [128]

From My Window [37]

Written by Olive Wong
Illustrated by Anna Rich

Hardcover: Silver
Published 1995

This brightly illustrated book of very few words features a thoughtful young boy peering out of his window. He watches the neighborhood activities until he is inspired to go outside to join in the wintertime play.

Furaha Means Happy!: A Book of Swahili Words [38]

Written and illustrated by Ken Wilson-Max

Hardcover: Hyperion
Published 2000

Moses and Wambui live in Kenya and speak the rhythmic Swahili language. In this bright picture book, they introduce young readers to the sounds of their native language. The story is written in English, but a number of common objects are identified with a picture and the English and Swahili words for children to learn. A companion book, *Halala Means Welcome!: A Book of Zulu Words* [46], is also available.

The Genie in the Jar [39]

Written by Nikki Giovanni
Illustrated by Chris Raschka

Hardcover: Henry Holt
Published 1996

A simple rhyme and lucent illustrations tell the dynamic story of the building of love and trust inside a single family and the entire black community. A mother and daughter tell their story together as they sing and dance and weave a blanket of love on a black loom, which represents their strong black neighborhood.

Et /Leo

Get the Ball, Slim [40]

Written by Marcia Leonard
Illustrated by Dorothy Handelman

Softcover: Scholastic
Published 1998

Tim and Jim are identical twins in this story featuring only simple words for new readers. The brothers play with their dog, Slim, in a series of photographic illustrations. The simple nature of the text is reminiscent of the "Dick and Jane" books for primary students.

The Girl Who Wore Snakes [41]

Written by Angela Johnson
Illustrated by James E. Ransome

Hardcover: Orchard
Published 1993

Ali was intrigued by the snakes that a zookeeper brought to her class. Ali was the first to volunteer to hold and pet the brown, yellow, and orange reptiles, which reminded her of the sun and the earth and everything in between. It wasn't long before she began to drape the snakes around her arms, neck, and ankles. Then she even began to wear the snakes to picnics, to school, and even on vacation. Young readers may or may not like snakes, but they will be surprised to learn how Ali acquired her love of the slithery creatures.

Give Me Grace: A Child's Daybook of Prayers [42]

Written and illustrated by Cynthia Rylant

Hardcover: Simon & Schuster
Published 1999

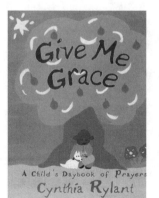

Seven poetic prayers are boldly printed and accompanied by childlike illustrations in this book of daily dedications for young children. This book offers children a structured way to give thanks for their blessings and to seek support from a higher source.

Good Night Baby [43]

BB

Written by Cheryl Willis Hudson
Illustrated by George Ford Jr. ☆ 76

Board Book: Cartwheel, Scholastic
Published 1992

A busy baby, exhausted from his active day, prepares for bedtime with a comforting bath and a bedtime story before being tucked in by his loving mom. Companion books include *Animal Sounds for Baby* [v1-5], *Good Morning Baby* [v1-40], and *Let's Count Baby.*

Grandfather's Work: A Traditional Healer in Nigeria [44]

Written and photographed by Ifeoma Onyefulu

Hardcover: Millbrook
Published 1998

A young Nigerian boy introduces young readers to his mother, a baker; his uncle, an attorney; his aunt, a pot maker; and other family members with proud professions. The boy is most interested in his grandfather, a traditional healer, who uses his knowledge of plants and herbs to work medical magic in the lives of his patients. The young boy shares his grandfather's commitment to healing and vows to learn the art and carry on the tradition. Four other books in the same style and format are *A Is for Africa* [v1-1], *Chidi Only Likes Blue: An African Book of Colors* [21], *Emeka's Gift: An African Counting Story* [v1-29], *Ogbo: Sharing Life in an African Village* [v1-247], and *A Triangle for Adaora: An African Book of Shapes.*

Greetings, Sun [45]

Easy Ger

Written by Phillis and David Gershator
Illustrated by Synthia Saint James

Hardcover: Richard Jackson, DK Publishing
Published 1998

Two young children enthusiastically start their new day by greeting everything from the new morning's sun and breeze to their clothes, breakfast, and school friends. Their appreciation continues through the day as they welcome the stars, moon, and nighttime rituals with the same greeting. Bold paintings illustrate this gentle poem, which was inspired by African praise songs.

Halala Means Welcome!: A Book of Zulu Words [46]

Written and illustrated by Ken Wilson-Max   J/Zulu/496/Wil

Hardcover: Hyperion Books for Children
Published 1998

Bold, bright illustrations picture Michael and Chidi, two South African boys, who speak the musical Zulu language. Young readers can learn the Zulu words for friend, bus, milk, and twenty-two other everyday words, which are pictured on the oversized pages. A glossary and pronunciation guide are included in the back of the book. A companion book, *Furaha Means Happy!: A Book of Swahili Words* [38], is also available.

Hansel and Gretel [47]

Written by Naomi Fox
Illustrated by Neal Fox

Softcover and audiotape: Confetti Entertainment
Published 1993

The Confetti Kids, members of a drama club, assume the roles of fairy tale characters to present traditional fairy tales. The book is accompanied by an audiotape on which the story is told in read-along style by actor Robert Guillaume. Other fairy tales in the Confetti Company series [v1-23] include *A Christmas Carol, Cinderella, A Different Kind of Christmas, The Frog Prince, Little Red Riding Hood* [67], *Rumplestiltskin, The Shoemaker and the Elves,* and *Sleeping Beauty.*

Happy to Be Nappy [48]

Written by bell hooks
Illustrated by Chris Raschka

Hardcover: Jump at the Sun, Hyperion
Published 1999

In this colorful book, young girls take pride in their "nappy" halos of hair, which they can "twist, plait, or just lie flat." The word "nappy" is used in an extremely positive way. The poetic text is printed in a handwritten script and illustrated with colorful abstract watercolor paintings of the confident young girls.

Honey Hunters [49]   J/3 98.24/Mar

Retold and illustrated by Francesca Martin

Hardcover: Candlewick
Published 1992

Once, all of the animals in the African bush lived together in peace and harmony, and they all loved honey. A little gray bird, known as the honey guide, was called upon by a little boy to help him find a sweet honeycomb. Soon a rooster, a bush cat, an antelope, a leopard, a zebra, a lion, and an elephant joined the honey-hunting procession, one by one. After a long search, the bird finally led the group to a tree where a honeycomb was found. The boy split the honeycomb into four pieces, to be shared among the animals. But greed prevailed, pitting one animal against the other. So that is why, even today, roosters and bush cats, antelopes and leopards, zebras and lions, and elephants and humans do not get along.

I Have a News: Rhymes from the Caribbean [50]

Collected by Walter Jekyll
Illustrated by Jacqueline Mair

Hardcover: Lothrop, Lee & Shepard
Published 1994

Thirteen lyrical poems collected from Jamaica are presented with eye-popping primary-color illustrations of the people and places of this Caribbean island. The simple poems can be set to the rhythmic cadence of the island music that appears in the back of the book. ***Caribbean dialect.***

I Have Heard of a Land [51]

Written by Joyce Carol Thomas   Coretta Scott King Honor: Illustrator
Illustrated by Floyd Cooper

Hardcover: Joanna Cotler, HarperCollins
Published 1998

Dramatically hued paintings trace an African American pioneer woman's journey to a new life in the Oklahoma Territory. She is joined by other men and women, both black and white, who are seeking the same land of promise. Their journey is long and hard, but their goal of reaching a new life in the promising new land keeps them moving forward.

I Make Music [52]

Written by Eloise Greenfield
Illustrated by Jan Spivey Gilchrist

Board Book: Black Butterfly
Published 1991

A sweet toddler makes joyful music for her mommy and daddy on a piano, drum, trombone, and xylophone as they lovingly encourage her. The young prodigy is delightfully illustrated with curly pigtails and a bright smile. Other books in this series include *Big Friend, Little Friend* [8]; *Daddy and I* [v1-24]; and *My Doll, Keshia* [78].

The Invisible Princess [53]

Written and illustrated by Faith Ringgold

Hardcover: Crown, Random House
Published 1999

A slave couple, Mama and Papa Love, wish for a child but are afraid to have one that will be subjugated to their cruel slave master, Captain Pepper. Finally their wish is granted by the Powers of Nature—Prince of the Night, Sun Goddess, Sea Queen, and others—who give the couple a child and then hide and protect her for years. When Captain Pepper's own daughter sees the invisible child in the fields, he realizes that the rumors of such a child are true. His threats against her parents are answered by the Powers of Nature, who come to the rescue again, liberating all the slaves on the plantation and transporting them to the invisible village of peace, freedom, and love.

Island in the Sun [54]

Written by Harry Belafonte and Lord Burgess
Illustrated by Alex Ayliffe

Hardcover: Dial Books for Young Readers, Penguin Putnam
Published 1999

Luminous illustrations of Jamaican island life are the perfect backdrop for the lyrics and music of a calypso favorite, "Island in the Sun," which was co-written, performed, and popularized by the esteemed singer Harry Belafonte.

THE CREATORS

Ruby Dee
AUTHOR

Ossie Davis
AUTHOR

"We think that those who write for the very young must anticipate the enormous challenges and changes in our universe in progress now and still to come. . . . We who write for children must, to paraphrase Dr. DuBois, try to encourage them to live life 'lit by some large vision of goodness and beauty and truth.'"

OUR FAVORITES

Ossie Davis:

Escape to Freedom: A Play about Young Frederick Douglass [vl-340]

Just Like Martin [vl-368]

Ruby Dee:

Tower to Heaven [vl-290]

Jafta [55]

Written by Hugh Lewin
Illustrated by Lisa Kopper

Reading Rainbow Review Book

Hardcover: Carolrhoda
Published 1983

Jafta, a young South African boy, compares his feelings to the characteristics of the animals that surround him. Sometimes he is as "strong as a rhino," and at other times he wants to "jump like an impala," or "nuzzle like a rabbit." Jafta's story is told in large type for young readers. He and the animals are pictured in sepia-toned illustrations. The Jafta series includes *Jafta's Mother* [57], *Jafta and the Wedding, Jafta's Father* [56], and *Jafta: The Town.*

Easy Lew

Jafta's Father [56]

Written by Hugh Lewin
Illustrated by Lisa Kopper

Reading Rainbow Review Book

Hardcover: Carolrhoda
Published 1983

Even though his father is working far away in the city, young Jafta thinks of him fondly in this sentimental story. Jafta recalls his father carrying him across the river on his shoulders, and the time that he built Jafta and his brother a log sailing raft. Warm sepia-toned illustrations of the father and son tell the story of their love and devotion to each other. The Jafta series includes *Jafta* [55], *Jafta's Mother* [57], *Jafta: The Town,* and *Jafta and the Wedding.*

Jafta's Mother [57]

Easy Lew

Written by Hugh Lewin
Illustrated by Lisa Kopper

Reading Rainbow Review Book

Hardcover: Carolrhoda
Published 1983

Jafta, a young South African boy, offers a loving tribute to his mother by recounting her many wonderful characteristics. She is, he says, "like the earth—full of goodness," and "like the sky, she's always there." Jafta's love and esteem for his mother, which she returns in kind, abound in this sentimental book. The Jafta series includes *Jafta* [55], *Jafta and the Wedding, Jafta's Father* [56], and *Jafta: The Town.*

Jamaica and the Substitute Teacher [58]

Written by Juanita Havill
Illustrated by Anne Sibley O'Brien

Easy Hav

Hardcover: Houghton Mifflin
Published 1999

Jamaica's shame turns to pride after she admits to her teacher that she copied from Brianna's spelling test paper. The teacher acknowledges Jamaica's confession but assures Jamaica that she is special and valued even if her work isn't perfect. Jamaica gains confidence and grows from the experience. The Jamaica series includes *Jamaica and Brianna* [v1-57], *Jamaica Tag-Along* [59], *Jamaica's Blue Marker* [60], and *Jamaica's Find* [v1-58].

Jamaica Tag-Along [59]

Easy Hav

Written by Juanita Havill
Illustrated by Anne Sibley O'Brien

Hardcover: Houghton Mifflin
Published 1989

Jamaica is hurt when her older brother refuses to let her tag along with him and his friends. Dejected, she goes to the sandlot to play by herself. When a toddler tries to join her, Jamaica becomes annoyed. When the younger child's mother scolds him, saying, "Big kids don't like to be bothered by little kids," Jamaica realizes the significance of her actions and invites the boy to play. The Jamaica series includes *Jamaica and Brianna* [v1-57], *Jamaica and the Substitute Teacher* [58], *Jamaica's Blue Marker* [60], and *Jamaica's Find* [v1-58].

Jamaica's Blue Marker [60]

Easy Hav

Written by Juanita Havill
Illustrated by Anne Sibley O'Brien

Hardcover: Houghton Mifflin
Published 1995

Jamaica is annoyed when her teacher makes her share her marker with Russell and he uses the marker to scribble all over her drawing. Resentful, Jamaica vows to never share with him again. She even refuses to make him a card for his going-away party. But then she figures out that Russell is only acting out his disappointment at having to move. In a gesture of good will, Jamaica gives Russell her blue marker as a farewell gift. Other books in the series include: *Jamaica and Brianna* [v1-57], *Jamaica and the Substitute Teacher* [58], *Jamaica Tag-Along* [59], and *Jamaica's Find* [v1-58].

Easy Fee

Jambo Means Hello: Swahili Alphabet Book [61]

Written by Muriel Feelings   **Caldecott Honor Book**
Illustrated by Tom Feelings   ***Reading Rainbow* Review Book**

Softcover: Puffin Pied Piper, Dial Books for Young Readers
Published 1974

Young readers are introduced to the Swahili language and learn interesting
facts about Africa in this alphabet book, including the fact that there is no Q
nor X in this dominant African language. Each of twenty-four letters is represented by an African object that is briefly described on a finely illustrated
page. A companion book is *Moja Means One: Swahili Counting Book* [v1-73].

Joe Can Count [62]

Written and illustrated by Jan Ormerod

Softcover: Mulberry, William Morrow
Published 1986

Joe, a typical little boy, demonstrates that he can count from one to ten by
numbering a series of fish, frogs, mice, chicks, turtles, snails, spiders, ants,
sheep, and pigs. As he counts each group, young readers will see a picture representation of the number as well as the numerals to help them understand the
correlation between the number of objects and the numeric symbol.

Joshua's Night Whispers [63]

Written by Angela Johnson
Illustrated by Rhonda Mitchell

Board Book: Orchard
Published 1994

From his bed, young Joshua tunes in to the sounds of the night. The scary
night whispers compel him to leave his room and walk down the hall to the
comforting arms of his daddy, who holds him warm and safe. Two other
books, *Mama Bird, Baby Birds* [69] and *Joshua by the Sea* [v1-61], are also
about the adventurous young Joshua.

Julius [64]

Easy Joh

Written by Angela Johnson
Illustrated by Dav Pilkey

Softcover: Scholastic
Published 1993

Maya's granddaddy brings her an unusual pet, a pig from Alaska named Julius, who becomes her best friend. Through the vibrant illustrations and simple words, young readers will enjoy Maya and Julius's frolicsome play.

Kofi and the Butterflies [65]

Written by Sandra Horn
Illustrated by Lynne Wiley

Softcover: Africa World
Published 1995

Kofi loves butterflies and spends hours watching their graceful flights through the park. One day, after saving a butterfly from the net of another boy, Kofi gets an extraordinary reward—the butterfly lights on his shoulder and invites him into the secret kingdom of the butterflies. Kofi is magically swept into the inner world, where he is surrounded by millions of the beautiful creatures. And then, just as suddenly, Kofi is returned to the park, and realizes that he must have had a fantastic dream . . . or did he?

Laney's Lost Momma [66]

Written by Diane Johnston Hamm
Illustrated by Sally G. Ward

Hardcover: Albert Whitman
Published 1991

Young Laney is accidentally separated from her mother while shopping. Frantic and upset, Laney heads for the door to check the parking lot, but then remembers her mother's important caution to never leave the store if she got lost. Remembering more of her mother's words, Laney calls upon a store employee to help her find her lost mother.

Little Red Riding Hood [67]

Adapted by Naomi Fox
Illustrated by Neal Fox

Softcover and audiotape: Confetti
Published 1993

The traditional story of Little Red Riding Hood is told again in this charming book/audiotape set. Young readers can read along as they hear the story told in the richly textured voice of actor Robert Guillaume. The Confetti Company series of fairy tales [v1-23] also includes *A Christmas Carol, Cinderella, A Different Kind of Christmas, The Frog Prince, Hansel and Gretel* [47], *Rumplestiltskin, The Shoemaker and the Elves,* and *Sleeping Beauty.*

Maebelle's Suitcase [68]

Written and illustrated by Tricia Tusa   ***Reading Rainbow* Review Book**

Hardcover: Macmillan
Published 1987

Maebelle is a wise but eccentric old lady of 108 years. She makes and wears kooky hats and lives in a tree house near her bird friends. As all of her bird neighbors begin to migrate south for the winter, one bird, Binkie, refuses to go. He insists that he cannot leave his belongings behind and begs Maebelle to lend him a suitcase for his long flight. Maebelle watches as the misguided bird fills the suitcase with branches, rocks, and a small pile of dirt. Of course, he is unable to fly with this load. Wisely, Maebelle figures out a way to relieve the bird of his burdensome treasures. The humorous story is perfect to share during story time.

 ## Mama Bird, Baby Birds [69]

Written by Angela Johnson
Illustrated by Rhonda Mitchell

Board Book: Orchard
Published 1994

Young Joshua and his sister find a nest of baby birds in their yard. As they watch the mother bird feed and tend her young, they are reminded of their own loving mother. Two other books, *Joshua by the Sea* [v1-61] and *Joshua's Night Whispers* [63], follow the adventures of this young boy.

The Many Colors of Mother Goose [70]

Adapted by Cheryl Willis Hudson
Illustrated by Ken Brown, Mark Corcoran, and Cathy Johnson

Hardcover and softcover: Just Us
Published 1997

Thirty-one Mother Goose favorites feature multicultural nursery rhyme characters. In this updated version, Little Miss Muffet is a sassy African American girl and Peter the Pumpkin Eater, also African American, puts his wife in the pumpkin shell, but then brings her a piece of sweet potato pie.

Max [71]

Written and illustrated by Ken Wilson-Max

Board Book: Hyperion
Published 1998

A little boy named Max plays with his pet pig in twelve colorfully illustrated pages. The bright, simple art will attract young readers, as will the manipulative tabs, wheels, and flaps designed for busy little hands. Other interactive books about the busy boy are *Max Loves Sunflowers* [72], *Max's Letter* [73], and *Max's Money* [74].

Max Loves Sunflowers [72]

Written and illustrated by Ken Wilson-Max

Board Book: Hyperion
Published 1998

Max, a cute round-faced boy, decides to plant a flower garden. Each step is pictured in large block illustrations with a series of manipulative pop-ups, flaps, and tabs that allow young readers to join in the fun. There are four other books about this character: *Max* [71], *Max's Letter* [73], *Max's Money* [74], and *Max Paints the House*.

Max's Letter [73]

Written and illustrated by Ken Wilson-Max

Board Book: Jump at the Sun, Hyperion
Published 1999

Young children will be amused by and spend hours with this interactive book. In the inside cover, they will discover a bag stuffed with a removable cardboard letter. In the following brightly colored pages they will find slotted boxes, bags, and mailboxes in which to deliver and redeliver their letter. Other titles about this character include *Max* [71], *Max Loves Sunflowers* [72], *Max's Money* [74], and *Max Paints the House.*

Max's Money [74]

Written and illustrated by Ken Wilson-Max

Board Book: Jump at the Sun, Hyperion
Published 1999

Little children will love this engaging interactive book. Each page features a pocket or a slot in the phone, wallet, bank, or bubble gum machine that will accept the cardboard coin that comes in the book. Other titles about this character include *Max* [71], *Max Loves Sunflowers* [72], *Max's Letter* [73], and *Max Paints the House.*

Messy Bessey's Closet [75]

Written by Patricia and Fredrick McKissack
Illustrated by Rick Hackney

Hardcover: Children's
Published 1989

Messy Bessey faces a challenge when she opens her closet door, revealing the mess inside. But the young girl thoroughly cleans her closet, hanging up her clothes and putting everything in its proper place. Now the only challenge is to decide what to do with the things that she never uses. Messy Bessey selflessly decides to give them away, sharing with other children who need her good, but discarded, things. Other stories about Bessey include *Messy Bessey, Messy Bessey's Garden, Messy Bessey's School Desk, Messy Bessey's Family Reunion, Messy Bessey's Holidays,* and *Messy Bessey and the Birthday Overnight.*

THE CREATORS

Diane Dillon
ILLUSTRATOR

Leo Dillon
ILLUSTRATOR

"Art in its many forms has survived to inform us of lives long gone. Art inspires, lifts our spirits, and brings beauty into our lives. We wish to pay homage to it and to the people who created it."

OUR FAVORITES

Listen Children: An Anthology of Black Literature [411]

Her Stories: African American Folktales, Fairy Tales, and True Tales [vl-359]

Honey, I Love: And Other Poems [vl-360]

Many Thousand Gone: African Americans from Slavery to Freedom [vl-378]

The People Could Fly: American Black Folktales [vl-393]

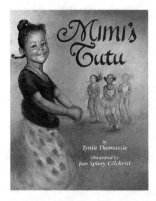

Mimi's Tutu [76]

Written by Tynia Thomassie
Illustrated by Jan Spivey Gilchrist

Hardcover: Scholastic
Published 1996

The first girl born into a family full of boys, Little Mimi was a cherished child. She was named M'bewe Iecine Magalee Isabella after her two grandmothers and two aunts, but they called her Mimi for short. Mimi's mother would often take her to her dance class, which the young girl enjoyed until the day that another young girl, the same age as Mimi, came wearing a beautiful, colorful tutu. All of a sudden Mimi felt inadequate and yearned for a tutu of her own. Once they found out, the grandmothers and aunts put their heads together and gave Mimi her own special dance skirt. It was a beautiful African lapa, a skirt wrap decorated with a belt of cowrie shells. The special skirt was just what Mimi needed to boost her spirits and her ancestral pride.

PB

My Aunt Came Back [77]

Written and illustrated by Pat Cummings

Board Book: HarperFestival, HarperCollins
Published 1998

Rhyming text and energetic illustrations will attract young readers to this entertaining story. A young girl tells about her aunt's travels to exotic destinations and the gifts she brought back. When Aunt went to Mandalay, she brought back a red beret. When she went to Beijing, she brought back a golden ring. Toddlers will love mimicking the catchy rhymes.

My Doll, Keshia [78]

Written by Eloise Greenfield
Illustrated by Jan Spivey Gilchrist

Board Book: Black Butterfly
Published 1991

A beautiful young girl cares lovingly for her doll, undoubtedly modeling the nurturing that she received from her own mother. Dressed in a bright pink dress with a poof of curls at the top of her head, the young girl plays with her doll, Keshia, before snuggling with her for a nap. Other titles in this board book series are *Daddy and I* [v1-24]; *Big Friend, Little Friend* [8]; and *I Make Music* [52].

My First Words [79]

Written by Patricia Hinds
Photographs by John Pinderhughes

Board Book: Essence, Golden Books
Published 1997

Fourteen different toddlers, each cute enough to eat up, are featured playing with their favorite things in this palm-size sculpted-edge book. Their bright, smiling faces demonstrate their love of life as they engage in the work of children—play! Three other books in the Shaped Little Nugget Book series are *Fingers, Nose, and Toes* [34]; *My Five Senses* [80]; and *Ring! Bang! Boom!* [91].

My Five Senses [80]

Written by Patricia Hinds
Illustrated by John Pinderhughes

Board Book: Essence, Golden Books
Published 1997

This palm-size book features bright, young toddlers taking in their world though their five senses. A young girl touches the soft hair of her dolls. A pensive boy hears his sister playing music, and a corn-rowed baby girl tastes a sweet mango. Three other books in the Shaped Little Nugget Book series are *Fingers, Nose, and Toes* [34]; *My First Words* [79]; and *Ring! Bang! Boom!* [91].

My Mama Needs Me [81]

Written by Mildred Pitts Walter ☆ 188   Coretta Scott King Award: Illustrator
Illustrated by Pat Cummings

Hardcover: Lothrop, Lee & Shepard
Published 1983

Sweet little Jason is so excited and feels so responsible when his mother brings his new baby sister home from the hospital that he sits steadfastly at home, knowing that his mama will need his help. As he sits and waits, all his mama and sister do is sleep . . . and sleep . . . and sleep. Still, he waits, knowing that at any moment he will be called upon to help. When Mama finally wakes up, she warmly acknowledges her son's devotion and then relieves him of his tough, self-imposed duty.

My Painted House, My Friendly Chicken, and Me [82]

Written by Maya Angelou
Photographs by Margaret Courtney-Clarke

Hardcover: Clarkson Potter, Crown
Published 1994

Eight-year-old Thandi invites young readers into her South African village, where the sights and sounds of her ancient African heritage are in contrast with her modern world. Thandi's best friend is a chicken that tours the village with the young tour guide as she shares the colorful paintings on the houses; the colorful, beaded tribal wear that she and her friends model; and her school, where the children wear their Western uniforms. This book is a companion to *Kofi and His Magic* [v1-216], another photographic essay about a village in Africa.

My Steps [83]

Written by Sally Derby
Illustrated by Adjoa Burrowes

Softcover: Lee & Low
Published 1996

The stoop and the five steps in front of a young girl's house are a world unto itself. As the seasons pass, the child and her friends play imaginatively on the steps, view the neighborhood activities, and clean the leaves and snow from the threshold to her home.

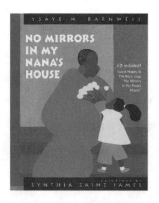

No Mirrors in My Nana's House [84]

Written by Ysaye M. Barnwell
Illustrated by Synthia Saint James

Hardcover: Harcourt Brace
Published 1998

There are no mirrors in her Nana's house, so this child's world is reflected in her Nana's eyes. In this uplifting poem, she sees her own beauty, a positive world, and plenty of love. Saint James's bold block-style paintings illustrate this self-affirming message. A CD of the spirited song, written by a member of the a cappella group Sweet Honey in the Rock, accompanies the book.

Octopus Hug [85]

Written by Laurence Pringle
Illustrated by Kate Salley Palmer

Softcover: Boyds Mills
Published 1993

Young Jesse and Becky are left home to play with Dad when Mom goes out for the evening. Dad is a virtual playing machine as he wrestles, rolls around, and plays on the floor with his two young ones. The two kids giggle away the evening as they frolic and tease with their loving father. The illustrations of this smiling family are bright and fun-inspiring, so don't read this to your young ones at bedtime!

1,2,3, Music! [86]

Written and illustrated by Sylvie Auzary-Luton

Hardcover: Orchard
Published 1997

Little Annie loves music. She listens and dances to music to the exclusion of everything else, which has a way of annoying her family and friends. Then she discovers a trunk full of musical instruments. As Annie blows and bangs and toots her new treasures she attracts her cousins, who join in to form a clamorous band. Young music lovers will enjoy the toe-tapping story and the chromatic illustrations.

Palampam Day [87]

Written by David and Phillis Gershator
Illustrated by Enrique O. Sanchez

Hardcover: Marshall Cavendish
Published 1997

In this whimsical story, young Turo is hungry but can't get anything to eat and drink. The coconuts in the tree chide him not to eat them, the frog in the barrel scolds him for dipping into the water, and the sweet potatoes turn him away when he tries to dig them up. Turo consults Papa Tata Wanga to try to understand why all the foods are talking. The mysterious event is explained as Palampam Day, "the day all things find their voice and say whatever they feel like saying." Papa Tata Wanga assures Turo that this strange event happens very rarely—only once in a blue moon. Turo goes to bed to wait for the new day, when everything will return to normal.

Easy Kea

Peter's Chair [88]

Written and illustrated by Ezra Jack Keats   ***Reading Rainbow*** **Review Book**

Softcover: Puffin, Penguin Putnam
Published 1967

Peter becomes concerned when his parents begin to pass all of his things on to his new baby sister. First they paint his cradle pink, and then his high chair and crib. When they begin eyeing his special chair, Peter takes the chair to his room for safekeeping. As he sits on the chair, pondering the situation, he reaches the mature conclusion that he is too big for the chair, and that he should pass it on to the new baby. Other books about Peter include *Goggles, Letter to Amy, Pet Show, The Snowy Day* [v1-98], and *Whistle for Willie*.

Easy Mac

Pickin' Peas [89]

Retold by Margaret Read MacDonald
Illustrated by Pat Cummings

Hardcover: HarperCollins
Published 1998

A little girl matches wits with a pesky rabbit in this retold folk tale. As she works in her garden, singing and planting her peas and looking forward to the delicious harvest, a rabbit, answering her in song, follows right behind her, eating them all up. She catches the rabbit and plans to keep him caged until her harvest is done, but he tricks her and gets away to do it all again another day. Music to the spirited song that the little girl and rabbit exchange is printed in the back and can be easily taught to young readers.

Red Light, Green Light, Mama and Me [90]

Written by Carl Best
Illustrated by Niki Daly

Hardcover: Orchard
Published 1995

Little Lizzie happily accompanies her mother to work for the day. The two walk hand in hand down the street and into the subway. They emerge across town at Mama's workplace—the public library. Lizzie spends the day as the center of attention, visiting with Mama's colleagues in this sweet mother-daughter story.

THE CREATORS

Sharon M. Draper

AUTHOR

"My goal as a writer is to show young people that books are accessible, valuable, and enjoyable. I want them to pick up one of my books, read page one, and be unable to put it down until it's finished. I want to make them thirsty for more. And I want to provide the material to quench their thirst."

Our Favorites

Jazzimagination: A Journal to Read and Write [396]

Ziggy and the Black Dinosaurs [vl-420]

Ziggy and the Black Dinosaurs: Lost in the Tunnel of Time [449]

Ziggy and the Black Dinosaurs: Shadows of Caesar's Creek [450]

Ring! Bang! Boom! [91]

Written by Patricia Hinds
Illustrated by John Pinderhughes

Board Book: Essence, Golden Books
Published 1997

Everything comes in twos in this palm-size, sculpted-edge book. Each photograph features a toddler engaging in an activity with a double sound: Honk-Honk of a horn, Bang-Bang on the pots and pans, and Pop-Pop of the popcorn! Three other books in the Shaped Little Nugget Book series are *Fingers, Nose, and Toes* [34]; *My First Words* [79]; and *My Five Senses* [80].

Robo's Favorite Places [92]

Written by Wade Hudson
Illustrated by Cathy Johnson

Softcover: Just Us
Published 1999

Robo's imagination runs wild when his teacher asks the class to tell about their favorite places. Robo considers his favorites—the skating rink, the neighborhood playhouse, the swimming pool. Then Robo remembers that his favorite place in the world is sitting at his computer working on the World Wide Web, which can take him anyplace in the world.

Sam [93]

Written by Ann Herbert Scott
Illustrated by Symeon Shimin

Hardcover: McGraw Hill
Published 1967

Sam becomes more and more depressed as, one by one, his family members reject him. First his mother sends him away because she is too busy in the kitchen. Then his big brother shoos him away because he is studying. His sister screams at him for playing with her doll. Finally, his father sends him away because he is too busy with his work. When Sam begins to cry, everyone realizes what they have done, and they stop to offer him the attention that he deserves.

Secret Valentine [94]

Written and illustrated by Catherine Stock

Hardcover: Bradbury
Published 1991

A very young girl and her mother make Valentine's Day cards for Grandma, Muffety (her cat), and the dear old lady who lives next door. They lovingly shop for the supplies, make the cards, and then mail them. Then on Valentine's Day she receives cards in return from Mommy and Daddy, Grandma, and even a card from Muffety. But one especially unique card is signed only "From Your Secret Valentine." Who could have sent it?

Seven Days of Kwanzaa: A Holiday Step Book [95]

Written by Ella Grier
Illustrated by John Ward

Hardcover: Viking, Penguin
Published 1997

Each of the seven days of Kwanzaa, the African American holiday, is poetically described and richly illustrated. Each page is bordered on the right with a kente cloth stripe, and the pages are cut in stair-step widths so that the edges come to together to form a larger kente pattern.

Shadow Dance [96]   J/398.21/Mol

Written by Tololwa M. Mollel
Illustrated by Donna Perrone

Hardcover: Clarion, Houghton Mifflin
Published 1998

Almost every culture has a version of this timeless folk tale. In this one, from Tanzania, young Salome helps to free a crocodile that is entwined in the gully. As soon as the ungrateful crocodile is free he turns on Salome and threatens to eat her unless she can persuade him otherwise. Salome pleads for her life but seems doomed until a wise pigeon, who was a witness to the whole episode, offers to arbitrate the argument. He tricks the crocodile into returning to the gully to demonstrate how he got caught in the first place. That done, Salome and her rescuer abandon the evil crocodile to his original fate.

Shaina's Garden [97]

Written by Denise Lewis Patrick ☆ 133
Illustrated by Stacey Schuett

Softcover: Aladdin, Simon & Schuster
Published 1996

Shaina, of the *Gullah Gullah Island* television series, is excited because she is planting her first garden today. But she is comically confused about the language of gardening. When Daddy suggests that they go to the nursery, Shaina imagines a baby's room. When her mother speaks of sowing seeds in the plant bed, Shaina envisions a needle and thread and a bed like her own. Nonetheless, Shaina figures it all out and completes the garden. Young readers can imagine what Shaina thought when she was told that she had a green thumb. Other books in the Gullah Gullah Island series include *Case of the Missing Cookies* [17]; *Happy Birthday, Daddy* [v1-46]; *Rain, Rain, Go Away*; and *Families, Phooey!*

Sharing Danny's Dad [98]

Written by Angela Shelf Medearis
Illustrated by Jan Spivey Gilchrist

Hardcover: Good Year, HarperCollins
Published 1995

His own daddy had to work today, but thank goodness his friend Danny is willing to share his dad for the day. Danny's dad generously tickles, plays ball with, and pushes both boys on the swing in this story of sharing.

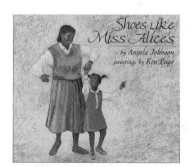

Shoes Like Miss Alice's [99]

Written by Angela Johnson
Illustrated by Ken Page

Hardcover: Orchard
Published 1995

Miss Alice brings a bag full of shoes when she comes to baby-sit for young Sara. The skeptical child is sad that Mama has left her with a babysitter until Miss Alice puts on her dancing shoes and entertains Sara with her twirls and spins. Then Miss Alice puts on her walking shoes and takes Sara for a long walk, and later puts on her fuzzy blue slippers for their nap. Sara's skepticism turns to appreciation for the fun-filled day she spent with her new friend.

THE CREATORS

Karen English

AUTHOR

"I want the children who read my books to recognize themselves dealing with the same everyday struggles as everyone else. I want them to see their world as a part of the world at large. I don't want them to feel their world circumscribed to just folktales and historical biographies."

OUR FAVORITES

Big Wind Coming [vl-130]

Francie [381]

Just Right Stew [222]

Neeny Coming, Neeny Going [vl-240]

Singing Black: Alternative Nursery Rhymes for Children [100]

Written by Mari Evans
Illustrated by Ramon Price

Softcover: Just Us
Published 1998

Twenty-two lyrical nursery rhymes are offered as alternatives to the traditional Western ones that are typically taught to our children. Each of these affirmative rhymes is inspired by black culture. For example, "Heroes" honors many of our black role models, and "Sweet Potato Pie" is a tribute to the dessert that follows a traditional soul food dinner.

The Singing Geese [101]

Retold by Jan Wahl
Illustrated by Sterling Brown

Hardcover: Lodestar, Dutton
Published 1998

Sam shoots a goose from a large flock of singing geese and brings it home for his wife to prepare for dinner. As she plucks the bird, each feather flies out of the window. Later that evening, as the couple sits down for their meal, the entire flock of geese swoops in through the window, each goose carrying a feather from their fallen friend. They reclaim the cooked but not eaten goose, leaving Sam and his wife wide-eyed with amazement.

Some of the Days of Everett Anderson [102]

Written by Lucille Clifton
Illustrated by Evaline Ness

Hardcover: Henry Holt
Published 1970

Young readers will be entertained by these brief poems about six-year-old Everett Anderson's view of everyday events that happen during his Monday morning, Tuesday all day, Saturday night, and other times. They may relate to his joy of being a six-year-old boy, his preference for getting wet rather than using an umbrella, or how he misses his daddy most on Sunday mornings. Other books about Everett Anderson include *Everett Anderson's 1-2-3,*

Everett Anderson's Christmas Coming, Everett Anderson's Friend [31], *Everett Anderson's Goodbye* [v1-167], *Everett Anderson's Nine Month Long* [32], and *Everett Anderson's Year* [33].

Song Bird [103]

J/398.2/Mol

Written by Tolowa M. Mollel
Illustrated by Rosanne Litzinger

Hardcover: Clarion
Published 1999

A bird escorts young Mariamu on a fantastic flight into the land of a gruesome, greedy beast to recover the cattle that the monster has stolen from her family. The bird's kindness is in exchange for Mariamu's agreement to not clear the field where she keeps her nest. The soft pastel illustrations are particularly inviting.

Sophie [104]

Written by Mem Fox
Illustrated by Aminah Brenda Lynn Robinson

Softcover: Voyager, Harcourt Brace
Published 1994

The passages of life are simply described in this book of few words. There was a time when there was no Sophie and then she was born and grew into a strong young girl. As Sophie grew up, she loved and was very close to her grandpa, who loved her too. But just as Sophie grew taller and stronger, her beloved grandpa grew smaller and weaker until he was gone. Sophie's story of life and death is pure and eloquent and expressed in a way that even young children will understand.

A South African Night [105]

Written and illustrated by Rachel Isadora

Hardcover: Greenwillow
Published 1998

Breathtaking watercolor paintings of South African nighttime scenes include lions and leopards out for their nightly hunt, hippos and elephants watering, and the sun setting on the savanna to prepare young readers for their bedtime.

Swinging on a Rainbow [106]

Written by Charles Perkins
Illustrated by Thomas Hamilton

Hardcover: Africa World
Published 1993

Patrice is a bright-eyed little girl who loves rainbows. One day, as she plays on her swing, she begins to wonder what it would be like to swing on a rainbow. Enthusiastically, Patrice shares her vision with friends, who consider the idea until a storm washes away their interest. Patrice's dampened spirit is re-energized when the sun comes up and she finds her swing washed in the colors of a rainbow. The lighthearted story is told in rhyme and vibrantly illustrated.

These Hands [107]

Written by Hope Lynne Price
Illustrated by Bryan Collier

Hardcover: Jump at the Sun, Hyperion
Published 1999

A young girl focuses on her hands and realizes how complicated and capable they are. Her miraculous hands allow her to touch and create, hug and pat, and pray or clap. The young girl is illustrated in a series of unique collage paintings.

Tiny's Hat [108]

Written and illustrated by Ann Grifalconi

Hardcover: HarperCollins
Published 1999

Little Tiny, like the blues legend Billie Holiday, who inspired this story, is the daughter of a traveling blues musician. Tiny's daddy leaves home often and stays away for long periods of time to pursue his musical career and to earn a living for his family. Tiny sadly mourns each of Daddy's departures. But then Daddy leaves her his bowler hat to remind her of him while he is away. One day the hat inspires Tiny to begin to sing out her own feelings, giving birth to her own blues, and a way of working out her pain.

Easy Gre

Water, Water [109]

Written by Eloise Greenfield
Illustrated by Jan Spivey Gilchrist

Hardcover: HarperFestival, HarperCollins
Published 1999

A young boy takes inventory of all the places where he finds water, from his fishbowl and drinking cup to streams, lakes, and fountains. Keep up the fun by challenging your young reader to add to this watery list.

When I'm Alone [110]

Easy Och

Written by Carol Partridge Ochs
Illustrated by Vicki Jo Redenbaugh

Hardcover: Carolrhoda
Published 1993

A delightful young girl with a vivid imagination has a difficult time convincing her mother that it was the ten aardvarks, nine lions, eight turtles, and other assorted creatures that visit her—only when she is alone—that messed up her room and bathroom. The rhythmic text of this fanciful counting story will amuse young readers.

When Will Sarah Come? [111]

Written by Elizabeth Fitzgerald Howard ☆ 82
Photographed by Nina Crews

Hardcover: Greenwillow
Published 1999

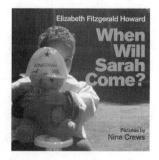

Sarah is off to school for the first time, but her little brother is left home to await her return. Photographic illustrations show the young preschooler playing with his toys as he patiently waits. But every time he hears a noise outside, he anxiously runs to the door to see if it is Sarah. When Sarah finally arrives, he is happy to have his playmate back at home.

Willie's Wonderful Pet [112]

E+/Ceb

Written by Mel Cebulash
Illustrated by George Ford Jr. ☆ 76

Softcover: Cartwheel, Scholastic
Published 1993

The other children bring their dogs, birds, fish, and rabbits to school for show-and-tell, but Willie brings something entirely different—a pet worm, in a paper cup filled with dirt. Nobody realizes what a worm can do until Willie gives them a demonstration of the worm's special talent.

You Are Here [113]   *Easy Cre*

Written and photographed by Nina Crews

Hardcover: Greenwillow
Published 1998

Take one rainy afternoon, two little girls, and a heaping dose of photo magic and you have an adventurous trip. In their own imagination-transformed dining room, the two sisters travel to far-off places and encounter giants, monsters, and treasures. They are happy, though, when the sun comes out and they can go outside and play.

You Are My Perfect Baby [114]

Written by Joyce Carol Thomas
Illustrated by Nneka Bennett

Board Book: HarperFestival, HarperCollins
Published 1999

A new mother offers a special poem of love to her new baby, acknowledging all of Baby's perfect features. Any parent can recite this poem to his or her little one as a special expression of love.

You Be Me, I'll Be You [115]

Written and illustrated by Phil Mandelbaum

Softcover: Kane/Miller
Published 1990

Anna laments to her white daddy that she doesn't feel pretty. She isn't happy about the color of her skin or the texture of her hair. She wishes that she looked more like him. Playfully, Daddy rubs coffee grounds onto his face and flour onto hers to show her that they each look better in their own skins. Then the two take a walk and observe people tanning themselves and having their hair curled, to get features that Anna has naturally. By the end of the day, Anna is more self-appreciative and secure in her own beauty.

Books for Early Readers

FTER YOUNG CHILDREN grasp the fundamentals of reading—the alphabet, phonics, and sight words—and become somewhat proficient at reading to themselves, the next step is to help them build their vocabulary, grammar, and comprehension skills. Therefore, the books you select should become increasingly longer and more complex. While the range of reading skills varies greatly between a five-year-old kindergartener and an eight-year-old third grader, all of the books in this chapter meet these criteria. Young students will find themselves following stories that require a longer attention span and closer attention to detail.

These young readers are also introduced to books that directly inform. Some are nonfiction selections, such as *Explore Black History with Wee Pals* [169], or easy biographies like *The Story of Jean Baptiste DuSable* [306]. Others teach through fictionalized accounts of real events, among them *If a Bus Could Talk: The Story of Rosa Parks* [202], or *Journey to Freedom: A Story of the Underground Railroad* [218].

Five- to eight-year-olds still need to be read to as much as they are encouraged to read on their own. Listening to you read will help them understand syntax, pronunciation, and the proper use of new words.

And, of course, these young readers are still very attracted by colorful illustrations and interesting visuals, which have the added value of increasing their comprehension of the story.

Children in this age group are usually encouraged to read for twenty to thirty minutes every evening, as homework, just to ensure that they are practicing their skills and building a reading discipline. What they read is not as important as *that* they read. We have selected a bevy of books that are just for fun. Young readers will enjoy, and identify with, *Jamela's Dress* [213], *Christopher, Please Clean Up Your Room!* [152], and similar books, since all kids get into mischief. They will also love books like *Shaq and the Beanstalk* [296], a book of fractured fairy tales featuring Shaquille O'Neal. *Cendrillon* [149] and *Leola and the Honeybears* [234] are based on the familiar stories of Cinderella and Goldilocks and the Three Bears.

Our children tend to be very familiar with Mother Goose and Grimm's fairy tales, but are not aware of the many stories from the African tradition. We have included a wonderful selection of African folktales, such as *The Hatseller and the Monkeys* [189], *Nobiah's Well* [269], and *Why the Sky Is Far Away* [340].

As they enter school, young children become less self-centered and more outwardly directed. We have selected an array of books that will help young readers adapt to a broader range of relationships and adopt a more positive social conscience.

A number of books, like those in the popular Little Bill series, will help young children learn positive values; we have included eight of those titles. *The Meanest Thing to Say* [246] and *My Big Lie* [258] teach very practical virtues. Other books—such as *Gettin' Through Thursday* [177], *Father's Day Blues* [171], and *In My Momma's Kitchen* [206]—reinforce the value of family. And still others, like *Palm Trees* [276] and *Pink Paper Swans* [282], are about the value of friendship with both peers and elders.

It is important to continue to build a young child's confidence and self-esteem, so please consider books like *Grandpa, Is Everything Black Bad?* [187], *I Love My Hair!* [200], and *I Want to Be* [201], which will remind them of their own inner beauty and strengths.

All Around the Town: The Photographs of Richard Samuel Roberts [116]

Written by Dinah Johnson
Photographs by Richard Samuel Roberts

Hardcover: Henry Holt
Published 1998

Acclaimed self-taught photographer Richard Samuel Roberts captured the lives of African American citizens of Columbia, South Carolina, in tens of thousands of photographs in the early 1900s. Thirty-six carefully selected handsome black-and-white and sepia-toned photographs are paired with simple but rich text to chronicle the lives and lifestyles of that place and time.

All the Magic in the World [117]

Easy Har

Written by Wendy Hartmann
Illustrated by Niki Daly

Hardcover: Dutton
Published 1993

Lena is known for her clumsiness, but all that is remedied when Joseph, the odd-job man, gives her a magic necklace made from odds and ends: pop bottle tops, string, and stones. Placing it around her neck, he tells her that whoever wears it becomes a princess. Full of new-found confidence, the once awkward child blooms and finds the magic within herself.

Always My Dad [118]

Easy Wye

Written by Sharon Dennis Wyeth ☆ 201
Illustrated by Raúl Colón

Reading Rainbow Feature Book

Softcover: Dragonfly, Knopf
Published 1995

A young girl longs wistfully for her dad, who travels from job to job and stays away for long periods of time. Then one evening Dad walks back into her life. She shyly embraces him, welcoming him home. The next days are magical, as she and Dad share each other's company. Then, just as suddenly as he appeared, he announces that it is time to go again. She sadly lets him go, knowing that wherever he is, he is always Dad and will always love her.

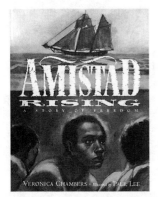

Amistad Rising: A Story of Freedom [119]

Written by Veronica Chambers
Illustrated by Paul Lee

J/Fiction/Chambers

Hardcover: Harcourt Brace
Published 1998

The story of the 1839 *Amistad* mutiny is told in a simple and straightforward manner in this historically correct picture book. Many children have by now heard of the *Amistad* because of the feature movie, but they may not really understand the emotionally charged case. The true tales of Cinque's frightening abduction from his African village, the cruel middle passage, and the violent mutiny are told. The complex legal case, political maneuvers, and John Quincy Adams's role in the final phases of the case are described in terms young readers can understand.

Anansi Finds a Fool [120]

Written by Verna Aardema
Illustrated by Bryna Waldman

Hardcover: Dial
Published 1992

Vibrant illustrations and descriptive text tell the story of Anansi, a lazy man who is humorously outsmarted by his would-be friend, Bonsu. Anansi plans to find a fool to join him in a new fishing business. He imagines tricking the fool into doing all the hard work, while he takes all the fish. But the tables are turned in this African tale that perfectly demonstrates the moral of the story: "When you dig a hole for someone else, you will fall into it yourself."

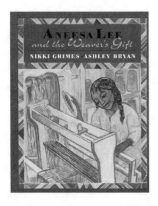

Aneesa Lee and the Weaver's Gift [121]

Written by Nikki Grimes
Illustrated by Ashley Bryan

Hardcover: Lothrop, Lee & Shepard
Published 1999

Thirteen related poems featuring Aneesa Lee, a biracial girl of African American and Japanese heritage, explore the fine art of weaving. The poetry uses the vernacular of the craft; a glossary and a diagram of a loom are included to help young readers. The poem about cloth making also represents the concept of weaving multicultural people into the fabric of one world.

An Angel Just Like Me [122]

Easy Hof

Written by Mary Hoffman
Illustrated by Cornelius Van Wright and Ying-Hwa Hu ☆ 181

Hardcover: Dial, Penguin USA
Published 1997

Young Tyler begins to ponder a problem as his family decorates their Christmas tree. Why do all the angel tree-toppers look like girls and why are none of them black? Tyler takes it upon himself to find a new angel for the family tree that looks like himself—a black boy. Tyler's search captures the need of children to see themselves reflected throughout their worlds. This touching and self-affirming story is beautifully illustrated.

Angel to Angel: A Mother's Gift of Love [123]

Written by Walter Dean Myers ☆ 119

Hardcover: HarperCollins
Published 1998

Forty years ago, when Walter Dean Myers wrote the title poem for his mother, neither he nor she imagined that it would one day be the cornerstone of a special book honoring mothers. Ten poems dedicated to loving African American families, especially mothers, are illustrated with dozens of century-old black-and-white and sepia-toned photographs of families. This heartfelt tribute follows the popular *Brown Angels* [v1-136] and *Glorious Angels.*

Angels [124]

Written by Eloise Greenfield
Illustrated by Jan Spivey Gilchrist

Hardcover: Hyperion
Published 1998

Visions of love, safety, and security are brought into focus in this lovely book about the angels that walk beside children every day. The seventeen short poems depict children doing everyday things—from playing in the snow or experiencing a time-out to napping and cuddling with Mom and Dad—as their angels look on. Fine pencil drawings illustrate the sweet words.

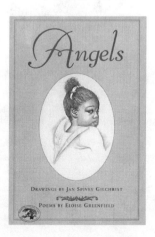

Easy Pin

Back Home [125]

Written by Gloria Jean Pinkney
Illustrated by Jerry Pinkney

Hardcover: Dial, Penguin
Published 1992

Eight-year-old Ernestine is excited to be taking a train back to Lumberton, North Carolina, to visit her aunt, uncle, and cousin on their farm, which was the childhood home of her mother. Ernestine is warmly welcomed by her Aunt Beula and Uncle June, but isn't sure about her cousin Jack. Even though she is fitted with a pair of old overalls and tries to keep up, he teases her unmercifully about her "citified" ways. It isn't until the end of her visit that Ernestine realizes that Jack's chiding is his expression of friendship. The sequel to this story is *The Sunday Outing* [v1-283].

A Band of Angels: A Story Inspired by the Jubilee Singers [126]

Written by Deborah Hopkinson
Illustrated by Raúl Colón

Hardcover: Atheneum, Simon & Schuster
Published 1999

This is the inspirational story of nine young people who in 1871 brought the Fisk School (later to become Fisk University) back from the brink of financial failure. Ella Sheppard, born into slavery in 1851, travels to Nashville after the emancipation to pursue her dream of attending Fisk. While there, she joins the choir. The group takes their show on the road, singing white songs to white audiences to try to earn money for the struggling school. Just when it seems that the school is going to fail, Ella decides to change the program, leading her peers in rousing black spirituals from their slave heritage. The audiences are so moved by the soulful sounds that word spreads and the group, who become known as the Jubilee Singers, becomes an international sensation, saving their school from bankruptcy.

The Barber's Cutting Edge [127]

Written by Gwendolyn Battle-Lavert
Illustrated by Raymond Holbert

Hardcover: Children's Book Press
Published 1994

While sitting in the barber's chair, Rashaad challenges his barber, Mr. Bigalow, to a vocabulary quiz, posing words like *abolish, idiosyncratic,* and *bewilderment.* Mr. Bigalow seems to have an excellent command of the words, defining each one perfectly. As Rashaad's admiration grows, Mr. Bigalow makes repeated trips to the back room, supposedly for a little more talcum powder, or to fix his hair clippers. When he disappears again, after the word *niche* is presented, Rashaad follows him and discovers Mr. Bigalow's cutting edge—a dictionary! Young readers will enjoy the artful illustrations, learn the definitions of some new words, and discover the power of a dictionary.

The Bat Boy and His Violin [128]

Written by Gavin Curtis ☆ 32   Coretta Scott King Honor: Illustrator
Illustrated by E. B. Lewis ☆ 93

Hardcover: Simon & Schuster
Published 1998

Young Reginald is a consummate musician who would rather play his violin than do anything else, much to his father's chagrin. His father, who manages the Dukes, a losing team in the Negro National Baseball League, decides to recruit Reginald as a bat boy for the team. Reginald is a disaster as a bat boy, but the team finds his violin music inspirational. As Reginald plays the music of Mozart, Beethoven, and Bach in the dugout during the games, the team begins to perform to new heights. Finally, the Dukes are in the position to win a pennant against the hottest team in the league. Win or lose, Reginald has made a difference, earning the respect of the team and the gratitude of his father.

Because You're Lucky [129]

Written by Irene Smalls ☆ 150
Illustrated by Michael Hays

Hardcover: Little, Brown
Published 1997

Kevin feels immediately at home when he comes to live with his aunt and her family. The young boy arrives at Aunt Laura's with nothing more than the clothes on his back. Aunt Laura immediately welcomes her nephew as a son, but her own son, Jonathan, is not so gracious. Jonathan isn't willing to share or to befriend his new roommate. But over time, the two bond and forge a brotherly relationship. Both Kevin and Jonathan come to understand how lucky they are to be blessed with family and each other.

J/ Ham

The Bells of Christmas [130]

Written by Virginia Hamilton   Coretta Scott King Honor: Author
Illustrated by Lambert Davis

Softcover: Harcourt Brace
Published 1986

Twelve-year-old Jason Bell and his family celebrate a traditional midwestern Christmas in the winter of 1890 with a visit from Uncle Levi and his family. All of their wishes come true: it snows, unexpectedly, so they have a white Christmas; there are plenty of pleasing presents under the tree; the holiday meal is fantastic; and Uncle Levi brings a special gift for Papa. This is a beautiful story of family life in a simpler time, but with all the timeless magic of Christmas.

E+/Cos

The Best Way to Play [131]

Written by Bill Cosby
Illustrated by Varnette P. Honeywood

Hardcover and softcover: Cartwheel, Scholastic
Published 1997

Little Bill and his friends are keen fans of the television show *Space Explorer,* so when Space Captain Zeke, the show's star, promotes a new video game based on the show, the friends all run home to ask their parents to buy it.

Only Andrew is successful in getting a copy of the game, but he is happy to share it with his friends. It doesn't take long before the kids have mastered the game and are bored again. That's when they turn to an imaginative game, pretending that they are Space Explorers, and discover that their play is far more fun than the video game. Other books in the Little Bill series are: *The Day I Saw My Father Cry, The Day I Was Rich* [160], *Hooray for The Dandelion Warriors!, The Meanest Thing to Say* [246], *Money Troubles* [255], *My Big Lie* [258], *One Dark and Scary Night* [272], *Shipwreck Sunday, Super-Fine Valentine* [317], *The Treasure Hunt* [325], and *The Worst Day of My Life*.

Bigmama's [132]

Written and illustrated by Donald Crews Easy Cre

Hardcover and softcover: Greenwillow
Published 1991

A grown man fondly reminisces about his family's annual trip to Cottondale, Florida, to visit Bigmama, his grandmother. She wasn't big; they called her Bigmama because she was their mama's mother. Visiting her farm was the highlight of his summers. Memories of playing on Bigmama's farm with his brothers and sisters and large family dinners are nostalgically presented. The sequel to this book is *Shortcut* [v1-275].

Billy and Belle [133]

Written and illustrated by Sarah Garland

Hardcover: Reinhardt, Viking Penguin
Published 1992

Little sister Belle is going to school with her big brother Billy today under a special arrangement because Mom and Dad are going to the hospital to deliver their new baby. It's a great day to take Belle because it is pet day at school and all of the children are bringing their favorite pets to show and tell. Everything is going fine until Belle, looking for her pet spider, opens and overturns all of the cages and boxes, releasing the chaotic menagerie of pets onto the playground. This fun, spirited story about a biracial family is illustrated in a colorful comic-strip style.

Billy the Great [134]

Written by Rosa Guy
Illustrated by Caroline Binch

Hardcover: Delacorte
Published 1991

As young Billy grows, his proud parents are amazed by everything he does and continually speculate on his great future. Perhaps he will become a doctor, a professor, or even a great soccer player. But Billy is already a great person, which he demonstrates when he makes friends with his new neighbor, Rod. Billy's parents consider Rod and his parents to be unsuitable as friends because they are a blue-collar family, and white. Billy, however, accepts and appreciates Rod for the fine person he is, setting an example of inclusion for his parents.

Birthday [135]

Written and illustrated by John Steptoe

Softcover: Henry Holt
Published 1972

Javaka Shatu is celebrating his eighth birthday. Before his birth, Javaka's parents immigrated from America to the town of Yoruba, where they thought that as black people, they could live a better life. Family, neighbors, and friends are all coming to a party in celebration of the special occasion. Javaka feels so positive about his home and the fellowship his family shares with their neighbors that, for his birthday, he wishes they could all live together forever.

Black Cowboy, Wild Horses: A True Story [136]

Written by Julius Lester
Illustrated by Jerry Pinkney

Hardcover: Dial, Penguin Putnam
Published 1998

The legendary Bob Lemmons rode his way to cowboy fame as a former slave who could track wild horses better than anyone. In this true story, young readers will ride with Bob as he methodically tracks a herd of wild mustangs, then slowly and patiently integrates himself into the herd until they hardly notice him. When the time is right, Bob and his own horse, Warrior, challenge the lead stallion for control of the herd. That battle won, Bob and Warrior lead the unwitting herd to the corral as the astonished crowd cheers the accomplishment. Intense watercolor paintings accompany the story.

> "*Throughout that day and the next he rode with the horses. For Bob there was only the bulging of the horses' dark eyes, the quivering of their flesh, the rippling of muscles and bending of bones in their bodies. He was now sky and plains and grass and river and horse.*"

Black Is Brown Is Tan [137]

Written by Arnold Adoff
Illustrated by Emily McCully

Hardcover and softcover: HarperCollins
Published 1973

The children of a black mother and a white father happily express their pride in themselves and their dedicated parents in this poetic text. They are neither black nor white, but wonderful shades of brown and tan. Their blended faces reflect both of their parents, who share a happy house that is full of love.

Boundless Grace [138]   *Easy Hof*

Written by Mary Hoffman   **Reading Rainbow** Review Book
llustrated by Caroline Binch

Hardcover: Dial
Published 1995

Grace is torn between excitement and apprehension as she prepares to visit her father, whom she barely remembers, and his new family in Africa. Once she arrives, her emotions are on a roller coaster—from insecurity about her place in her father's home to guilt for having left her mother back in the United States and finally, mistrust of her stepmother. Over time, Grace adjusts to her dual-family situation and learns that she has control over her role in each family. Vibrant illustrations of Grace in Africa are a picture journal of her adventure. This book is the sequel to *Amazing Grace* [v1-121] and is followed by *Starring Grace*, a chapter book.

J/398.47/San

The Boy and the Ghost [139]

Written by Robert D. San Souci
Illustrated by J. Brian Pinkney

Hardcover: Simon & Schuster
Published 1989

> "*The ghost led the little boy to a lonely spot far from the house. Stopping under a huge sycamore tree, the ghost pointed with his right hand to the ground near its roots. 'Dig there,' he commanded.*"

Young Thomas leaves his parents' farm to find work to earn money for his struggling family. His parents offer him two simple pieces of advice as he departs: First, to always be polite and generous to everyone, and second, to always be brave and honest. When Thomas meets an old man along the way, he politely invites the other traveler to join him and then generously shares his small meal with the old fellow. The old man tells Thomas that he can earn a fortune if he is able to spend an entire night, from sunset to sunrise, in a haunted house on the hill. Thomas goes to the house and is confronted by the ghost, but remembers his parents' second lesson. Through his bravery and honesty, Thomas helps the ghost find eternal peace and wins the ghost's treasure.

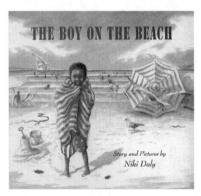

The Boy on the Beach [140]

Written and illustrated by Niki Daly

Hardcover: Margaret K. McElderry, Simon & Schuster
Published 1999

Young Joe accompanies his parents on a trip to the beach. The three enjoy an afternoon splashing and frolicking in the surf until Joe becomes bored and decides to run down the beach in search of something new. Before long he discovers an old abandoned boat, half buried in the sand, that becomes the stage for his imaginative adventure. But before he knows it, Joe looks up and realizes that he is lost among the sand dunes. His cries for help are answered by a new friend, who helps him reunite with his parents.

The Boy Who Didn't Believe in Spring [141]

Written by Lucille Clifton
Illustrated by Brinton Turkle

Softcover: Puffin, Penguin Putnam
Published 1973

King Shabazz is a very hip, street-wise kid. Based on his urban experience, he just doesn't believe in spring, the season of renewal. When he is told that spring is just around the corner, he decides to take a walk around the block with his best friend, just to see if he can find it. As the two walk the city streets, there is no trace of spring until they happen upon an empty lot, a very unlikely place to find spring. But evidence of the coming season abounds, changing the young boy's mind. ***Nonstandard English.***

Brothers of the Knight [142]

Easy All

Written by Debbie Allen
Illustrated by Kadir Nelson

Hardcover: Dial Books for Young Readers
Published 1999

Reverend Knight is unable to unravel a mystery in his own household. Every night his twelve sons go to bed behind a locked door and presumably sleep through the night. Yet every morning he finds twelve pairs of filthy, worn-out shoes at the foot of their beds. It takes a whimsical new nanny to solve the mystery. Young readers will enjoy this witty retelling of "The Twelve Dancing Princesses," narrated by the family dog, and the hip, colorful imagery of the illustrations.

> **"**T*he brothers danced their way 'cross the rooftops. Steppin' and stompin'. The moon gave everything a magical glow, as if they were dancing on the Milky Way."*

The Bus Ride [143]

Written by William Miller
Illustrated by John Ward

Hardcover: Lee & Low
Published 1998

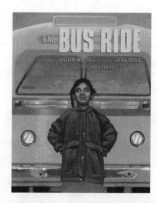

Rosa Parks wrote a short, inspiring introduction to this story, which is loosely based on her own historic actions. In this story, young Sara does not understand why she, her mother, and other African Americans cannot ride in the front of the bus as the white people do. One day, out of curiosity, she walks to the front of the bus just to see what's so special. Then, out of defiance, she stays there until she is bodily removed by a police officer. Her brave action sets the wheels in motion for a boycott by black riders and the political and social changes that follow.

THE CREATORS

George Ford Jr.

ILLUSTRATOR

"For an illustrator whose subject is the portrayal of black life and black children, it is important to use the story as a beginning, an opportunity to arouse in himself, and express to his readers, those broader human qualities that have helped us to survive this long—those qualities that are positive, full of energy and enthusiasm. All of these things I hope come out automatically, and inspire, and uplift, the young people who read the books."

OUR FAVORITES

Bright Eyes, Brown Skin [vl-16]

Good Night Baby [43]

The Story of Ruby Bridges [vl-280]

Wild, Wild Hair [vl-306]

Willie's Wonderful Pet [112]

Bye, Mis' Lela [144]

Written by Dorothy Carter
Illustrated by Harvey Stevenson

Hardcover: Frances Foster Books, Farrar, Straus and Giroux
Published 1998

A little girl affectionately known as Sugar Plum to her baby-sitter enjoys the security of Mis' Lela's care while her mama goes to work. Mis' Lela is a kind and warm-hearted woman who lovingly cares for the child day after day. When Mis' Lela passes away, the young girl learns that death means no more hearing, no more seeing, no more eating, and no more toiling. Even though Mis' Lela has passed into her long sleep, the sensitive child remembers her fondly for the love they shared.

Can I Pray with My Eyes Open? [145]

Written by Susan Taylor Brown
Illustrated by Garin Baker

Hardcover: Hyperion
Published 1999

A young girl wonders how and when it is appropriate to pray. Her questions, presented in verse, seem to be addressed to God. This girl, who is depicted in a series of extraordinary paintings, has a real need to know if it is okay to pray while she roller blades, builds castles on the beach, or even climbs a tree. The answer for her and all children is "There's no wrong time or place to pray."

> "*I wondered how and when and where was the perfect way to say a prayer. Must every prayer be one that's spoken? And can I pray with my eyes open?*"

Carolina Shout! [146]

Easy Sch

Written by Alan Schroeder
Illustrated by Bernie Fuchs

Hardcover: Dial Books for Young Readers, Penguin
Published 1995

Young Delia is enchanted by the sounds of her city that blend together to make music. From her house in Charleston, South Carolina, she can hear the background "Shack-a-lack-a-lack" of the railroad workers, the "Whomp, bidda-bay!" of the carpenters, and the "Chickama, Chickama, Craney Crow" of the jump ropers. Then the cries of the street vendors harmonize together to create the familiar melodies of the city. While these sounds are from an era long past, the sepia-toned illustrations and the phonetic descriptions of the sounds will help young readers imagine this place and time.

Jane Resh Thomas · ILLUSTRATED BY Raul Colón

Celebration! [147]

Written by Jane Resh Thomas
Illustrated by Raul Colón

Easy Tho

Hardcover: Hyperion Books for Children
Published 1997

Young Maggie's grandmother, uncles, aunts, and many cousins gather in her backyard for the annual Fourth of July family picnic. There is plenty of food, drink, gossip, swimming, and games for everyone. But Maggie's favorite event comes at the end of the evening, when they light their sparklers.

Celebration Song [148]

Written by James Berry
Illustrated by Louise Brierley

Hardcover: Simon & Schuster
Published 1994

The Virgin Mary, a young Caribbean woman, celebrates the first birthday of her precious son, Jesus, with a lyrical song about his wondrous birth. The simple words tell the jubilant story, and the paintings of Mary and her baby in a Caribbean setting are unusual but special.

J/398.2/San

Cendrillon: A Caribbean Cinderella [149]

Written by Robert D. San Souci
Illustrated by Brian Pinkney

Hardcover: Simon & Schuster
Published 1998

The tale of Cinderella is told with a Caribbean twist from the point of view of the godmother, a washerwoman. This version parallels the traditional tale, except that Cendrillon loses and later reclaims an embroidered slipper rather than a glass one. The vibrant illustrations of the colorful Caribbean characters help capture the magic of the story.

Children of Color Storybook Bible [150]

Interpreted and illustrated by Victor Hogan

Hardcover: Thomas Nelson
Published 1997

More than sixty stories from the Old and New Testament are told in contemporary English for young readers. Each story is three to five pages long, and the biblical characters—Adam and Eve, Moses, Ruth and Naomi, and even Jesus—are black. The stories are simply told to help foster an early understanding of the Bible and appreciation for the life lessons it teaches. Each story is footnoted with scriptural references so young readers or parents can easily refer to the biblical text. This book is equally suited for Sunday school study or bedtime storytelling.

Children of Long Ago [151]

Written by Lessie Jones Little
Illustrated by Jan Spivey Gilchrist

Hardcover: Philomel Books
Published 1988

Delicate watercolors are the perfect complement to this selection of poems about the life and times of children in the early 1900s. Today's children may be interested to know about a child's life in simpler times when there were no televisions, video games, or other modern amusements. The children in these seventeen poems made paper dolls, played with the farm animals, and read by lantern light.

Christopher, Please Clean Up Your Room! [152]

Written by Itah Sadu
Illustrated by Roy Condy

Softcover: Firefly
Published 1993

In this jovial story, young Christopher's room is such a mess that even the roaches won't go in. Despite pleas and warnings from his parents, Christopher steadfastly refuses to clean up his "funky" space. Finally, the goldfish, who live in a bowl of stagnant water in his room, make a pact with the roaches to convince Christopher to clean up his act. One night the roaches come by the thousands to Christopher's room. They cover him and his bed and then arrange themselves to spell out their instructions, "Christopher, tidy up your room now!" Terrified by the event, Christopher immediately jumps into action, cleaning, clearing, and picking up the mess.

Cocoa Ice [153]

Written by Diana Appelbaum
Illustrated by Holly Meade

Hardcover: Orchard
Published 1997

A little girl in Santo Domingo in the late 1800s describes the slow process that her family goes through to make chocolate from the cocoa beans that grow on their land. They patiently wrap the beans in banana leaves, dry them in the sun, roast them, and finally crush them into a fine chocolate powder. At the same time, a little girl in Maine details her family's painstaking ice-making process. They tap the ice freezing in the river, scrape snow from the river's frozen crust, and cut the blocks of ice. Yankee trading schooners bring the ice to the Caribbean island in exchange for the chocolate, which provides the ingredients of a special treat for the girls in both countries—chocolate ices.

Come On, Rain! [154]

Easy Hes

Written by Karen Hesse
Illustrated by Jon J. Muth

Hardcover: Scholastic
Published 1999

It has been three long weeks since it rained in the city, and young Tess and her neighbors are hoping that the rain will come soon and bring relief from the oppressive heat. Tess may have been the one to inspire the rain that finally falls by getting her girlfriends together, all in their swimsuits. When the rain comes they are ready to skip, jump, and sing in celebration of the long-awaited event.

The Coming of Night: A Yoruba Tale from West Africa [155]

Written by James Riordan
Illustrated by Jenny Stow

Hardcover: Millbrook Press
Published 1999

Aje, the daughter of the river goddess, Yemoya, leaves her watery home to marry a chief on the earth. There is only daylight on the earth—no night!

Aje misses the darkness that she knew in the river and begs her husband to find night for her. The compliant chief dispatches Crocodile and Hippopotamus to the bottom of the river to get night from Yemoya. They return with a sack full of night—a whole new world of darkness that includes insects, moths, and bats. And that, according to this traditional tale, is how nighttime came to be.

The Conjure Woman [156]

Written by William Miller
Illustrated by Terea D. Shaffer

Hardcover: Atheneum
Published 1996

People fear the conjure woman, Madame Zina, because of her mysterious, magical ways. But when the doctors and preachers cannot help, people inevitably call on Madame Zina for healing. In this richly illustrated book, Madame Zina receives a young boy, fallen ill with fever, to help cure him. Magically, Madame Zina and the boy rise above the earth and are whisked into the night, over the fields and the ocean, back to their homeland in Africa. There, in a village, the young boy is surrounded by the healing rituals and medicines of his ancestors. When he returns home, he is well, with only a vague memory of his experience. Or was it just a dream?

Courtney's Birthday Party [157]

Written by Dr. Loretta Long
Illustrated by Ron Garnett

Softcover: Just Us
Published 1998

Best friends Courtney and Diana live in the same town, go to the same school, are in the same class, and like all the same things. But they are different. Courtney is white and Diana is black, a fact that never affected either of them until Courtney begins to plan her seventh birthday party. Courtney's mom tries to keep Courtney from inviting Diana to the party because of the difference. Diana's mother understands that bigotry is in action and tries to protect and comfort her deeply disappointed daughter. But the girls' friendship and commitment to each other prevails when they both insist on sharing the special occasion together.

THE CREATORS

Elizabeth Fitzgerald Howard

AUTHOR

"I read voraciously, constantly. As a fifth and sixth grader my favorite book was *Little Women*. I became Jo and at the same time she was my best friend. Books showed me I could fly. But what a loss that I couldn't soar with Angela Johnson's or Virginia Hamilton's feisty protagonists as best friends, too."

OUR FAVORITES

Mac and Marie and the Train Toss Surprise [vl-223]

Papa Tells Chita a Story [278]

Virgie Goes to School with Us Boys [334]

What's in Aunt Mary's Room? [337]

When Will Sarah Come? [111]

The Crab Man [158]

Written by Patricia E. Van West
Illustrated by Cedric Lucas ☆ 98

Hardcover: Turtle, Group West
Published 1998

Young Neville has a crisis of conscience when he discovers that the hermit crabs that he has been trapping for the crab man are being raced for the entertainment of tourists at a local resort. Dismayed by the cruelty, he steals back the crabs and chooses to let them go. His actions cost Neville his one dollar per day fee but buy him the knowledge that he did the right thing.

Cumbayah [159]

Illustrated by Floyd Cooper

Hardcover: William Morrow
Published 1998

The words and music to this well-known folk song are accompanied by poignant illustrations of children. The word *cumbayah,* translated as "come by here," comes from the dialect of the Gullah people of the Georgia Sea Islands. The song, a classic in the American music repertoire, can now be attributed to its African roots.

The Day I Was Rich [160]

E+/cos

Written by Bill Cosby
Illustrated by Varnette P. Honeywood

Hardcover and Softcover: Cartwheel, Scholastic
Published 1999

Little Bill is rich, if only for a day, when he discovers a huge glittering stone at the playground. He and his friends examine the huge gem and decide that it must be the largest diamond in the world, worth tens of millions of dollars. Since Little Bill has offered to share his wealth with his friends, they each imagine what they will do with their share. As it turns out, the discovery is only a glass paperweight, but the thrill of the possible was enough to make their day. Other books in the Little Bill series include *The Best Way to Play* [131], *Hooray for the Dandelion Warriors!, The Day I Saw My Father Cry, The Meanest Thing to Say* [246], *Money Troubles* [255], *My Big Lie* [258], *One Dark and Scary Night* [272], *Shipwreck Sunday, Super-Fine Valentine* [317], *The Treasure Hunt* [325], and *The Worst Day of My Life.*

Day of Delight: A Jewish Sabbath in Ethiopia [161]

Written by Maxine Rose Schur
Illustrated by Brian Pinkney

Hardcover: Dial Books for Young Readers, Penguin
Published 1994

This finely illustrated book offers a glimpse into the village life of a group of black Jews known as the Beta Israel, who have lived for thousands of years in the high country of Ethiopia. This important picture book opens up the world for young readers by describing the customs and practices of this obscure group of black people as they prepare for the Jewish Sabbath, the Day of Delight.

Dear Willie Rudd, [162]

Written by Libba Moore Gray
Illustrated by Peter M. Fiore

Hardcover: Simon & Schuster
Published 1993

In this poignant story, Miss Elizabeth, a white woman, remembers back fifty years to her childhood, when Willie Rudd was her family's housekeeper. She sits down to write a letter to finally say thank you to the black woman who was so special to her at the time. Willie Rudd will never receive the letter, because she has passed away, but Miss Elizabeth flies the letter to the skies on the tail of a kite, satisfied that she has made her peace with the special older woman.

Don't Be My Valentine: A Classroom Mystery [163]

Written by Joan M. Lexau
Illustrated by Syd Hoff

Softcover: HarperTrophy, HarperCollins
Published 1999

Amy Lou is a bit of a know-it-all with her classmates, especially Sam, who resents her for her meddling. When the teacher instructs the class to make Valentine's Day cards to exchange the next day, Sam makes a particularly mean one for Amy Lou. But somehow the offensive card is delivered to the teacher instead. Sam is embarrassed by the mix-up and confused about how it all happened, but learns a valuable lesson about civility and kindness. The book is in the I Can Read series for new readers, featuring large, well-spaced print and simple words.

Down the Road [164]

Easy Sch

Written by Alice Schertle
Illustrated by E. B. Lewis ☆ 93

Hardcover: Browndeer, Harcourt Brace
Published 1995

The first time her parents trust her to go down the road to buy eggs for breakfast, little Hetty plans to be a model of responsibility. She plots her path to avoid any obstacles that may cause her to stumble and break the eggs. She walks smoothly down the road, over a log, and through a stream to protect her precious cargo, until, almost home, she is distracted by a tree full of crisp, fresh apples. As she reaches to pick the apples, the worst happens—all the eggs break. Humiliated, Hetty climbs up the tree to pout. When she doesn't return home on time, her parents go looking for her and find her in the tree. In a pure act of love they join her in the tree for a moment of family unity.

Duke Ellington: The Piano Prince and His Orchestra [165]

Written by Andrea Davis Pinkney
Illustrated by Brian Pinkney

Caldecott Honor Book
Coretta Scott King Honor: Illustrator

Hardcover: Hyperion
Published 1998

J/B/ Ellington

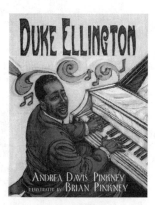

King of the Keys, Piano Prince, and Edward Kennedy Ellington are all names associated with the one and only Duke Ellington. This picture-book biography presents an overview of Ellington's magical career from his early days as a pianist in New York honky-tonks to his triumph as a composer and orchestra leader. Brightly colored scratchboard paintings help tell the story of the musical icon.

Easter Parade [166]

Written by Eloise Greenfield
Illustrated by Jan Spivey Gilchrist

Hardcover: Hyperion
Published 1998

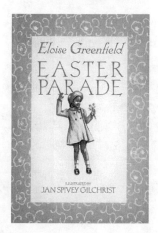

Two young cousins—one in Washington, D.C., and the other in Chicago—prepare for Easter parades in their respective cities. Neither child is quite sure of what to expect, since their concepts of parades involve marching bands, floats, and balloons, but each is excited about the preparations. The two and their mothers make new dresses and get shiny black shoes to wear on Easter Sunday, when they will join in the procession of finely dressed church-goers.

J/Rosen

Elijah's Angel: A Story for Chanukah and Christmas [167]

Written by Michael J. Rosen
Illustrated by Aminah Brenda Lynn Robinson

Hardcover: Harcourt Brace Javonovich
Published 1992

Elijah, an eighty-year-old black barber, and Michael, a nine-year-old Jewish boy, are two unlikely friends in this unusual holiday story. Young Michael is intrigued by the beautiful wooden carvings that Elijah, an ex-slave, creates in his workshop. When Elijah offers the boy a wooden angel, Michael is disturbed because he believes the angel will be regarded as a "graven image" by his Jewish family. His parents help Michael understand that the angel need not have any religious significance and that he can accept it as simply a token of his friendship with the old man. This story is based on an event in the life of Elijah Pierce (1892–1984), an African American folk artist whose work is exhibited in the Columbus Museum of Art.

Enid and the Dangerous Discovery [168]

Written by Cynthia G. Williams
Illustrated by Betty Harper

Hardcover: Broadman & Holman
Published 1999

Enid's awareness is heightened when a schoolmate is suspended for bringing a toy gun to school. Even though it is only a toy, the school authorities enforce their "zero tolerance" policy. Later the same day, Enid and several of her friends find a real gun in the alley. They are cautioned not to touch it, and the police are called to remove it. The story is an important one for young readers in this day and age, reminding them of the danger guns pose and teaching responsible gun behavior.

Explore Black History with Wee Pals [169]

Written and illustrated by Morrie Turner

Softcover: Just Us
Published 1998

The Wee Pals, comic-strip characters who first appeared in *Ebony* and *Black World* magazines in 1964, are the vehicle for delivering a dose of African

American history to young readers. The accomplishments of over seventy prominent African Americans from all walks of life, including Angela Davis, Jesse Jackson, Thurgood Marshall, and James Farmer, are discussed by the Wee Pals in a series of short comic strips. The format and brevity of each vignette are sure to attract young readers.

Faraway Drums [170]

Written by Virginia Kroll
Illustrated by Floyd Cooper

Hardcover: Little Brown
Published 1998

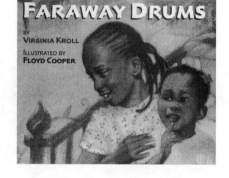

Jamila is left to baby-sit for her younger sister, Zakiya, while their mother goes to work. When the sounds of their urban neighborhood scare little Zakiya, Jamila helps her translate the sounds into an African fantasy. The young child is comforted by imagining the sound of screamin' brakes and trumpetin' horns as elephants coming to a watering hole and the screechin' sirens as monkeys playing in the treetops. Jamila is the picture of a loving and responsible big sister. ***Nonstandard English.***

Father's Day Blues: What Do You Do about Father's Day When All You Have Are Mothers? [171]

Written by Irene Smalls ☆ 150
Illustrated by Kevin McGovern

Hardcover: Longmeadow
Published 1995

Cheryl Blues has to write a composition about Father's Day but finds it difficult, since her dad doesn't live with her. As she struggles with the assignment, Cheryl consults her grandmother, her aunt, and her mother, who each offer a different philosophical explanation for her missing father. But Cheryl isn't satisfied until she realizes that she is special and loved in the context of her own family situation. She also clearly recognizes that her father's absence has nothing to do with her, an understanding that many children in single-family homes may need.

First Palm Trees [172]

Written by James Berry
Illustrated by Greg Couch

Hardcover: Simon & Schuster
Published 1997

The king has offered a sizable reward to the one who can create tall palm trees in his land. Anancy, the spider man, goes into partnership with the sun spirit, but then must recruit the water spirit, earth spirit, and air spirit to help him. He is determined to win the reward, but disappointed that he must share it with so many partners. Anancy waits and waits for the spirits to deliver the promised trees. When they finally do, thirty other villagers step forward to claim the reward. Since neither Anancy nor his competitors can prove that they were the one who brought the trees to the land, the king withdraws the reward and invites everyone to join in a feast. Yet according to this traditional African folk tale, everyone knows that it was Anancy who brought the first palm trees to earth.

Five Brave Explorers [173]

Written by Wade Hudson
Illustrated by Ron Garnett

Softcover: Scholastic
Published 1995

The accomplishments of five African Americans are told in short stories detailing their daring explorations and contributions to their fields. Esteban Dorantes was a Spanish explorer who was one of the first to explore America in the early 1500s. Matthew A. Henson was a fearless early explorer of the North Pole. James Pierce Breckworth was an American trailblazer. Jean DuSable was the founder of Chicago, and Mae Jemison was the first African American woman in space. Two other books in the Great Black Heroes series are *Five Brilliant Scientists* and *Five Notable Inventors* [v1-188].

Fly, Bessie, Fly [174]

J/B/ Coleman

Written by Lynn Joseph
Illustrated by Yvonne Buchanan

Hardcover: Simon & Schuster
Published 1998

Bessie Coleman dared to dream of the impossible until she found a way to make her dream a reality. The story of Bessie's monumental accomplishment is told in this inspiring book. Bessie overcame the financial shortcomings, cynicism, sexism, and racial barriers that stood between her and her dream of learning to fly. Her tenacity led her to become, in 1921, the first black woman aviator in the world, and the first black American ever to earn a pilot's license.

Fly, Eagle, Fly: An African Tale [175]

J/ 398.2 / Gre

Retold by Christopher Gregorowski
Illustrated by Niki Daly

Hardcover: Simon & Schuster
Published 2000

A profound tale with a strong moral is shared in this beautiful picture book. A farmer rescues a lost eagle chick and takes it home to live among his own chickens in the chicken yard. The bird behaves like a chicken—walking like one, clucking like one, thinking like one, and even eating like one. But when the eagle is taken away from the other chickens in the yard, high into the mountains, it spreads its wings and soars like the eagle it is.

Follow the Drinking Gourd: A Story of the Underground Railroad [176]

Written by Bernardine Connelly
Illustrated by Yvonne Buchanan

Hardcover: Rabbit Ears, Simon & Schuster
Published 1997

Eleven-year-old Mary and her family flee their Southern plantation in search of freedom. With the help of Peg Leg Joe they follow their own wits, the Little Gourd constellation, and the natural landmarks that were identified in the lyrics of a slave escape song. Expressive watercolor illustrations vividly portray the daring escape.

Gettin' Through Thursday [177]

Written by Melrose Cooper
Illustrated by Nneka Bennett

Hardcover: Lee & Low
Published 1998

Money is always tight by the time Thursday comes along, because Mama doesn't get paid until Friday. Every Thursday is the same—the family always runs out of something and Mama has to help them find a way to make do, like the time she taught them to use baking soda when the toothpaste ran out. When André brings home an honor roll report card on a Thursday, he is disappointed because he knows that there will be no money to sponsor the celebration of his accomplishment. But Mama comes through with her most creative and loving improvisation to save the day.

Ginger Brown: The Nobody Boy [178]

J/Wyeth

Written by Sharon Dennis Wyeth ☆ 201
Illustrated by Cornelius Van Wright and Ying-Hwa Hu ☆ 181

Softcover: First Stepping Stone, Random House
Published 1997

Young Ginger Brown becomes a tentative friend of an even younger boy while they each visit their neighboring grandfathers' farms during the summer. When the two fall out over a silly misunderstanding, their grandfathers try to mend the relationship. The only problem is that the grandfathers had fallen out with each other decades before over an equally silly misunderstanding. Young readers can judge this situation for themselves in this easy-to-read chapter book. This book is a sequel to *Ginger Brown: Too Many Houses* [179].

Ginger Brown: Too Many Houses [179]

J/Wyeth

Written by Sharon Dennis Wyeth ☆ 201
Illustrated by Cornelius Van Wright and Ying-Hwa Hu ☆ 181

Softcover: First Stepping Stone, Random House
Published 1996

Young Ginger Brown's life is being turned upside down because her parents are getting a divorce. She and her mommy are staying with her grandparents for a while until they can get their own apartment. Daddy is still in the family home, but he will be getting a new apartment, too. Ginger even spends a few weeks in the summer with her other grandparents on their farm. Sadly, there are just too many houses for one little girl who just wants one home and one family. This easy-to-read chapter book simply explores one of the problems of divorce from a child's perspective. *Ginger Brown: The Nobody Boy* [178] is a sequel to this book.

Girls Together [180]

Written by Sherley Anne Williams
Illustrated by Synthia Saint James

Hardcover: Harcourt Brace
Published 1999

Five friends from the city get together on a Saturday afternoon. They leave the projects, where they live, to get away from their pesky little brothers and to see the suburbs, where, unlike their own neighborhood, there are houses and lots of trees. The story is simply told in large text and embellished with brightly colored block illustrations.

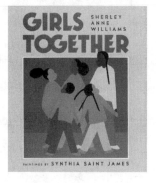

Glo Goes Shopping [181]

Written by Cheryl Willis Hudson
Illustrated by Cathy Johnson

Softcover: Just Us
Published 1999

Glo, a thoughtful young girl, goes on a shopping expedition to the local mall to find a birthday gift for her friend, Nandi. She considers everything from plants and pets to skates and shoes, but she knows that whatever she selects must be both practical and fun. Glo finally settles on a perfect gift that young readers will discover at the end of this colorfully illustrated, easy-to-read story.

God Inside of Me [182]

Written by Della Reese
Illustrated by Yvonne Buchanan

Hardcover: Jump at the Sun, Hyperion
Published 1999

Kenisha is totally exasperated by her little brother's dawdling on the way to church. Then her patience is tested even further by her animated toys. Rabunny, her stuffed animal, is lazy. Rockeroon, a doll, asks too many questions. Clown is too wishy-washy. As Kenisha reaches the end of her rope, Dolly Dear, her favorite doll, reminds her of the lessons she has learned at Sunday school and helps her apply the virtues of patience and understanding to her own life.

J/811/ Hop

Good Rhymes, Good Times [183]

Written by Lee Bennett Hopkins
Illustrated by Frané Lessac

Hardcover: HarperCollins
Published 1995

Twenty-one poems and vibrant illustrations capture some of the fleeting thoughts and feelings of children. In "Valentine Feelings," a child expresses a "flippy, fizzy, whoopy, whizzy" feeling when she thinks of her valentine. In "Nighttime," a child wonders how dreams know when to creep into your head, and in "Winter," a child acknowledges that there is no need to quarrel with winter because winter always wins.

Granddaddy's Gift [184]

Written by Margaree King Mitchell
Illustrated by Larry Johnson

Hardcover: BridgeWater
Published 1997

Little Joe lives through a life-changing experience when she witnesses her granddaddy's stand against racial discrimination. Granddaddy is the first black to register to vote in their rural Mississippi town, and he and the family endure humiliation and threats from the townspeople as a result of his action. Little Joe's love and respect for her granddaddy deepen as a result of the experience, but more importantly, Little Joe begins to appreciate the value of education and standing up for what is right.

THE CREATORS

E. B. Lewis

ILLUSTRATOR

"In this industry I think that we, as children's book illustrators and others, paint a sensitive and accurate picture of all the various cultures we portray whether it be with our brushes or our pens."

OUR FAVORITES

The Bat Boy and His Violin [128]

Down the Road [164]

The Jazz of Our Street [214]

The Magic Tree: A Folktale from Nigeria [242]

Virgie Goes to School with Us Boys [334]

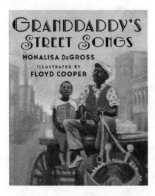

Granddaddy's Street Songs [185]

Written by Monalisa DeGross
Illustrated by Floyd Cooper

Hardcover: Jump at the Sun, Hyperion
Published 1999

Roddy joins his grandfather, a street produce vendor (an "arabber"), for a day on the streets of Baltimore. As they travel their route, calling out their lyrical songs to attract customers, "Wa-a-a-ter-melons, I got wa-a-a-termelons. Come git my wa-a-ter-melons," Roddy enjoys looking at an old photo album and hearing stories from Granddaddy about the good old days. The affection between the two is apparent in the soft watercolor illustrations. ***Nonstandard English.***

Grandma's Hands [186]

Written and illustrated by Dolores Johnson

Hardcover: Marshall Cavendish
Published 1998

A young boy is delivered to his Grandma's farm by his mother when she decides that she must leave him for a while to "get herself together." At first the transition is difficult. He misses his mother, and Grandma is coarse and doesn't smile very often. But over time the grandmother and child bond through shared meals, chores, and meaningful talks. When his mother comes to get him many months later, he feels that he is being torn away again, from a home he has come to love and from Grandma's rough but loving hands.

Grandpa, Is Everything Black Bad? [187]

Written by Sandy Lynne Holman
Illustrated by Lela Kometiani

Hardcover: Culture Co-Op
Published 1998

"*Be proud of your dark skin. It represents a proud people and black is truly a beautiful color. It was passed down to you by Africans who lived before and your heritage is like no other.*"

Young Montsho becomes insecure about his own blackness when he observes that the color black seems to represent the worst—black and scary, black for funerals, black cats, and black sheep. He asks his grandpa, "Is everything black bad?" Grandpa wisely affirms Montsho by telling him about their proud black heritage, rooted in Africa, including stories about the dark-skinned Africans who developed writing, mathematics, calendars, astronomy, and religion and who built the great pyramids.

Haircuts at Sleepy Sam's [188]

Written by Michael R. Strickland
Illustrated by Keaf Holliday

Hardcover: Boyds Mills
Published 1998

Three attractively illustrated brothers get a delightful surprise when they take their weekly trip to Sleepy Sam's Barber Shop. Every week their mom gives them each a note, directing Sam to give them an Afro-cut. But Afro-cuts are old-fashioned, and the boys want a fresher look. Today is their day, when Sleepy Sam takes the initiative to update their look to the more popular bald fade.

The Hatseller and the Monkeys [189]

Easy Dia

Written and illustrated by Baba Wagué Diakité

Hardcover: Scholastic
Published 1999

BaMusa, a West African hatseller, uses a little monkey psychology when a group of the mischievous creatures threatens his business. While he rests under a mango tree, a family of monkeys descends upon the sleeping merchant and steals all of the hats he intends to sell at the market. When he discovers his loss, he yells up at the monkeys, but they just yell back. He throws a branch and then stones at them, but they just throw mangoes back. Cleverly BaMusa decides upon a plan of action to retrieve his merchandise. Young readers will laugh at BaMusa's dilemma, which can easily be play-acted for more fun. Colorful Afrocentric illustrations accompany this delightful tale.

The Hired Hand: An African American Folktale [190]

Retold by Robert D. San Souci
Illustrated by Jerry Pinkney

J/398.21/San

Hardcover: Dial
Published 1997

Young Sam is shiftless, lazy, and no help to his father, Old Sam, at their saw mill. He is so worthless that Old Sam hires a man to pick up the slack. Young Sam treats the new hired hand badly, ordering him around and criticizing his work. But one day young Sam witnesses the hired hand performing a miraculous deed, magically returning an old man to his youth. Young Sam tries to use the secret incantation for his own profit, but the results are disastrous. This original African American folktale offers a dramatic lesson of virtue for young readers. **Nonstandard English.**

> "Young Sam wouldn't lift a finger. He put all the work on the hired man, then called him lazy and yelled at him to work faster."

> "Sometimes the truth is told at the wrong time or in the wrong way, or for the wrong reasons. And that can be hurtful. But the honest-to-goodness truth is never wrong."

The Honest-to-Goodness Truth [191]

Written by Patricia C. McKissack
Illustrated by Giselle Potter

Easy Mck

Hardcover: Atheneum
Published 2000

Little Libby vows never to tell a lie, after being caught in one she told to her mama. So all day she tells the painful truth to everyone. She tells everyone, out loud, that Ruthie Mae has a hole in her sock, that Willie hasn't done his homework, and that Daisy forgot her Christmas speech and cried in front of the entire audience. Her friends are totally dismayed at her true but thoughtless announcements. After a little heart-to-heart with Mama, Libby finally understands that although the honest-to-goodness truth is important, it should be told at the right time, in the right way, and for the right reasons. **Nonstandard English.**

Hoops [192]

Written by Robert Burleigh
Illustrated by Stephen T. Johnson

Hardcover: Silver Whistle, Harcourt Brace
Published 1997

Even if you have never played basketball, you will know exactly how it feels to hold the ball and run the court after reading this articulate poem about the game. Young readers will feel the tension, the excitement, and the physical actions of a player through the crisp text and the action-filled illustrations of the game in play.

Hope [193]

Written by Isabell Monk
Illustrated by Janice Lee Porter

Hardcover: Carolrhoda
Published 1999

> "You have your mother's beautiful brown eyes. You have the noble shape of your father's face. Your skin is the color of delicious things."

Young Hope is dismayed when an insensitive neighbor is overheard referring to her as "mixed." Aunt Poogee lovingly explains that as a mixture of her black mother and white father, Hope embodies the joining of two proud heritages—European immigrants and African slave descendants. Hope and other biracial children can take tremendous pride in themselves with this poignant understanding of their roots.

The House with No Door: African Riddle Poems [194]

Written by Brian Swann
Illustrated by Ashley Bryan

J/811/Swa

Hardcover: Brown Deer, Harcourt Brace
Published 1998

Vivid illustrations contain clues and the answers to fourteen poetic riddles that were collected by the author from a variety of African sources. Young readers are challenged to solve the riddles, each of which may have more than one correct answer, through their powers of observation.

How Many Stars in the Sky? [195]

Easy Hor

Written by Lenny Hort
Illustrated by James E. Ransome

Reading Rainbow Review Book

Hardcover: Tambourine
Published 1991

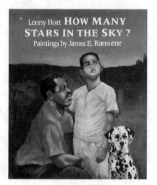

A curious young boy tries to count the stars in the sky from his suburban home, but the task is too overwhelming. So Daddy takes him for a long ride, through the glare of the city lights, into the country where the view is better. The two share a special night during their impossible task, but the experience bonds them in countless other ways in this richly illustrated, warm story.

I Am African American [196]

Written by Ruth Turk

Hardcover: Rosen
Published 1997

Stories from the African American heritage are told in single-page descriptions of various events in black history and cultural topics. Each topical entry—Slavery, Kwanzaa, and Soul Food, for example—is laid out in a dictionary-style format, defining and detailing the item in easy-to-read large print, and is accompanied by a photographic illustration.

THE CREATORS

Cedric Lucas

ILLUSTRATOR

"Books that accurately reflect accounts and experiences of their culture are critical to folklore and preservation of that culture. Children need a truthful relationship with their past to know what the future holds. My drawings serve to enhance the text by creating a mood, an atmosphere that cannot be expressed in words."

OUR FAVORITES

Big Wind Coming [vl-130]

The Crab Man [158]

Frederick Douglass: The Last Days of Slavery [vl-344]

Night Golf [267]

What's in Aunt Mary's Room? [337]

I Can Do It by Myself [197]   J/Lit

Written by Lessie Jones Little and Eloise Greenfield
Illustrated by Carole Byard

Hardcover: Thomas Y. Crowell
Published 1978

Donny is going shopping today for his mother's birthday gift. On his way out he was offended by his older brother's offer to go with him, as if he wasn't old enough to go shopping alone. Then his mother seemed anxious when he announced he was going out. Then two old ladies on the street called him cute, as if he was a baby. Finally, the clerk at the stored demeaned him by calling him "kid." Donny would have taken it all again, if any one of them had been there when, on the way back from the store, he was confronted by a bulldog. But instead he had to stand up and deal with this threatening situation like a big boy!

I Have a Dream: Dr. Martin Luther King, Jr. [198]

Written by Martin Luther King Jr.
Illustrated by various artists

Hardcover: Scholastic
Published 1997

Martin Luther King Jr.'s moving "I Have A Dream" speech is revisited in this beautiful commemorative book. Exquisite illustrations by fifteen talented winners of the Coretta Scott King Award—including Ashley Bryan, Tom Feelings, Pat Cummings, and James Ransome—bring Dr. King's speech to life for young readers, who may be reading these thirty-year-old words for the first time. Coretta Scott King has written a beautifully simple foreword introducing her husband's 1963 speech, and at the back of the book, each illustrator describes his artistic depiction of scenes from the Martin Luther King Jr. era.

> "*I* have a dream that my four little children will one day live in a nation where they will not be judged by the color of their skin but by the content of their character. I have a dream today!"

I Have Another Language: The Language Is Dance [199]

Written and illustrated by Eleanor Schick

Hardcover: Maxwell Macmillan
Published 1992

A young girl expresses her thrill and excitement as she prepares for her first dance recital. Young readers will feel her mounting excitement as she stretches and exercises at dance class and then returns to the theater for makeup and costume. Then, as the music begins and the curtain rises, she expresses in dance the feelings that she cannot express in words. Fine black-and-white pencil drawings further illustrate her joy.

I Love My Hair! [200]

Easy Tar

Written by Natasha Anastasia Tarpley
Illustrated by E. B. Lewis ☆ 93

Hardcover: Little, Brown
Published 1998

Young Keyana is totally satisfied with her head of thick, soft hair. Even as she endures the sometimes painful combing and brushing process, she understands that her hair is special. It can be woven, braided, or beaded into beautiful styles that she loves and that fill her with pride.

Easy Mos

I Want to Be [201]

Written by Thylias Moss
Illustrated by Jerry Pinkney

Softcover: Picture Puffin, Puffin Pied Piper
Published 1993

After careful thought, a little girl knows in infinite detail what she wants to be when she grows up. Her insights and wisdom are beyond her years as she poetically recites the physical characteristics as well as the talents and character traits that she hopes will be hers when she grows up. Soft watercolor illustrations convey the girl's hope and the sense of her possibilities.

If a Bus Could Talk: The Story of Rosa Parks [202]

Written and illustrated by Faith Ringgold J/Bio/Parks

Hardcover: Simon & Schuster
Published 1999

In an imaginative biographical story, young Marcie boards a bus and experiences an eerie event. The bus has no driver, but it is full of riders who are celebrating Rosa Parks's birthday. The riders tell Marcie the story of Rosa's life from childhood through the events that followed her courageous refusal to give up her seat on this very same bus. Marcie's enlightening bus ride climaxes when she actually meets Mrs. Parks, leaving her with a full understanding of why Rosa Parks is known as the mother of the civil rights movement.

If I Only Had a Horn: Young Louis Armstrong [203]

Written by Roxane Orgill
Illustrated by Leonard Jenkins   J/B/Armstrong

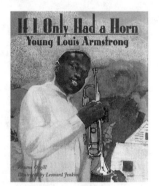

Hardcover: Houghton Mifflin
Published 1997

Some kids know from a very early age what they want to be. Louis Armstrong was one of those, and this story tells about his journey from juvenile delinquent to legendary musician. Louis's interest was born from the streets of New Orleans, where he grew up, and then brought to fruition in a detention center for boys, where he was a member of the band. The illustrations in this book are superbly presented with sharp imagery on muted backgrounds.

Imani and the Flying Africans [204]

Written by Janice Liddell
Illustrated by Linda Nickens

Hardcover: Africa World
Published 1994

While on a road trip from Detroit to Savannah to visit his grandparents and great-grandmother, Imani's mama tells him the incredible story of the Flying Africans. The story, which is still a well-known myth among the African Americans of Georgia's Sea Islands, is about the rebellious African slaves who escaped slavery by actually flying away to Africa. During the telling of the story, Imani learns for the first time that his great-grandmother was once a slave, a revelation that leads him to a surreal dream adventure and encounter with the wise old woman.

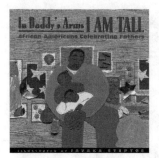

In Daddy's Arms I Am Tall: African Americans Celebrating Fathers [205] J/811/Ind

Written by various poets

Coretta Scott King Award: Illustrator

Illustrated by Javaka Steptoe

Hardcover: Lee & Low
Published 1997

The special bond between fathers and their children is artfully explored by a talented group of African American writers and poets including Carole Boston Weatherford and Dakari Hru. The twelve sensitive poems reflect the love, esteem, and respect that children hold for their fathers. Each poem is interestingly illustrated with a creative torn-paper collage that is embellished with found objects like buttons, burlap, seashells, and tin.

In My Momma's Kitchen [206] Easy Nol

Written by Jerdine Nolen ☆ 126

Illustrated by Colin Bootman

Hardcover: Lothrop, Lee & Shepard
Published 1999

"*And when I finally start to yawn, I know for sure that everything good that happens in my house happens in my momma's kitchen.*"

In eight stories, a delightful little girl reminisces about all the wonderful things that have taken place right in her Momma's kitchen. "First in Line" is about the day her sister received a college scholarship letter, which they read and celebrated in the kitchen. "Nighttime Serenades" is about the sleepless family's late-night gatherings in the kitchen where they all indulged in midnight snacks and each other's company. The heartwarming stories are supported by realistic illustrations.

In the Rainfield Who Is the Greatest? [207]

J/398.2/Ola

Written by Isaac O. Olaleye

Illustrated by Ann Grifalconi

Hardcover: Blue Sky, Scholastic
Published 2000

Wind, Fire, and Rain argue about which of them is the greatest and most powerful. Finally, they agree to a contest to prove once and for all which of them is superior. Wind competes first, blowing across the earth in a destructive fury. It is impressive, but when Fire lights the earth up in flames, Wind cannot put out the inferno. Fire is clearly stronger than Wind. But Rain proves that she is the strongest of all when she sprinkles her gentle but steady waters over the earth, extinguishing the fire. Luminous collage illustrations of the elements, pictured as strong, beautiful black people, give a mythical quality to the story.

In the Time of the Drums [208]

Written by Kim L. Siegelson
Illustrated by Brian Pinkney

Coretta Scott King Award: Illustrator

Hardcover: Jump at the Sun, Hyperion
Published 1999

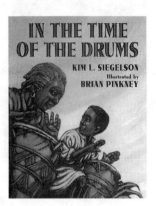

In this story, passed down through the oral tradition of the Sea Island Gullahs, an African-born slave woman, Twi, takes a young boy, Mentu, under her wing. Twi loves and mentors Mentu as if he were her very own. She teaches him about his African heritage, including the music of the drums, and implores him to grow into a strong man who will never let go of his culture. When a slave ship full of Ibo tribesmen lands, Twi joins the rebellious Ibos, leading them into the water for their long walk, across the ocean floor, back to their homeland. Mentu is left behind to testify to the events and to keep the African traditions alive for his people.

Irene and the Big, Fine Nickel [209]

Written by Irene Smalls ☆ 150
Illustrated by Tyrone Geter

Easy Sma

Softcover: Little, Brown
Published 1991

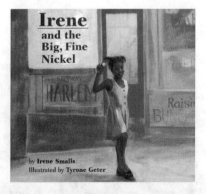

Seven-year-old Irene and her three friends—Lulabelle, Charlene, and Lulamae—have the run of their Harlem neighborhood as they play during a lazy Saturday morning. Then, something happens to make this the "best day ever." Irene spots a shiny nickel in the gutter. Now the four must decide how to spend their small fortune. This urban story, set in the 1950s, is a fine expression of friendship and sharing.

Isn't My Name Magical?: Sister and Brother Poems [210]

Written by James Berry
Illustrated by Shelly Hehenberger

Hardcover: Simon & Schuster
Published 1991

Dreena and Delroy, sister and brother, share a series of exuberant poems that express their unique perspectives on the world. In the first section, full of richly textured illustrations, Dreena's poems range from subjects like "Mom" and "Dad" to observations about her own name in "Isn't My Name Magical?" The next section contains the poetic expressions of her brother, Delroy, an energetic youngster who is the featured character in "Delroy and the Skateboard Roller" and "Delroy the Dance-Explorer."

It's Raining Laughter [211]

Written by Nikki Grimes
Photographs by Myles C. Pinkney

Hardcover: Dial Books for Young Readers, Penguin
Published 1997

This is a captivating photographic essay of children caught in the act of being children. African American kids are shown in their quiet private times, in their vulnerable moments, and as they play. Each picture helps to convey the feelings expressed in the eleven brilliantly simple and sometimes humorous poems. Young readers will love phrases like "goofy giggler" and "good-mood maker" found on these attractive pages.

Jackson Jones and the Puddle of Thorns [212]

Written by Mary Quattlebaum
Illustrated by Melodye Rosales

J/ Fiction/Quattlebaum

Hardcover: Delacorte, Bantam Doubleday Dell
Published 1994

Instead of the basketball he expected, Jackson Jones is given a garden patch for his tenth birthday. What is a ten-year-old boy supposed to do with a garden patch? Jackson's entrepreneurial spirit, however, is quickly aroused as he realizes that he can grow flowers and sell them, thereby earning enough money to buy himself the basketball. But there are problems along the way— jealous friends, a taunting bully, and gardening problems. Young readers will enjoy Jackson's challenges and how he rises to the occasion in this witty story.

Jamela's Dress [213]

Written and illustrated by Niki Daly

Easy Pal

Hardcover: Farrar, Straus & Giroux
Published 1999

Jamela, a young girl in South Africa, gets herself into big trouble. Mama just bought a beautiful piece of fabric to make herself a special-occasion dress. After prewashing the fabric and hanging it to dry, Mama asks Jamela to watch the fabric and to keep the dog from jumping on it. Instead, Jamela begins handling, then draping, then wearing the fabric, and finally parading down the street with the fabric trailing behind her. Needless to say, the fabric is ruined, Mama is angry, and Jamela is remorseful. But young readers will be delighted by the happy ending.

The Jazz of Our Street [214]

Written by Fatima Shaik
Illustrated by E.B. Lewis ☆ 95

Hardcover: Dial Books for Young Readers
Published 1998

A young brother and sister run from their house to join the neighbors and friends who are parading behind a New Orleans marching jazz band. Young readers will feel the beat through the rhythmic text. The impromptu spirit of the occasion is conveyed in expressive watercolor illustrations.

Jewels [215]

Written by Belinda Rochelle
Illustrated by Cornelius Van Wright and Ying-Hwa Hu ☆ 181

Hardcover: Lodestar, Dutton
Published 1998

Young Lea Mae visits her great-grandparents for the summer and is entertained by oral accounts of her family heritage. Her great-grandmother, known as 'Ma dear, tells about relatives from past generations like James, who was led to freedom by Harriet Tubman, and Harold, a buffalo soldier who fought in the Civil War. Lea Mae also hears stories about the family's more recent past, like how her own grandmother was born at home because blacks were not allowed to be treated in hospitals. Watercolor illustrations portray the love and affection of the family members as they bond through these meaningful moments.

"You and I are Africa's daughters. . . . My father told me once that Africa's daughters are the children of the sun; the sun has touched us. Our darkness is proof of its blessings."

Jezebel's Spooky Spot [216]

Written by Alice Ross and Kent Ross
Illustrated by Ted Rand

Hardcover: Dutton, Penguin Putnam
Published 1999

As Papa prepares to go off to war, he makes a pact with young Jezebel when she expresses fear about his safety. They both agree to look fear in the eye whenever either of them gets that "googery-boogery-creepy-crawly feeling." True to her word, Jezebel takes control of her fears by claiming a particularly scary spot in the woods as her own. In spite of the terrifying spiders, snaky weeds, fog ghosts, and pixie lights, Jezebel is drawn to this place, where she holds her own against both real and imagined threats. It is only after Papa's safe return that she learns that her special spot is also his.

Jonkonnu: A Story from the Sketchbook of Winslow Homer [217]

Written by Amy Littlesugar
Illustrated by Ian Schoenherr

Hardcover: Philomel, Putnam Grossett
Published 1997

In 1876, as our country prepared to celebrate its centennial, one white artist traveled bravely into the South to capture paintings of America's newest, but least privileged, citizens. In one small rural southern town, the blacks lived far from the whites, down a red clay road. Winslow Homer walked down that road to visit and paint the blacks who lived there. His famous painting, *Dressing for the Carnival,* captures the carnival known as Jonkonnu, a holiday remnant from the days of slavery, a day when slaves pretended to be free.

Journey to Freedom: A Story of the Underground Railroad [218]

Written by Courtni C. Wright
Illustrated by Gershom Griffith

Hardcover: Holiday
Published 1994

Barefoot and threadbare, young Joshua and Nathan and their parents travel the Underground Railroad with Harriet Tubman as their conductor. For twenty treacherous days and nights the group treks from their Kentucky plantation to freedom in Canada, eluding slave catchers, coping with hunger and fear, and braving the season's first snow. The family's passion for each other and for their freedom motivates them to push ahead with the challenging journey.

> "When the first joy and excitement of freedom are over, Miss Tubman leads us in a prayer of thanksgiving to God."

Juma and the Honey Guide: An African Story [219]

Written by Robin Bernard
Illustrated by Nneka Bennett

Hardcover: Silver Press
Published 1996

Bakari and Juma, father and son, travel through the African bush to find honey. They carefully track and follow the honey-guide bird, which will lead them to their sweet reward. The bird leads them to an acacia tree bearing a huge beehive. The two patiently smoke out the bees and remove the hive full of honey. As they prepare to go home, Bakari admonishes Juma to put a piece of the honeycomb back in the tree for the bird as a reward for helping them find the hive. Juma selfishly refuses until his father gives him a profound reason to obey, and young readers a reason to snicker.

Jump Rope Magic [220]   *Easy / Scr*

Written by Afi Scruggs
Illustrated by David Diaz

Hardcover: Blue Sky, Scholastic
Published 2000

Young Shameka and her friends love to double Dutch. Their joyous songs are annoying to old Miss Minnie, who runs to the street to stop their noisy play. But she is caught up in the magical cadence of the ropes and begins to jump rope, too. In facts, she jumps to heaven, where she looks down upon the girls and listens for their good-bye song. Whimsical illustrations of the rope-jumping girls accentuate the rhyming verse.

THE CREATORS

Sharon Bell Mathis

AUTHOR

"As a school librarian (now retired) and grandmother, I am ecstatic about the quality and quantity of African American children's books available today. Themes and topics are diverse and varied; prose and poetry alike are often extraordinarily eloquent—winning both acclaim and major awards in the field of children's literature. The effect of this is that African American children, today, have opportunities to explore fiction and nonfiction that affirm their lives and in which characters with a familiar array of skin tones and facial features explore both real and imaginary worlds. I do hope my writing adds to this growing body of lovely books celebrating the African American experience—which is also universal."

OUR FAVORITES

The Hundred Penny Box [vl-361]

Red Dog, Blue Fly: Football Poems [vl-397]

Running Girl: The Diary of Ebonee Rose [429]

Sidewalk Story [vl-400]

Jump Up Time: A Trinidad Carnival Story [221]

Written by Lynn Joseph
Illustrated by Linda Saport

Hardcover: Clarion, Houghton Mifflin
Published 1998

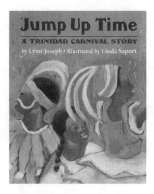

Little Lily is jealous. The whole family has been fussing for weeks over a carnival costume for her older sister, Christine. Not only is Lily missing her share of the attention, but she is too young to get a costume of her own. Christine is going to perform in the children's carnival as a hummingbird, adorned in a colorful, feathery costume. When Christine's excitement turns to stage fright just before her debut, Lily forgets her own disappointment and offers encouragement to her sister. This is a warm story of family affection, illustrated with the bold colors of the island celebration. ***Caribbean dialect.***

Just Right Stew [222]

Written by Karen English ☆ 57
Illustrated by Anna Rich

Hardcover: Boyds Mills
Published 1998

Mama and Aunt Rose are planning a birthday surprise for Big Mama's birthday. They plan to replicate Big Mama's favorite recipe for oxtail stew to serve at the family dinner. No one is quite sure of the seasonings, so in a series of episodes Mama, Aunt Rose, and other female relatives put in a pinch of cumin, a dash of lemon pepper, a shake of dill, and a little of this-'n-that. But still the stew is not quite right. Only Big Mama and young Victoria know the secret, which they quietly add when no one else is watching. Young readers will also learn the secret in this entertaining story. ***Nonstandard English.***

K Is for Kwanzaa: A Kwanzaa Alphabet Book [223]

Written by Juwanda G. Ford
Illustrated by Ken Wilson-Max

Hardcover: Cartwheel, Scholastic
Published 1997

An object represented by each letter of the alphabet from "A is for Africa," the original continent of our African American heritage, to "Z is for Zawadi," a gift exchanged at Kwanzaa time, is simply defined and colorfully illustrated in this Kwanzaa primer.

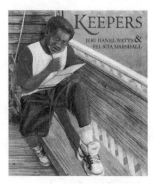

Keepers [224]

Written by Jeri Hanel Watts
Illustrated by Felicia Marshall

Hardcover: Lee & Low
Published 1997

Young Kenyon lives with his father and Little Dolly, his almost ninety-year-old grandma, who often entertains Kenyon with stories that she has carried down from the past generations. As a keeper of stories, she is looking for someone she can trust from the succeeding generation to be the next keeper. Kenyon would love the job, but he betrays a trust when he misappropriates the money that was set aside for Little Dolly's birthday party. Determined to make amends, Kenyon creates a handmade book of Little Dolly's stories, demonstrating that he can be a trusted keeper.

Kele's Secret [225]

Written by Tololwa M. Mollel
Illustrated by Catherine Stock

Hardcover: Lodestar
Published 1997

Yoanes, a young Tanzanian boy, is motivated by the treat he will earn if he helps his grandmother find the eggs that her chicken, Kele, is laying. The secretive chicken has been laying her eggs all over the farm—in the loft, the barn, and even the outhouse. Grandmother is anxious to find all of the eggs so she can take them to market to sell. Yoanes follows the fowl all day, watching her every move, until he discovers her secret place, a scary shed overgrown with vines. Yoanes must overcome his fears, which are fed by an overactive imagination, to enter the dark place to find Kele's nest.

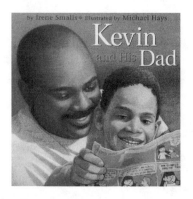

Kevin and His Dad [226]   *Easy Sma*

Written by Irene Smalls ☆ 150
Illustrated by Michael Hays

Hardcover: Little, Brown
Published 1999

Kevin spends a special day with his dad while his mom is away. The two spend a day full of shared activities like vacuuming, cleaning windows, and laundering. But there is still time after their chores to play. The two play ball and even take in a movie. This story, told in rhyme, sets an excellent example of male responsibility and male bonding.

Koi and the Kola Nuts: A Tale from Liberia [227]

Written by Verna Aardema
Illustrated by Joe Cepeda

J/398.21/Aar

Hardcover: Atheneum Books for Young Readers
Published 1999

Young Koi, the son of a chief, strikes out to explore the world with his only inheritance, a bag of kola nuts. He encounters a snake, an army of ants, and a crocodile, all in need of his nuts to solve their own problems. Koi gives the nuts freely, even though they are all he has. Later Koi enters a village and accepts the village chief's challenge to perform three impossible tasks. If he is successful, he will win the hand of the chief's daughter; if not, he will die. Koi's earlier kindness is rewarded when the creatures he once helped return to help him, proving the adage, "Do good and good will come back to you—in full measure and overflowing."

Kwanzaa [228]

J/394.261/Cho

Written by Deborah M. Newton Chocolate   **Reading Rainbow** Review Book
Illustrated by Melodye Rosales

Softcover: Children's Press
Published 1990

Warm illustrations of a loving family celebrating Kwanzaa help to tell the story of the traditional African American celebration. Young readers will learn the seven principles of the week-long holiday that is a time of kinship for African American families and an opportunity to focus on our origin and heritage.

Kwanzaa [229]

J/394.261/Por

Written by A. P. Porter
Illustrated by Janice Lee Porter

Hardcover: Carolrhoda
Published 1991

The African American holiday of Kwanzaa is described in simple but complete detail in this elementary level reader. This book is somewhat different from others on the subject because it offers a broader historical perspective on the African American conditions that led the holiday's founder, Ron Karenga, to create the seasonal celebration. The book includes descriptions of the seven principles and traditions of the holiday and a checklist of things young readers will need to practice the celebratory customs.

Kwanzaa [230]

Written by Janet Riehecky
Illustrated by Lydia Halverson

Hardcover: Children's Press
Published 1993

The African American holiday of Kwanzaa, which is celebrated between December 26 and January 1, is described in this easy-to-read book. A loving family preparing for their holiday celebration is illustrated throughout the thirty pages to help express the spirit of the season. This book, more than others on the same subject, stresses the importance of reflecting on the contributions of African Americans and on racial pride. Three activities show young readers how to prepare their own Kwanzaa celebration.

Lake of the Big Snake: An African Rain Forest Adventure [231]

Written by Isaac Olaleye
Illustrated by Claudia Shepard

Hardcover: Boyds Mills
Published 1998

Two Nigerian boys, Ada and Tayo, are best friends. In this engaging story, the two are threatened by a water snake as they frolic in the river. Their mothers had warned them not to leave the village, and their disobedience has led them into this dangerous situation. The two friends try to outsmart the snake, but it takes all of their wits to get away. Nothing, however, will save them from their scolding mothers when they return to the village.

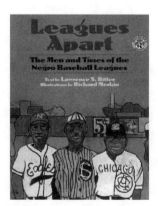

Leagues Apart: The Men and Times of the Negro Baseball Leagues [232]

J/796.357/Rit

Written by Lawrence S. Ritter
Illustrated by Richard Merkin

Softcover: Mulberry, William Morrow
Published 1995

The stories of twenty of baseball's African American trailblazers, most of whom never had the chance to play in the major leagues because they were black, are briefly outlined in this book for young sports fans. Each of the historical characters, who played for the love of the game, is illustrated with a simple description of his game attributes.

Lemonade Sun: And Other Summer Poems [233]

Written by Rebecca Kai Dotlich   J/811/Dot
Illustrated by Jan Spivey Gilchrist

Hardcover: Wordsong, Boyds Mills
Published 1998

Thirty short poems capture the essence of summer with impressions of "Fireworks," "Barefoot," "Ladybugs," and other seasonal topics. Colorful watercolors punctuate the poetry and the summertime theme.

Leola and the Honeybears: An African-American Retelling of Goldilocks and the Three Bears [234]

Written and illustrated by Melodye Benson Rosales

Hardcover: Scholastic
Published 1999

Little Leola gets lost in the woods and, just like Goldilocks in the traditional telling of this story, takes comfort in the house of the three bears. In fact, the entire story follows the original, but instead of eating the bear's porridge, Leola eats Papa Honeybear's plum pie, Mama Honeybear's rose petal cobbler, and L'il Honey's huckleberry tart. Young readers will be delighted, as always, with this story and will especially enjoy the spectacular illustrations of cute-as-a-button Leola and her reluctant hosts.

Let Freedom Ring: A Ballad of Martin Luther King, Jr. [235]

Written by Myra Cohn Livingston
Illustrated by Samuel Byrd

Hardcover: Holiday
Published 1992

Profound quotes from some of the many famous speeches made by Martin Luther King Jr. are poetically woven together into a ballad telling the story of the civil rights leader's life. The refrain, "From every mountain, let freedom ring," captures the essence of King's life work. Provocative illustrations of King with both his supporters and his antagonists are deeply reminiscent of his time.

Little Cliff and the Porch People [236]

Easy Tau

Written by Clifton L. Taulbert
Illustrated by E. B. Lewis ☆ 93

Hardcover: Dial
Published 1999

Little Cliff was supposed to go straight up the road to Miz Callie's house to buy a pound of special butter for Mama Pearl. Mama Pearl was going to turn ordinary sweet potatoes into her famous candy potatoes with the right ingredients and a little of her magic. Along the way, each of Cliff's neighbors stops the young boy for a chat and to offer him another ingredient for Mama Pearl to add to the potatoes—vanilla, nutmeg, and fresh fat. Cliff finally completes his mission, and Mama Pearl keeps her promise to make him the sweetest, softest candied potatoes ever. Then Cliff happily shares them with his good neighbors. **Nonstandard English.**

Little Eight John [237]

J/398.2/ Wah

Written by Jan Wahl   Coretta Scott King Honor: Illustrator
Illustrated by Wil Clay

Hardcover: Lodestar, Dutton
Published 1992

Little Eight John is full of mischief, disobeying every caution that his mother and father give him. Superstitiously, they warn him that bad luck will befall the family if he sits backward on the chair, counts his teeth, or sleeps with his head at the foot of the bed. But the rebellious youth does all these things and more, to the regret of his family, who suffer the aftermath of each action. It is only when Little Eight John faces his own hard consequences that he accepts his parents' wisdom and agrees to change his ways.

Little Muddy Waters: A Gullah Folk Tale [238]

Written by Ronald Daise
Illustrated by Barbara McArtor

Hardcover: G.O.G. Enterprises
Published 1997

Little Muddy Waters, so named in the Gullah tradition because of his good looks and dark skin, is a "don't-listen-to-anybody, do-whatever-he-wanted-to-do little child." His frustrated grandparents often chide Little Muddy Waters to "respect yo elders and do what's right." But he goes out of his way to disobey the good advice. Sometimes his mischief is downright mean, as when he purposely violates a household superstition and brings bad luck upon his entire family. The boy finally learns his lesson, the hard way, when he is rude to an old man. Young readers will enjoy the story told in colorful Gullah dialect about this mischievous young boy and the day he meets his match. *Nonstandard English*.

The Longest Wait [239]

Written by Marie Bradby
Illustrated by Peter Catalanotto

Hardcover: Orchard
Published 1998

Young Thomas is left at home to worry about his father, a mail carrier who is out in a blizzard delivering the mail. Daddy is gone for a long time in the treacherous storm, while Thomas and the rest of the family worry about him. Eventually Daddy does return, but he becomes deliriously ill from exposure to the weather. All night Thomas worries, hoping that Daddy will recover. In the morning Thomas knows that it will be all right. Daddy awakens and the two are able to go out to sled in the brilliant newly fallen snow. *Nonstandard English*.

Madelia [240]

Easy Gil

Written and illustrated by Jan Spivey Gilchrist

Hardcover: Dial, Penguin
Published 1997

Madelia is frustrated because she has to go to church, where her father is the minister, on Sunday morning instead of staying home to play with her new paint set. During his sermon, her father comes down from the pulpit and addresses the sermon directly to her. He paints such a dramatic and vivid picture with his words that Madelia can actually see and feel what he is talking about. After the sermon, Madelia is so inspired by the images her father has conjured up that she knows she will be able to go home and recreate that picture with her own paints.

Madoulina: A Girl Who Wanted to Go to School [241]

Written and illustrated by Joël Eboueme Bognomo

Softcover: Boyds Mills
Published 1999

Young Madoulina wants to go to school more than anything. But, as the daughter of a poor, struggling single mother, she must spend her days in her African village selling fritters to help make a living for the family. One day a compassionate teacher takes an interest in Madoulina and visits her mother to explain the value of education, even for a girl. Her mother disagrees until the young teacher arranges to buy Madoulina's fritters for the school every day, thereby guaranteeing the family their daily income. Young readers will appreciate that their opportunity for an education is a precious gift.

The Magic Tree: A Folktale from Nigeria [242]

Written by T. Obinkaram Echewa
Illustrated by E. B. Lewis ☆ 93   J/398.2/ Ech

Hardcover: William Morrow
Published 1999

Mbi, an orphan boy, lives with his unkind relatives in an African village. He is overworked, underloved, and underfed by his family and the other villagers, and called upon only when there is work to do. As Mbi sits under an udara tree, it magically begins to bear delicious, but unseasonable, fruit for him to eat. When he plants the seeds from the fruit, another full-grown, fruit-laden tree grows within minutes. Mbi discovers that he is able to direct the tree to grow, bear more fruit, or raise and lower its branches with a magical song. He also discovers that he can command a new respect from the villagers with his new-found powers.

Malcolm X [243]   J/B/ X

Written by Arnold Adoff
Illustrated by John Wilson

Hardcover: HarperTrophy, HarperCollins
Published 1970

The life and times of Malcolm X are explored in elementary terms for young readers. The brief biography touches on Malcolm's life from his birth to Reverend and Mrs. Earl Little in 1925 through his assassination in 1965. Young readers will understand the political and spiritual journey that motivated Malcolm and distinguished him as an African American icon.

Mama Rocks, Papa Sings [244]

Written by Nancy Van Laan
Illustrated by Roberta Smith

Hardcover: Apple Soup, Alfred A. Knopf
Published 1995

This lyrical poem tells the tale of two missionaries, Dan and Kathy Blackburn, who worked among the poor people of Haiti. The Blackburns took in dozens of children who were left at their doorsteps and adopted them as their own. The text is full of the sounds and alliterations of the French Caribbean island. **Caribbean dialect.**

Matthew and Tilly [245]

Easy Jon

Written by Rebecca C. Jones
Illustrated by Beth Peck

Softcover: Puffin Unicorn, Penguin
Published 1991

Matthew and Tilly are very good friends. They play together all the time, until one day Matthew accidentally breaks Tilly's crayon. The two quarrel about this mishap and angrily go their separate ways. Each tries to play alone, but they quickly learn that it's no fun, and they reconcile. Young readers may learn that patience and understanding are an important part of friendship.

The Meanest Thing to Say [246]

E+/Cos

Written by Bill Cosby
Illustrated by Varnette P. Honeywood

Hardcover and softcover: Cartwheel, Scholastic
Published 1997

Little Bill learns a valuable lesson in interpersonal skills and self-control when he refuses to be drawn into a game of "playing the dozens" with a new boy at school. The new boy, Michael, tries to taunt Little Bill into an angry reaction, but Little Bill exercises a simple nonconfrontational strategy that sees him through the experience. Later, Little Bill shows more strength of character when he invites Michael to play, even after the embarrassing showdown. Other books in the Little Bill series include *The Best Way to Play* [131], *The Day I Saw My Father Cry*, *The Day I Was Rich* [160], *Hooray for the Dandelion Warriors!*, *Money Troubles* [255], *My Big Lie* [258], *One Dark and Scary Night* [272], *Shipwreck Sunday*, *Super-Fine Valentine* [317], *The Treasure Hunt* [325], and *The Worst Day of My Life*.

Meet Martin Luther King, Jr.: A Man of Peace with a Dream for All People [247]

Written by James T. deKay

Softcover: Bullseye, Random House
Published 1993

The story of Dr. Martin Luther King Jr. is revealed to young readers in this elementary-level chapter book. Dr. King's life is told from his childhood, when racist experiences had already begun to shape his thinking, through his assassination in 1968. Virtually every major milestone in Dr. King's life and career is simply shared in this comprehensive book, which answers most of the questions regarding his life's work as a civil rights leader.

A Million Fish . . . More or Less [248]

Written by Patricia C. McKissack
Illustrated by Dena Schultzer

Hardcover: Alfred A. Knopf
Softcover: Dragonfly, Alfred A. Knopf
Published 1992

Young Hugh didn't know whether to believe Papa-Daddy and Elder Abbajon or not when they told him that they caught a five-hundred-pound turkey, more or less, and other incredible tales about their adventures in the Bayou Clapateaux. And the two old men didn't know whether to believe Hugh when he returned home after a fishing trip in the bayou with only three fish but an equally incredible story about the one million fish, more or less, that he caught and then lost. Young readers will be left to sort out fact from fantasy in this fun-loving story.

Misoso: Once Upon a Time Tales from Africa [249]

Retold by Verna Aardema
Illustrated by Reynold Ruffins

Hardcover: Apple Soup, Alfred A. Knopf
Published 1994

Twelve favorite African tales are humorously retold in this read-aloud book. Each tale is richly illustrated with the sights and colors of Africa. A glossary of terms and an afterword is included for each selection. Two favorite selections are "Leelee Goro," which is about how crying came into the world, and "The Cock and the Jackal," a short story with an important moral.

THE CREATORS

Walter Dean Myers

AUTHOR

"What I think I'm doing now is rediscovering the innocence of children that I once took for granted. I cannot relive or reclaim it, but I can expose it and celebrate it in the books I write. I really like people— I mean I really like people—and children are some of the best people I know."

OUR FAVORITES

Angel to Angel: A Mother's Gift of Love [123]

At Her Majesty's Request: An African Princess in Victorian England [358]

The Journal of Joshua Loper: A Black Cowboy, The Chisholm Trail, 1871 [397]

Me, Mop, and the Moondance Kid [vi-381]

The Righteous Revenge of Artemis Bonner [426]

Miss Tizzy [250]

Written by Libba Moore Gray
Illustrated by Jada Rowland

Hardcover: Simon & Schuster
Published 1993

Miss Tizzy is an eccentric old woman with a heart of gold. Wearing her purple hat and green high-top tennis shoes, she plays with the neighborhood children every day, Monday through Saturday. They bake cookies, make puppets, draw, play dress-up, and more—to the constant refrain, "And the children love it." Then on Sunday, Miss Tizzy's day to rest, the children live up to the example of kindness that she has set by singing her a comforting song as she prepares to sleep—"and she loved it."

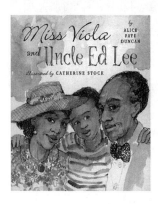

Miss Viola and Uncle Ed Lee [251]

Written by Alice Faye Duncan
Illustrated by Catherine Stock

Hardcover: Atheneum
Published 1999

Young Bradley is the unlikely matchmaker between his two senior citizen neighbors, Miss Viola and Uncle Ed Lee. Bradley has his work cut out for him, because even though Uncle Ed Lee would like to make friends with Miss Viola, the two are as opposite as night and day. Miss Viola is as neat and orderly as a pin, while Uncle Ed Lee is messy, disorderly, and sometimes even trifling. With Bradley's encouragement, Uncle Ed Lee cleans up his home and yard and successfully attracts Miss Viola.

Miz Berlin Walks [252]

Written by Jane Yolen
Illustrated by Floyd Cooper

Hardcover: Philomel, Putnam & Grosset
Published 1997

This poignant story, illustrated with rich oil-wash paintings, is both beautiful and sad. Young Mary Louise cautiously approaches her elderly white neighbor, Miz Berlin, who is thought to be a little bit crazy. The old woman takes a walk every day, talking and singing to herself. The curious Mary Louise at first just follows Miz Berlin, listening to her fantastic stories, but soon becomes comfortable enough to walk side by side, and then hand in hand, with her new friend. One day, Miz Berlin becomes disabled by a fall. Unable to enjoy her daily walk, her spirit broken, Miz Berlin dies, leaving behind a young friend who was happy to have known her.

Miz Fannie Mae's Fine New Easter Hat [253]

Written by Melissa Milich
Illustrated by Yong Chen

Hardcover: Little, Brown
Published 1997

Fannie Mae accompanies her father to town to select a special Easter bonnet for her mama. They choose an extraordinary hat, one that they can barely afford, because it is perfect. Mama wears the hat to Easter service and gets more attention than expected when the tiny bird eggs that decorate the bonnet begin to hatch. The baby birds entering the world in their bonnet-nest cause jubilation and a real sense that a miracle has occurred. Expressive watercolor paintings of the loving family and their Easter adventure accentuate the humorous tale.

Momma, Where Are You From? [254]

Written by Marie Bradby
Illustrated by Chris K. Soentpiet

Hardcover: Orchard
Published 2000

When a young girl asks her momma where she's from, Momma reaches into her memory and defines her home as being the things that she does, such as washing clothes, buying fish, and picking beans. Then she defines that place from her warm memories of growing up in her childhood home. Momma's answers reflect the thoughts of a self-assured, mature adult who appreciatively embraces her own life. Momma sets a fine example for her young daughter, who later answers the same question for herself. The illustrations are so deep that young readers will fall into the scenes.

"I am that morning-washing, bean-snapping, wagon-swinging, Miss Mary-waving, brown bus-riding, clothes-sprinkling, croaker-eating, Red Light–playing, finger-popping, star-dreaming girl. That's where I'm from."

F+/cos

Money Troubles [255]

Written by Bill Cosby
Illustrated by Varnette P. Honeywood

Hardcover and softcover: Cartwheel, Scholastic
Published 1998

Little Bill is determined to buy a telescope that costs $100, but he only has $47.87. Industriously, he washes and waxes neighbors' cars and collects soda cans in an attempt to earn the rest of the money. After he competes with another boy for empty soda cans in the park, he notices that the other boy obviously needs the money more than he does. With that realization, Little Bill sacrifices all of his cans to the other boy and donates his $47.87 to a food drive. This is a story of selflessness that may inspire young readers to see beyond themselves. Other books in the Little Bill series include: *The Best Way to Play* [131], *The Day I Saw My Father Cry*, *The Day I Was Rich* [160], *Hooray for the Dandelion Warriors!*, *The Meanest Thing to Say* [246], *My Big Lie* [258], *One Dark and Scary Night* [272], *Shipwreck Sunday*, *Super-Fine Valentine* [317], *The Treasure Hunt* [325], and *The Worst Day of My Life*.

Monkey Sunday: A Story from a Congolese Village [256]

Written and illustrated by Sanna Stanley

Hardcover: Frances Foster, Farrar, Straus & Giroux
Published 1998

Young Luzolo is preparing to go to church with her parents to celebrate Matondo, a celebration of thanksgiving. Her father, who will be preaching for the first time in his village, admonishes Luzolo to sit still during the service, a feat that is very challenging for the energetic young girl. But once in church, her task becomes even more difficult when the service is disturbed by a puppy, chickens, goats, and even a monkey, which all come to join the celebration.

The Music in Derrick's Heart [257]

Written by Gwendolyn Battle-Lavert
Illustrated by Colin Bootman

Hardcover: Holiday
Published 2000

Young Derrick spends his entire summer taking harmonica lessons from his dear Uncle Booker T. Derrick spends his days listening to the sultry, soulful sounds that Uncle Booker T. makes on the mouth harp, and he goes to bed every night with the harmonica, trying to play his own music. Uncle Booker T. admonishes him to "slow down and take his time." Months later, after tenacious dedication, Derrick blows a tune, from the heart, for his uncle.

My Big Lie [258]

E+/Cos

Written by Bill Cosby
Illustrated by Varnette P. Honeywood

Hardcover and softcover: Cartwheel, Scholastic
Published 1999

Little Bill digs himself into a deep hole when he tries to avoid responsibility for a mistake by telling one little lie. The fabrication snowballs, requiring another lie and then another, until his story takes on a life of its own. Bill's story will remind young readers that one hard truth is better than a series of easy lies. Other books in the Little Bill series include *The Best Way to Play* [131], *The Day I Saw My Father Cry*, *The Day I Was Rich* [160], *Hooray for the Dandelion Warriors!*, *The Meanest Thing to Say* [246], *Money Troubles* [255], *One Dark and Scary Night* [272], *Shipwreck Sunday*, *Super-Fine Valentine* [317], *The Treasure Hunt* [325], and *The Worst Day of My Life*.

My Heroes, My People: African Americans and Native Americans in the West [259]

Written by Morgan Monceaux and Ruth Katcher
Illustrated by Morgan Monceaux

Hardcover: Frances Foster, Farrar, Straus & Giroux
Published 1999

Over thirty African American and Native American personalities from the Old West are profiled in this collection. The subjects, both male and female, range from fur traders, cowboys, and buffalo soldiers to stagecoach drivers, outlaws, and lawmen. A brief synopsis of each person's life is accompanied by a colorful portrait. An interesting aspect of this book is that it features both African American and Native Americans as people of color, and one section, "Black and Red United," discusses the integration of the two groups.

My Mama Sings [260]

Written by Jeanne Whitehouse Peterson
Illustrated by Sandra Speidel

Hardcover: HarperCollins
Published 1994

"By myself I try singing all of Mama's old songs, but they don't sound the same. So I make up a song—a special song for Mama."

A young boy is often entertained and comforted by the songs his mama sings to him. While she has no new songs, she does have a special song for every occasion—for bedtime, for doing the laundry, for playing in the leaves on a fall day. But one day, Mama has a terrible day and loses her job. She comes home with no songs at all. The loving young boy decides to cheer her up with his own self-composed ditty. Mama can't help but respond to his loving gesture.

My Man Blue [261]

Written by Nikki Grimes
Illustrated by Jerome Lagarrigue

Hardcover: Dial, Penguin Putnam
Published 1999

Fourteen artfully illustrated poems describe the relationship forged between a young boy, Damon, and his single mother's new boyfriend, Blue. Damon and Blue grow together, bonding in an endearing best friend, father-son-like relationship. The poetic chapters of their story include "Fearless," an expression of love and support from Blue to Damon, and "Like Blue," a tribute to Blue from Damon, who hopes to grow up like his role model.

My Mom Is My Show-and-Tell [262]

Written and illustrated by Dolores Johnson

Hardcover: Marshall Cavendish
Published 1999

Young David is a nervous wreck, worrying about his mother's appearance at his class's parent career day. As they walk to school together, David admonishes her to not call him Pumpkin, not hold his hand in front of his friends, not tell any silly jokes, and more. In spite of his early jitters, he proudly introduces his mother, his show-and-tell, when the time comes.

My Rows and Piles of Coins [263]   *Easy Mol*

Written by Tolowa M. Mollel   Coretta Scott King Honor: Illustrator
Illustrated by E. B. Lewis ☆ 93

Hardcover: Clarion
Published 1999

An industrious young Tanzanian boy, Suruni, secretly saves the coins that his mother gives him every Saturday to spend at the marketplace. Instead of buying treats, Suruni saves to buy a new bike. He sorts, piles, and counts his savings every day, but his high hopes turn to disappointment when he realizes that he is still a long way from his goal. Even so, the virtuous young boy gets a bike from his supportive parents, who have known of the secret savings plan all along.

> "*I emptied the box, arranged the coins in piles and the piles in rows. Then I counted the coins and thought about the blue and red bicycle.*"

NBA Game Day: From Morning Until Night Behind the Scenes in the NBA [264]   *J/ 796. 323/ Lay*

Written by Joe Layden and James Preller
Photographs by Gary Gold

Hardcover: Scholastic
Published 1997

This photographic journal chronicles the lives of NBA players preparing for and playing their game. Candid color photographs reflect all aspects of the players' professional lives—from pregame preparation, practice, and game action to autograph signing. The text is minimal, but the pictures of many of the game's stars will tell the story for young fans.

A Net to Catch Time [265]

Written by Sara Harrell Banks
Illustrated by Scott Cook

Hardcover: Alfred A. Knopf
Published 1997

Young Cuffy is going crabbing with his father off the Georgia barrier islands, where they live. Young readers have a treat in store as they read this warm story about Cuffy's fishing expedition—from first fowl crow (about 5:30 A.M.) until sundown (about 6:30 P.M.) and his evening activities during Plat-eye Prowl (about 8:30 P.M. to midnight). The story is told in Cuffy's colorful Gullah language, especially the descriptive terms that mark the time of day. All the unfamiliar terms are defined in a glossary. **Nonstandard English**.

THE CREATORS

Jerdine Nolen

AUTHOR

"What do I hope to accomplish with my writing? I hope to continue to promote and cause one to wonder; to foster the love of the written and spoken word; and to contribute and add to the wonder and joy of it all because of the need we humans have to tell and hear each other's stories. To connect, we need to have something to believe in with others."

OUR FAVORITES

In My Momma's Kitchen [206]

Raising Dragons [288]

Nettie Jo's Friends [266]

Written by Patricia C. McKissack
Illustrated by Scott Cook

Softcover: Dragonfly, Knopf
Published 1989

This masterful example of southern storytelling is about young Nettie Jo, who is desperate to find a sewing needle so she can make a new dress for her doll, Annie Mae, to wear to cousin Willadeen's wedding. As Nettie Jo searches, she finds a ribbon, a horn, and a hat—in fact, almost everything but a needle. Along the way, Nettie Jo seeks the help of Miz Rabbit, Fox, and Panther. They each need something from Nettie Jo but have no time to help her in return, until the whirlwind ending.

Night Golf [267]

Written by William Miller
Illustrated by Cedric Lucas ☆ 98

Hardcover: Lee & Low
Published 1999

Young James finds his passion the day he discovers the game of golf. It is something he knows he can do, if only he is given the chance to play. But in the 1950s, golf was a game for "rich, white men," not for young black boys. So James becomes a caddy to be near the game he loves. He is befriended by an older, wiser caddy who invites him back to the course at night to play in the moonlight. James's story is a true representation of real events in African American sports history.

The Night Has Ears: African Proverbs [268]

Selected and illustrated by Ashley Bryan

Hardcover: Atheneum Books for Young Readers, Simon & Schuster
Published: 1999

A series of profound one-line African proverbs, ascribed to the Ashanti, Yoruba, Zulu, and other African tribes, are presented with visually stimulating paintings. Ancient sayings, such as "A man with a cough cannot conceal himself," offer timeless bits of wisdom for young and old alike.

Nobiah's Well: A Modern African Folktale [269]

Written by Donna W. Guthrie
Illustrated by Rob Roth

Hardcover: Ideals Children's Books
Published 1993

Nobiah, a young African boy, embarks on a mission to fetch water for his family. Their village is parched, and the precious water is needed to drink and to water the few surviving plants that are their food. But on his way home, Nobiah gives in to his heart, offering the water to the thirsty hedgehog, hyena, and bear that he meets. To his mother's dismay, Nobiah's jar is empty by the time he arrives home. That night, the appreciative animals come to Nobiah's village and help him dig a well that is "as deep as his heart and as wide as his thirst."

The Old Cotton Blues [270]

Written by Linda England
Illustrated by Teresa Flavin

Hardcover: Margaret K. McElderry, Simon & Schuster
Published 1998

Young Dexter is enthralled by the riveting sound of Johnny Cotton's clarinet. Through the music Dexter can feel the "blue-down blues and the deep-down shaking, slow, laughing feel-goods." He wants to learn to play the clarinet himself, but his Mama cannot afford to buy him a clarinet. Johnny Cotton introduces Dexter to the harmonica, assuring him that, with a little practice, he will be able to express his blues just as well on the mouth harp. And later, Dexter does just that.

On Mardi Gras Day [271]

Written by Fatima Shaik
Illustrated by Floyd Cooper

Hardcover: Dial Books for Young Readers, Penguin Putnam
Published: 1999

Through lyrical text and shimmering paintings, young readers will experience the parades, the pageantry, the costumes, and the customs of the traditional annual New Orleans Mardi Gras celebration.

One Dark and Scary Night [272] *F+/Cos*

Written by Bill Cosby
Illustrated by Varnette P. Honeywood

Hardcover and softcover: Cartwheel, Scholastic
Published 1999

Little Bill faces the demons that are, at one time or another, in every child's room at bedtime. He sees strange flashes of light, hears threatening thumps, and just knows that something is in his closet. He runs to Mom and Dad for safety, but they return him to his bed. Then he runs to Alice the Great, his great-grandmother, who wisely uses a little child psychology to calm his shattered nerves. Other books in the Little Bill series include *The Best Way to Play* [131], *The Day I Saw My Father Cry*, *The Day I Was Rich* [160], *Hooray for the Dandelion Warriors!*, *The Meanest Thing to Say* [246], *Money Troubles* [255], *My Big Lie* [258], *Shipwreck Sunday*, *Super-Fine Valentine* [317], *The Treasure Hunt* [325], and *The Worst Day of My Life*.

One Round Moon and a Star for Me [273]

Written by Ingrid Mennen
Illustrated by Niki Daly

Hardcover: Orchard
Published 1994

A young boy watches in amazement as his family celebrates the birth of his new sibling. His grandmother and aunts bring gifts for the baby. The village prepares to welcome their newest member. His father catches a falling star for his new child, whom he proudly declares as his own. Through it all the boy begins to question his place in the family and finally asks if he, too, is his father's child. In an endearing scene, Papa reassures the boy of his love and promises to catch a star for him, too.

> "*H*e puts his arms around me and says, 'Tonight, when the moon is big and round and the stars light up God's great sky, I'll show you, there is also a star for you.'"

The Origin of Life on Earth: An African Creation Myth [274]

Written by David A. Anderson/Sankofa   Coretta Scott King Award: Illustrator
Illustrated by Kathleen Atkins Wilson

Hardcover: Sights Productions
Published 1991

Lavish watercolor illustrations embellish this Yoruban story of creation that has been handed down from generation to generation for the past thousand years. In this tale, developed over time by ancient people in an attempt to explain the mystery of life, all that existed in the beginning were the skies above and the waters below. A collection of deities banded together to create the earth and living beings to inhabit the new world they formed.

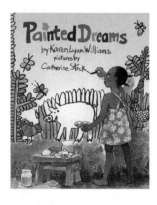

Painted Dreams [275]

Written by Karen Lynn Williams
Illustrated by Catherine Stock

Hardcover: Lothrop, Lee & Shepard
Published 1998

Eight-year-old Ti Marie is creative in more ways than one. She is an aspiring young artist, but her Haitian family is too poor to buy her the art supplies she needs. So she improvises, using a moss-covered wall as a canvas, goat hairs and feathers as brushes, and brick dust and charcoal for paints. When she paints a colorful mural near her parents' small vegetable stand, their sales increase because so many delighted villagers come to admire the work.

Palm Trees [276]

Written and illustrated by Nancy Cote

Hardcover: Four Winds
Published 1993

Young Millie faces the challenge of combing her own hair, which is full, thick, and very difficult to manage. But she is able to arrange her hair into two neat sections on either side of her head. Millie's pride in her accomplishment turns to humiliation when her best friend, Renee, looks at the hairdo and declares that it looks like two palm trees. Embarrassed, Millie runs away, determined to cut off her offensive locks. Just in time to save Millie's hair and their friendship, Renee arrives with her own hair arranged in *three* neat sections that look like palm trees. The two are able to laugh at themselves and at each other, an important lesson for young readers.

Papa Lucky's Shadow [277]   *Easy Dal*

Written and illustrated by Niki Daly

Softcover: Aladdin, Simon & Schuster
Published 1992

Papa Lucky loves to dance and can't give up his passion, even in his later years. With his young granddaughter as his shadow, Papa Lucky takes his dancing to the street. The two dance for coins on the sidewalk, but it's not the money that motivates them. It is their shared love of dancing and their special bond with each other.

Papa Tells Chita a Story [278]

Written by Elizabeth Fitzgerald Howard ☆ 82
Illustrated by Floyd Cooper

Hardcover: Simon & Schuster
Published 1995

Chita's father tells her a story—one that she has obviously heard over and over again—about his heroic actions during the Spanish-American War. As Papa tells the story, Chita interrupts to make sure that he doesn't forget a single detail of the story she loves. It is tough to tell how much of the action-packed tale is truth and how much fiction, but it is clear that Papa did complete an important and dangerous mission and was awarded a medal for his accomplishment. This book is the sequel to the popular *Chita's Christmas Tree* [v1-145].

The Piano Man [279]   *E/cho*

Written by Debbi Chocolate
Illustrated by Eric Velasquez

Hardcover: Walker
Published 1998

A young girl proudly shares the story of her piano-playing grandfather's musical career, which parallels the history of American musical theater. He began as an accompanist for silent pictures, then played for the Ziegfeld Follies and jammed with Jelly Roll Morton and Scott Joplin, and finally performed in vaudeville. Ultimately her grandfather returned to play for the silent movies until the "talkies" displaced him. The story is well told and lushly illustrated.

Picking Peas for a Penny [280]

Written by Angela Shelf Medearis
Illustrated by Charles Shaw

Softcover: Blue Ribbon, Scholastic
Published 1993

A penny went a long way in the 1930s, so two young children help their family pick peas for the penny a pound their grandpa promises to pay them. Although the work is hard in the sun-drenched pea fields, the two approach their work in good spirits, competing in the pea-picking races, and picking to rhythmic rhymes that help them keep up the pace.

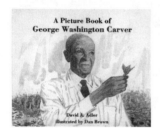

A Picture Book of George Washington Carver [281]

Written by David A. Adler
Illustrated by Dan Brown

J/Bio/Carver

Hardcover: Holiday
Published 1999

Despite his beleaguered beginnings, George Washington Carver, born a slave in 1864, became one of the most important agriculturists in history. His work on plant rotation and peanut products breathed new life into Southern farming practices. Carver's legacy belongs to the African American family and is proudly shared in this elementary biography. Other subjects of this picture book biography series are Martin Luther King Jr., Harriet Tubman, Jesse Owens, Frederick Douglass, Rosa Parks, Sojourner Truth [v1-257], Jackie Robinson, and Thurgood Marshall.

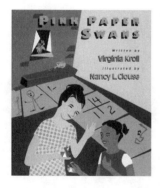

Pink Paper Swans [282]

Written by Virginia Kroll
Illustrated by Nancy L. Clouse

Hardcover: William B. Eerdmans
Published 1994

Eight-year-old Janetta Jackson and her neighbor, Mrs. Tsujimoto, forge an unlikely partnership. Mrs. Tsujimoto has intrigued Janetta all summer long with her extraordinary origami figures, but the old woman's arthritis makes it difficult for her to continue with her craft and trade. At Janetta's urging, Mrs. Tsujimoto teaches her to make the folded paper figures, which the two then sell in partnership. Young readers will appreciate the relationship between young Janetta and her older friend and can learn to make their own origami creations from the directions in the back of the book.

THE CREATORS

Denise Lewis Patrick

AUTHOR

"With my writing I hope to give African American kids a sense that books and fiction can be 'theirs.' I hope to help them realize that they can pursue a creative professional life; and I'd like all kids to understand that stories driven by African American characters can hold their interest just as well as any other character."

OUR FAVORITES

Adventures of Midnight Son [350]

Case of the Missing Cookies [17]

The Longest Ride [412]

Red Dancing Shoes [vl-265]

Poppa's Itchy Christmas [283]

Written by Angela Shelf Medearis
Illustrated by John Ward

Hardcover: Holiday
Published 1998

Young George can hardly contain his disappointment when both he and Poppa each receive an ugly knit muffler and a pair of bright red, itchy long johns for Christmas. His only satisfying gift is a pair of new ice skates. When George goes to try out the new skates, he falls through the cracked ice and almost perishes until he is rescued by Poppa, who ingeniously uses the knit muffler to pull George to safety. Poppa, Big Mama, Grandma Tiny, and Aunt Viney are all reprised characters in this winsome sequel to *Poppa's New Pants* [v1-259].

The Princess Who Lost Her Hair: An Akamba Legend [284]

Written by Tololwa M. Mollel
Illustrated by Charles Reasoner

Hardcover: Troll
Published 1993

A vain princess is cursed when she refuses to give a bird a few strands of her hair for its nest. The princess is punished harshly for her selfishness, losing her entire head of hair. Meanwhile a young beggar, who has very little, graciously shares his meager resources with the bird. The bird rewards the young man with the secret to restoring the princess's hair and to instilling a kinder heart in her.

Quotes for Kids: Words for Kids to Live By [285]

Compiled by Katura J. Hudson
Illustrated by Howard Simpson

Softcover: Just Us
Published 1999

This collection of thoughtful sayings and quotes is arranged in six topical chapters ranging from "Listening to Elders" to "Believing in Yourself." The timeless quotes and sayings are from the African tradition, the Bible, and even the contemporary wisdom of prominent men and women like Muhammad Ali, Mae Jemison, and Michael Jordan, who is quoted as saying, "I can accept failure. Everyone fails at something. But I cannot accept not trying."

Ragtime Tumpie [286]

Written by Alan Schroeder
Illustrated by Bernie Fuchs

Hardcover: Little, Brown
Published 1989

Young Tumpie began dreaming about becoming a famous honky-tonk dancer at a very early age. Growing up in the early 1900s, she was always engrossed by the exuberance of ragtime music, taking every opportunity to dance to the "syn-co-pa-tion." Tumpie fulfilled her dream many years later and became a world-famous entertainer. This upbeat story is about the love of music and dancing that inspired young Tumpie, who went on to become the legendary Josephine Baker.

Rainbow Joe and Me [287]

Written and illustrated by Maria Diaz Strom

Hardcover: Lee & Low
Published 1999

Young Eloise tells Rainbow Joe, a blind neighbor, about the colorful animals that she creates with her paints. She describes to Joe how she mixes the colors to create other colors, like mixing black and yellow to make olive-colored elephants. Rainbow Joe promises that one day he will mix some special colors for Eloise, but she doesn't understand how a blind person can mix colors. Rainbow Joe shows Eloise a whole new way to see when he pulls out his saxophone and begins to play a colorful song. Through his expressive music, she can see the rainbow of colors he plays, mixing the sounds of green, blue, red, and yellow.

Raising Dragons [288]

Written by Jerdine Nolen ☆ 126   Easy/No1
Illustrated by Elise Primavera

Hardcover: Silver Whistle, Harcourt Brace
Published 1998

A little farm girl finds the most amazing thing—a dragon egg—in a cave near her house. A fire-breathing dragon hatches from the egg and becomes a special companion to the child, who loves and nurtures him from infancy to adulthood. The two enjoy a number of unusual adventures, including the time that Hank, the dragon, breathes fire over the cornfields, turning all the kernels into popcorn. This imaginative story is illustrated in soft, dreamy pastels.

Read for Me, Mama [289]

Written by Vashanti Rahaman
Illustrated by Lori McElrath-Eslick

Hardcover: Boyds Mills
Published 1997

This sensitive story about a hard-working single mother and her loving son will touch young readers. Joseph loves to read and checks two books out of the library—one that he can read by himself and another, more difficult one for his Mama to read to him. But every day Mama has a reason to avoid reading. On Mondays there was grocery shopping to do; on Tuesdays, housecleaning; on Wednesdays, choir practice; on Thursdays, laundry. And on Fridays Mama claimed to be too tired. Joseph finally learns in a dramatic climax that Mama cannot read. But she is eager to learn, and Joseph is more than happy to support her efforts.

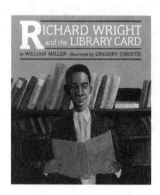

Richard Wright and the Library Card [290]

Written by William Miller
Illustrated by Gregory Christie

Hardcover: Lee & Low
Published 1997

Richard Wright, a young black boy in Mississippi in 1908, yearned to learn to read. In this fictionalized account of the famous writer's early days, he did learn and was on a constant quest for more reading material. He devoured everything he could, but as a black person in the old South, he was denied access to the library. Richard was befriended by his white employer, Mr. Falk, who understood Richard's hunger for books and allowed Richard to use his library card. Of course, they both had to pretend that the books Richard checked out were for Mr. Falk. Richard continued to be inspired by what he read until he was able to write his own novels. In 1940, his novel *Native Son* was published, followed by his autobiography, the acclaimed *Black Boy,* in 1945.

The Riddle Streak [291]

Written by Susan Beth Pfeffer
Illustrated by Michael Chesworth

Hardcover: Henry Holt
Published 1993

Young Amy, a third grader, is frustrated because her older brother Peter beats her at everything, including Ping-Pong, checkers, and hide-and-seek. Amy figures that Peter will always be "two years bigger, stronger, and smarter" than she is, so she begins to lose faith that she will ever win. But the determined young girl finally finds a way to get the best of her superior brother. Amy challenges Peter with a series of her own original riddles and finally breaks her losing streak.

Sam and the Tigers: A New Retelling of Little Black Sambo [292]

Easy Les

Written by Julius Lester
Illustrated by Jerry Pinkney

Hardcover: Dial
Published 1996

The story of Little Black Sambo is retold in this entertaining and politically correct version. The offensive racial stereotypes of the original story are gone, and what is left is the humorous tale of a young boy, Sam, who lives in the town of Sam-sam-sa-mara with his mother and father, both also named Sam. Sam the boy comes face to face with a group of tigers and is forced to give them his hip new suit of clothes in exchange for his life. But the clever boy finds a way to outsmart the not-so-smart tigers. It may seem that there are too many Sams in this engaging story, but young readers will love reading it to the delightful end.

> "*There was a little boy in Sam-sam-sa-mara named Sam. Sam's mama was also named Sam. So was Sam's Daddy. In fact, all the people in Sam-sam-sa-mara were named Sam.*"

The Secret of the Stones [293]

J/398.2/San

Retold by Robert D. San Souci
Illustrated by James Ransome

Hardcover: Penguin Putnam
Published 2000

John and Clara, a childless farm couple, take home two small white stones they find by the creek. From that day forward, magical things begin to happen. Every evening when they return home, they find their small cabin in perfect order—the clothes washed and ironed, the firewood cut and stacked, and the floor and porch swept clean. John and Clara can't figure out who performs these tasks until Aunt Easter, a visionary, has a dream that reveals that the two stones are actually orphan children, caught under a conjure-man's spell. When they are alone, the children appear and do the work, but they become stones again whenever John and Clara are present. In a dramatic confrontation with the conjure-man, the couple defeat him and fulfill their dream of breaking the spell so they can raise the two orphans as their own. *Nonstandard English.*

Senefer: A Young Genius in Old Egypt [294]

Written by Beatrice Lumpkin
Illustrated by Linda Nickens

Softcover: Africa World
Published 1992

Ancient Egyptian base-ten counting principles, which are the basis of modern mathematics, are ingeniously embedded in this story of a young Egyptian boy who grew up to become a famous mathematician and engineer in this early civilization. Young readers may embrace the principles illustrated in several counting, equation, and word problems throughout the story. Additionally, the science of mathematics is correctly credited to African people.

Shake It to the One That You Love the Best: Play Songs and Lullabies from Black Musical Traditions [295]

Collected by Cheryl Warren Mattox   **Reading Rainbow** Review Book
Illustrated by Varnette P. Honeywood and Brenda Joysmith

Hardcover: JTG of Nashville
Published 1989

The words and music to twenty-six childhood songs from the African, African American, Creole, and Caribbean cultures are presented in this book/audiotape set. The collection includes well-known favorites such as "Mary Mack" and "Hambone," as well as lesser known songs like "There's a Brown Girl in the Ring." The selections can be used for ring games, line games, or double Dutch, or sung as lullabies. A companion set, *Let's Get the Rhythm of the Band* [v1-67], explores the potpourri of African American music styles, including folk, ragtime, and jazz.

Shaq and the Beanstalk: And Other Very Tall Tales [296]

Written by Shaquille O'Neal   J/Fiction/Oneal
Illustrated by Shane W. Evans

Hardcover: Cartwheel, Scholastic
Published 1999

NBA star turned story-teller Shaquille O'Neal serves up six well-known fairy tales with his own twist. In each of the fun-loving fractured tales, such as "Shaq and the Beanstalk" and "Shaq and the Three Bears," Shaq himself takes the leading role. The stories are told with plenty of hip language, and many of the colorful illustrations contain the sports hero's likeness. Young basketball fans won't mind this digression into early childhood fairy tales with Shaq as their guide.

Silver Rain Brown [297]

Written by M. C. Helldorfer
Illustrated by Teresa Flavin

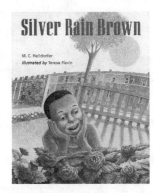

Hardcover: Houghton Mifflin
Published 1999

An expectant mother and her son endure a summer heat wave. It is so hot and water is so scarce that they can't even use water to wash cars or water the flowers. Momma's new baby is born the night that it finally rains, cooling the neighborhood and watering the earth. The new baby is appropriately named Silver Rain, a name descriptive of the rain that fell on the night of her birth.

Singing Down the Rain [298]

Written by Joy Cowley
Illustrated by Jan Spivey Gilchrist

Hardcover: HarperCollins
Published 1997

Today "the grass is green, the corn is yellow ripe and the river runs sweet down to the pool." But it wasn't always this way. A little while ago the town was in the middle of a terrible drought. Then a rain singer came into town and sang for rain. Her one voice wasn't enough, so soon the crickets, the frogs, and the blue jays joined in. Then the children, full of faith, added their voices. Finally the dubious adults joined the song and brought the rain.

Sister Anne's Hands [299]

Written by Marybeth Lorbiecki
Illustrated by K. Wendy Popp

Hardcover: Dial Books for Young Readers
Published 1998

In the early 1960s, when she is seven, Anna is exposed to a teacher who touches her life profoundly. The teacher, Sister Anne, a nun, is the first African American whom Anna had ever known. When faced with racial mockery by her students, Sister Anne turns the occasion into an opportunity to expose the children to some of the glory, as well as the pain and suffering, in African American history. Anna is impressed by the combination of Sister Anne's gentleness and strength and embraces both qualities in her own life.

Sky Sash So Blue [300]

Written by Libby Hathorn
Illustrated by Benny Andrews

Hardcover: Simon & Schuster
Published 1998

A young slave girl, Susannah, cherishes a prized possession, a blue sash. As her sister prepares for her marriage to a free man, their Ma'am collects scraps of fabric from wherever she can to create a special patchwork "all over" wedding dress for the older daughter. After the wedding, the dress must be taken apart to return the fabric swatches to their places, and the married sister prepares to move north with her new husband. Susannah selflessly offers her sister the sash to symbolically tie their lives together. In keeping with the theme, fine fabric collages illustrate this sensitive story.

Solo Girl [301]

J/Pinkney

Written by Andrea Davis Pinkney
Illustrated by Nneka Bennett

Softcover: Hyperion
Published 1997

> "*The secret of the fives is taking hold. And to make it stick, you gotta practice. Do it over and over, till it's dancing in your head. . . . Same thing with rope jumping, over and over till your feet are dancing with the sidewalk.*"

Cass is blessed with the gift of numbers. She knows her multiplication tables better than any other third grader and recites them rhythmically with the accompaniment of her whistle. But Cass can't jump rope, something she desperately wants to do. Pearl, on the other hand, is the best jumper in the Fast Feet Four, a neighborhood jump-rope team, but is challenged by math. When the two girls meet, they immediately appreciate each other's strengths and become supportive friends, helping each other to grow.

Something Beautiful [302]

Written by Sharon Dennis Wyeth ☆ 201
Illustrated by Chris K. Soentpiet

Hardcover: Doubleday
Published 1998

A young girl searches for something beautiful in her inner-city neighborhood, surrounded by graffiti, homelessness, broken glass, and trash. Through her neighbors she begins to recognize the small things in life that are beautiful, such as good meals, friends, a small neighborhood garden, and the special love of her mother. Her mother has no trouble seeing the beauty in her own child, whose beaming face is seen on the book's cover.

Somewhere in Africa [303]

Easy Men

Written by Ingrid Mennen and Niki Daly
Illustrated by Nicolaas Maritz

Softcover: Puffin Unicorn, Puffin
Published 1992

A young boy named Ashraf lives in Africa, but not the Africa that might come to mind when young readers think about that continent. Ashraf's home is a big city teeming with skyscrapers, bustling with cars, and alive with the energy of any large metropolitan area. Ashraf's only view of the wilder side of Africa comes from books, whose pictures of lions, zebras, and crocodiles fascinate him. Your young reader's vision of Africa will broaden with the new knowledge that Africa has more than jungles and wild animals.

Stevie [304]

Easy Ste

Written and illustrated by John Steptoe

Hardcover: Harper & Row
Published 1969

During the week, while his mother works, little Stevie stays with Robert and his family. Robert is dismayed because Stevie plays with all of Robert's toys, messes up his bed, and generally makes a pest of himself. There seems to be nothing good about having Stevie around until the care-giving arrangement comes to an end, and then Robert reminisces about the good times that he and Stevie shared. **Nonstandard English.**

The Stories Julian Tells [305]

Written by Ann Cameron
Illustrated by Ann Strugnell

Hardcover: Pantheon Books
Softcover: Alfred A. Knopf
Published 1981

Julian tells six short stories, including the one about the time he and his brother, Huey, eat up all the lemon pudding that their father made from scratch. When their dad discovers that the pudding is gone, he threatens them with "There's going to be some whipping and beating here now!" And there is! Julian and Huey whip cream and beat eggs to exhaustion, to make a new pudding. There are more stories about Julian in *Julian, Dream Doctor; Julian, Secret Agent; Julian's Glorious Summer* [v1-364]; and *More Stories Julian Tells.*

Harriette Gillem Robinet

AUTHOR

"It is important to provide historical and contemporary fiction that places black children as heroes in American society along with other races.
I think children need a sense of self-acceptance, rising to self-respect, and ending in a celebration of self. It is a life-long process."

OUR FAVORITES

Forty Acres and Maybe a Mule [380]

If You Please, President Lincoln [vl-449]

Mississippi Chariot [vl-459]

The Story of Jean Baptiste DuSable [306]

Written by Robert H. Miller
Illustrated by Richard Leonard

Hardcover: Silver, Paramount
Published 1995

Jean Baptiste DuSable, a black French immigrant, is fully credited in this story
as the founder of Eschikagoo, a trading post on the banks of Lake Michigan
in 1772. Young readers will learn that the city DuSable established is now
known as Chicago. Other books in the series include *Buffalo Soldiers: The
Story of Emanuel Stance* [v1-138], *The Story of Nat Love,* and *The Story of
"Stagecoach" Mary Fields* [v1-281].

The Story of Lightning & Thunder [307]   J/ 398.26 /Bry

Written and illustrated by Ashley Bryan

Hardcover: Antheneum
Softcover: Aladdin, Simon & Schuster
Published 1993

Ma Sheep Thunder and her son, Ram Lightning, used to live on earth among
the people of an African kingdom. The two were often called upon to use
their lightning and thunder to summon their friend Rain. All was well until
Ram Lightning's repeated impetuous, destructive antics caused the king to
move them farther and farther from the kingdom until they finally resided in
the sky. This masterfully told tale, perfect for read-a-long storytelling, is
accompanied by vibrant mosaic-style illustration.

A Strawbeater's Thanksgiving [308]

Written by Irene Smalls ☆ 150
Illustrated by Melodye Benson Rosales

Hardcover: Little, Brown
Published 1998

Traditionally, during the harvest time in late November, slaves were permitted
to celebrate the end of their work. The gaiety would include corn-husking
contests, singing, dancing, and other frivolities. One year, seven-year-old Jess
decides that he is old enough to serve as the "strawbeater," the boy who
stands behind the fiddler and reaches around to beat the fiddle strings while
the fiddler plays. But Jess would have to wrestle the much older, much larger
Nathaniel for that honor. The vivid and expressive illustrations put young
readers in the middle of the action of this lively story. ***Nonstandard English.***

A Street Called Home [309]

Written and illustrated by Aminah Brenda Lynn Robinson

Hardcover: Harcourt Brace
Published 1997

This unusual book is both visually and tactilely stimulating. Each page is a colorful mural depicting 1940s African American life on Mt. Vernon Avenue in the heart of a housing development in Columbus, Ohio, that had once been a shantytown called Blackberry Patch. In the midst of each mural is a lift-and-see flap, under which a particular character from the street is featured. Young readers will learn about the sockman, the umbrellaman, the brownyskin man, and the chickenfoot woman, who all practice their trades on this street.

Strong to the Hoop [310]

Written by John Coy
Illustrated by Leslie Jean-Bart

Hardcover: Lee & Low
Published 1999

James's time has finally come. He has always had to watch his older brother play basketball from the sidelines, but now one of the players is injured and James is called in to play. James is smaller and younger, but he has everything to prove in this high-stakes neighborhood game. His determination and raw energy are evident in the description of the play-by-play action. The text is street real, and the action is captured in snapshot illustrations.

Subira Subira [311]

J/398.22/Mol

Written by Tololwa M. Mollel
Illustrated by Linda Saport

Hardcover: Clarion
Published 2000

Tatu, a young Tanzanian girl, is charged with the care of her younger brother, Maulidi, after their mother dies. Their relationship is contentious and difficult, as Maulidi fights his sister at every turn. Tatu consults MaMzuka, the old spirit woman, for a spell to improve her relationship with her brother. The old woman sends Tatu into the bush to pluck three whiskers from a lion to use in the spell. Tatu bravely goes into the night to find a lion, but he will not allow her to get close to him. Patiently, Tatu returns night after night, creeping closer each time, until the lion allows her to not only approach him, but to pluck his whiskers. When Tatu returns with the whiskers, the old woman throws them away, telling Tatu that all she needs to tame her young brother is the same patience that she used to tame the lion.

Summer Wheels [312]   *J/Fiction/ Bunting*

Written by Eve Bunting
Illustrated by Thomas B. Allen

Softcover: Voyager, Harcourt Brace
Published 1992

The good-hearted Bicycle Man fixes up bikes and allows the neighborhood kids to ride them. There were only a few rules that the kids had to live by. The first was that bikes be returned by four o'clock and the second was that the kids were responsible for fixing any damage to the bikes they rode. Most of the neighborhood kids respected the rules, especially Brady and his friend. But when a new boy, Leon, comes and blatantly disregards the rules, the two veterans take matters into their own hands. Twice they deliver Leon and his missing bikes to Bicycle Man, but they cannot understand why Bicycle Man continues to extend his kindness to the errant boy. The wise Bicycle Man seems to understand that Leon is crying out for attention and support, which he is more than willing to extend.

Summertime: From Porgy and Bess [313]

Written by George Gershwin, DuBose Heyward,
  Dorothy Heyward, Ira Gershwin
Illustrated by Mike Wimmer

Hardcover: Simon & Schuster
Published 1999

The well-known song "Summertime," from *Porgy and Bess,* is expressively illustrated in this beautiful book. Each painting brings summertime images to life as young readers read the words to the ageless song. The music is included on the last page.

Sunday Week [314]

Written by Dinah Johnson
Illustrated by Tyrone Geter

Hardcover: Henry Holt
Published 1999

There is no question that Sunday is the best day of the week. The Monday-through-Saturday activities of a small community are described as relatively mundane. But things come alive on Sunday, when all the people dress in their finery for church, the church choir rocks, the Sunday feast is spread, and they all go for Sunday drives. At the end of the day everyone is left to eagerly await the next Sunday.

Sundiata: Lion King of Mali [315]

Written by David Wisniewski
Illustrated by Lee Salsbery

Hardcover: Clarion
Published 1992

Bright cut-paper illustrations help add drama to this African story of deceit and political intrigue. Sundiata, who was both lame and mute, was named heir to his father's throne in the great empire of Mali. But when the time came for Sundiata to ascend to the throne, the council of elders passed him over in favor of his older half-brother. Over time, the weak half-brother lost the empire to an evil sorcerer king, who brought the great empire to ruin. While in exile, Sundiata rose to the challenge of saving his nation. He gained not only his voice, but the physical strength and cunning necessary to conquer his enemy and restore his homeland to its former greatness.

Sunflower Island [316]

Written by Carol Greene
Illustrated by Leonard Jenkins

Hardcover: HarperCollins
Published 1999

Young Polly was watching the day that the *Sunflower* ferryboat sank halfway into the river. Over the generations that followed, Polly watched as the *Sunflower* was surrounded by sand, silt, and driftwood and evolved into an island. Years later the island actually became a pleasure place where people went to fish or picnic. Still years later, the sands shifted and the island became unstable until finally the power of the river washed away the island and the old *Sunflower*.

Super-Fine Valentine [317]

E+/Cos

Written by Bill Cosby
Illustrated by Varnette P. Honeywood

Hardcover and softcover: Cartwheel, Scholastic
Published 1998

In a typical third-grade experience, Little Bill is insecure and shy about his crush on Mia. His friends have noticed that he likes her and tease him about it, and his brother has exposed Little Bill's feelings to their parents. Now it is Valentine's Day and Little Bill has to decide whether or not to give Mia the card that he has made especially for her. After a wrenching process, Little Bill finally gives her the card and decides that it is best to show people you like them. Other books in the Little Bill series include *The Best Way to Play* [131], *The Day I Saw My Father Cry*, *The Day I Was Rich* [160], *Hooray for the Dandelion Warriors!*, *The Meanest Thing to Say* [246], *Money Troubles* [255], *My Big Lie* [258], *One Dark and Scary Night* [272], *Shipwreck Sunday*, *The Treasure Hunt* [325], and *The Worst Day of My Life*.

Tailypo! [318]

J / 398.21 / Wah

Retold by Jan Wahl
Illustrated by Wil Clay

Hardcover: Henry Holt
Published 1991

An old man who lives alone in the woods strikes out at a creature that he finds in his cabin. He cuts off the creature's tail and eats it for dinner. But the creature retaliates by returning time and time again, demanding the return of his "tailypo." Each time the old man sends his dogs to chase the creature away. Eventually, the creature confronts the old man and devours him to get back the tailypo. The tale is fast-paced and intriguing, but suitable only for young readers who can handle the dark story line.

Tambourine Moon [319]

Written by Joy Jones
Illustrated by Terry Widener

Hardcover: Simon & Schuster
Published 1999

Walking in the moonlit night, Granddaddy tells young Noni the story of the tambourine moon and the night that he met his wife, her grandmother. Walking alone in the dark, he had become lost. Then he heard the singing of a church choir, with one particularly beautiful voice rising above the rest. He followed the music until he came upon a church, where the choir was practicing. When the choir members emerged, Granddaddy introduced himself to the songstress, his bride to be, and walked her home, carrying her tambourine for her. After seeing her home, he felt alone and frightened in the dark night, but he still had her tambourine. Magically, the tambourine jumped from his hand into the sky, where it became the glowing moon that lit his way home.

Tanya's Reunion [320]   *Easy Flo*

Written by Valerie Flournoy
Illustrated by Jerry Pinkney

Hardcover: Dial, Penguin
Published 1995

Tanya has the unexpected pleasure of going with her grandma, ahead of her parents, to the family farm, where she will help prepare for the upcoming family reunion. But Tanya is disillusioned; the farm doesn't look anything like she imagined it, and there isn't very much to do. Sensing Tanya's disappointment, Grandma shares her fond memories of living on the farm, giving Tanya an appreciation for the significance of their family home. With her new perspective Tanya discovers a special memento that will hold special meaning for her loving grandma. This story is the sequel to *The Patchwork Quilt* [v1-256].

Three Wishes [321]

Written by Lucille Clifton
Illustrated by Michael Hays

Hardcover: Doubleday for Young Readers
Published: 1992

New Year's Day is Zenobia's lucky day when she finds a penny that was minted in her birth year. Everyone knows that that means you will get three wishes, and Zenobia looks forward to fulfilling her good luck. She accidentally wastes one wish when she makes an incidental comment about the weather, wishing it were warmer. She loses another when she thoughtlessly wishes that her best friend, Victor, would go away after they have a little spat. Zenobia begins to miss her friend and then realizes that there is only one way to spend her third and final wish. She wishes that she and Victor were still good friends.

Tiny and Bigman [322]

Written by Phillis Gershator
Illustrated by Lynne Cravath

Hardcover: Marshall Cavendish
Published 1999

Tiny is a large woman with a booming voice, stronger than every man she meets. That's why she doesn't have a husband. Bigman is a small, weak fellow but is secure enough to recognize Tiny's inner beauty. The two fall in love and get married. As they await the birth of their first baby, a vicious hurricane is bearing down on their West Indian island. Tiny isn't about to let the storm destroy their home, so she uses her extraordinary strength to keep their house and home together. This delightful, brightly illustrated book is a read-aloud treat.

To Be a Drum [323]

Easy Col

Written by Evelyn Coleman
Illustrated by Aminah Brenda Lynn Robinson

Hardcover: Albert Whitman
Published 1998

Young Matt and Martha's daddy tells them about their African ancestors who were so in tune with the earth that they captured its beat and translated it through their bodies onto their drums. When they were torn from their land and brought into slavery, their drums were taken away. But the people never lost their beat. Richly textured mixed-media paintings embellish the thought-provoking message.

THE CREATORS

Irene Smalls

AUTHOR

"My goal as a writer is to produce classic children's books that will last for one hundred years or more. I aim as a writer to be clear and beautiful in my use of language."

OUR FAVORITES

Because You're Lucky [129]

Dawn and the Round To-It [vI-157]

Father's Day Blues: What Do You Do about Father's Day When All You Have Are Mothers? [171]

Irene and the Big, Fine Nickel [209]

Kevin and His Dad [226]

A Strawbeater's Thanksgiving [308]

Too Much Talk [324]

Easy Med

Written by Angela Shelf Medearis
Illustrated by Stefano Vitale

Hardcover: Candlewick
Published 1995

An African farmer out harvesting his crop reels from shock when a yam talks to him. He is jolted again when his dog speaks to him. The farmer flees in fright until he meets a man with a fish and shares his incredible story. The man does not believe him until the fish speaks to both of them. In fear, the two run until they meet a weaver, whose cloth speaks, and then a swimmer, who is addressed by the water. The tormented group runs to the chief, who bans them from the village for spreading their disturbing story. The tale comes to a quick and humorous end when the chief's chair speaks to him.

The Treasure Hunt [325]

Written by Bill Cosby
Illustrated by Varnette P. Honeywood

Hardcover and softcover: Cartwheel, Scholastic
Published 1997

Little Bill is in a quandary after he realizes that he has no special treasure. His father is engrossed in his album collection. His mother seems to care a great deal about her china, and his brother is into his baseball card collection. While Bill is in his room looking for his own treasure, his Great-Grandmother Alice comes in and wisely prods Little Bill to tell her a story. He makes up an incredibly creative and funny story that makes Great-Grandmother laugh. In the process he realizes his own treasure—storytelling. Other books in the Little Bill series include *The Best Way to Play* [131], *The Day I Saw My Father Cry, The Day I Was Rich* [160], *Hooray for the Dandelion Warriors!, The Meanest Thing to Say* [246], *Money Troubles* [255], *My Big Lie* [258], *One Dark and Scary Night* [272], *Shipwreck Sunday, Super-Fine Valentine* [317], and *The Worst Day of My Life*.

> "**M**y treasure hunt is over. I learned what was special to me—telling stories and making people laugh. . . . You can't polish or dust or sort my special things. You can only enjoy them."

Tree of Hope [326]

Written by Amy Littlesugar
Illustrated by Floyd Cooper

Hardcover: Philomel, Penguin Putnam
Published 1999

An old, twisted tree that stood in front of the Lafayette Theatre in Harlem was a symbol of hope for the actors who performed there. The Depression closed the theater, and many of the actors had to give up their acting careers and find other work. Young Florrie's father was one of those actors, and he always hoped to return to the stage. Florrie makes his wish come true by wishing on the old tree. Suddenly, the theater is reopened for the first time in years by a director named Orson Welles, who goes to Harlem to stage *Macbeth*. Florrie's father's role is small but significant. This production of the play, with its setting changed from Scotland to Haiti, and starring black actors, was a true event that helped revitalize the black arts for the first time since the Harlem Renaissance.

Trina's Family Reunion [327]

Written by Roz Grace
Illustrated by James Melvin

Hardcover: BMF Press
Published 1994

Seven-year-old Trina is flying off for her summer vacation. She is going to Durham, North Carolina, to visit her grandparents and to enjoy the annual family reunion. Trina describes the fun of fishing and picnicking with her grandparents and the joy of getting together with her cousins.

Turtle Knows Your Name [328]

Written and illustrated by Ashley Bryan

Hardcover: Atheneum, Macmillan
Published: 1989

Upsilimana Tumpalerado has a long and difficult name, but not as long as his grandmother's, whom he has always just called Granny. One evening Granny challenges young Upsilimana to discover her correct name. He circulates throughout the village, unsuccessfully seeking anyone who may know her given name. He finally meets Turtle, who tells him that she is named Mapaseedo Jackalindy Eye Pie Tackarindy. It seems that Turtle knows all of the villagers' names in this clever, tongue-twisting tale.

Two and Too Much [329]

Easy Wal (handwritten)

Written by Mildred Pitts Walter ☆ 188
Illustrated by Pat Cummings

Hardcover: Bradbury, Macmillan
Published 1990

Seven-year-old Brandon has his hands full when he agrees to watch his two-year-old sister, Gina, while his mother does the housework. Gina is everything two-year-olds are reputed to be—too busy, too uncooperative, and much too negative. Her favorite word, of course, is "No!," which challenges young Brandon's patience as a big brother.

Two Mrs. Gibsons [330]

Written by Toyomi Igus
Illustrated by Daryl Wells

Hardcover: Children's Book Press
Published 1995

A young girl reflects on the traits of two very different women who share the same name, Mrs. Gibson. One is tall and chocolate-dark; the other small and vanilla-colored. One is loud and cheery, the other quiet and reserved. They like different foods and different activities, and have different talents. Despite their differences, the child loves them both, since one is her African American grandmother and the other her Japanese mother.

Ty's One-Man Band [331]

Written by Mildred Pitts Walter ☆ 188
Illustrated by Margot Tomes

Reading Rainbow Feature Book

Softcover: Scholastic
Published 1980

Young Ty meets an intriguing stranger, a one-legged man who claims he is a one-man band. At the stranger's bidding, Ty collects a washboard, two wooden spoons, a tin pail, and a comb from his dubious family members, promising them a concert in return. Late in the evening the stranger shows up and keeps his promise, to the enjoyment of the entire community. Then, just as mysteriously as he came, the stranger disappears back into the night.

> "*B*oys and girls, mothers and fathers, even the babies clapped their hands. Some danced in the street. Whenever the music stopped, everybody shouted, 'More.'"

Under the Breadfruit Tree: Island Poems [332]

Written by Monica Gunning
Illustrated by Fabrico Vanden Broeck

Hardcover: Wordsong, Boyd Mills
Published: 1998

Thirty-six poems offer poignant views of a Jamaican child's life. The selections are about everyday island subjects like "Tell the Truth," "High Tea," and "My Parents." Each selection is illustrated with strong black-and-white scratchboard drawings.

Vacation in the Village: A Story from West Africa [333]

Written and illustrated by Pierre Yves Njeng

Softcover: Boyds Mills
Published 1999

Young Nwemb is skeptical about his family's summer vacation to a village outside their city. Concerned that he will be bored in the country, away from city life and without his friends, Nwemb boards the train for the journey. Despite his worries, Nwemb finds a new friend and a summer full of fun in the village and looks forward to his next visit.

Virgie Goes to School with Us Boys [334]

Written by Elizabeth Fitzgerald Howard [82]   Coretta Scott King Honor: Illustrator
Illustrated by E. B. Lewis [93]

Hardcover: Simon & Schuster
Published 2000

Inspired by a true story about the author's grandfather, this book is about the Fitzgerald family, who grew up near Jonesborough, Tennessee, seven miles from the Warner Institute. The Institute was established by the Quakers during the Reconstruction period as a school for black children. Young Virgie longs to go to school with her six brothers. But she is always denied the chance for a variety of reasons: she is too young for the long walk, she would be homesick for Mama during their five-day stay at the school, and because "girls don't need school." Finally Virgie gets her chance and accompanies the boys to the place of her dreams and an opportunity to receive an education.

We Had a Picnic This Sunday Past [335]   *Easy Woo*

Written by Jacqueline Woodson
Illustrated by Diane Greedseid

Hardcover: Hyperion
Published 1997

Teeka and her family had a big party last Sunday. Everyone was there, except Cousin Martha, who is known for her dry pies. Cousin Luther was there, playing his usual tricks, like sprinkling plastic flies on the corn. Auntie Kim, the second-grade teacher who never married, was there, too. Even Sister Carol and Reverend Luke came. And naturally, Grandma was there with her wonderful chicken and biscuits and wagging her tongue about Cousin Martha's dry pie. This exuberant bunch is your family, my family, every family.

The Wedding [336]

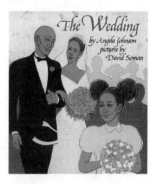

Written by Angela Johnson
Illustrated by David Soman

Hardcover: Orchard
Published 1999

Young Daisy reflects on her older sister's wedding from shopping for the wedding gown, site selection, and food tasting to the day of the ceremony with its food, music, and dancing. She also comments wistfully on the loss of her sister, but seems to take pleasure in the fact that she will be in the wedding.

What's in Aunt Mary's Room? [337]

Written by Elizabeth Fitzgerald Howard ☆ 82
Illustrated by Cedric Lucas ☆ 98

Hardcover: Clarion, Houghton Mifflin
Published 1996

Young Sarah and her sister have always been curious about what is behind the locked door of their late Aunt Mary's bedroom. They know that their great-great-aunt, Aunt Flossie, keeps treasures in there, and when Aunt Flossie invites them to visit the locked room, they discover a room full of old lamps, mirrors, newspapers, and an old sewing machine. The real treasure, though, is an old family Bible that once belonged to their great-great-great grandpa and contains the family records. The two sisters proudly enter their names and birth dates to bring the heirloom Bible up to date. This book is the sequel to *Aunt Flossie's Hats (and Crab Cakes Later)* [v1-123].

Easy Aar

What's So Funny, Ketu? [338]

Written by Verna Aardema
Illustrated by Marc Brown

Hardcover: Dial
Published 1982

An African villager, Ketu, rescues a small snake and is rewarded with a special gift or a curse, depending upon how you look at it. Ketu has been given the ability to hear the thoughts of animals but is forbidden, under threat of death, to tell anybody else about his new talent. Ketu overhears the thoughts of a mosquito, a rat, and a cow, which sends him into fits of laughter. Nobody, especially his frustrated wife, understands Ketu's odd behavior. The village elders are finally called upon to judge Ketu's actions, forcing him to divulge his secret or face death. An unexpected twist in the story saves Ketu's life and will bring a giggle to young readers.

Easy Orm

Who's Whose? [339]

Written and illustrated by Jan Ormerod

Hardcover: Lothrop, Lee & Shepard
Published 1998

The fun begins when four parents, one grandmother, eight kids, two guinea pigs, one dog, and one stray cat from three neighboring families come together in this story of relationships and interactions. Challenge young readers to follow the trail of activities and interactions from school to soccer, piano practice, cooking, and more to unravel the question, "who's whose?"

J/398. 2/Ger

Why the Sky Is Far Away: A Nigerian Folktale [340]

Written by Mary-Joan Gerson
Illustrated by Carla Golembe

Hardcover and softcover: Little, Brown
Published 1992

There was a time when the sky was very close to the earth and was the source of food for all the people. Since food was so plentiful, there was little work to do, so people spent their time in more artistic pursuits. But then the sky looked down and realized how wasteful the people were. The ungrateful humans took chunks of the sky and then left large, uneaten pieces wasted on garbage heaps throughout the village. Sky warned the king, who urgently cautioned the people that the wastefulness must stop. Despite the warnings, one day a greedy woman took more sky than she could eat. She desperately tried to share the large, leftover piece, but couldn't find any takers. With that, the sky moved far away from the people, and from that time on, they had to work and toil for their food.

Wiley and the Hairy Man [341]

Retold by Judy Sierra
Illustrated by Brian Pinkney

Hardcover: Lodestar, Dutton
Published 1996

In this African American folktale from Alabama, young Wiley encounters the frightening Hairy Man, who is known to gobble up young children. Wiley keeps his cool and uses his wits to outsmart the beast and escape. Having done so once, all Wiley has to do is outsmart Hairy Man two more times and the monster will never bother him again. The second time Wiley and the creature meet, he tricks Hairy Man into using his own conjurer talents against himself. Young readers will enjoy this suspenseful tale and the creative trick that Wiley uses in his third and final encounter with Hairy Man.

Wilhe'mina Miles: After the Stork Night [342]

Written by Dorothy Carter
Illustrated by Harvey Stevenson

Hardcover: Frances Foster, Farrar, Straus and Giroux
Published 1999

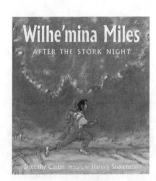

Eight-year-old Wilhe'mina overcomes both her disappointment that her daddy can't come home from his far-away job and her fears when Mama asks her to go out in the night. Wilhe'mina must run in the moonlit night through all of the scary nighttime obstacles to get the midwife to help Mama on her "stork night." The next morning Wilhe'mina is gratified by the sight of her beautiful new baby brother in the arms of their loving mama.

Willie Jerome [343]

Written by Alice Faye Duncan
Illustrated by Tyrone Geter

Reading Rainbow **Review Book**

Hardcover: Macmillan
Published 1995

> "*So Mama loosens up her frown and takes a seat by me on the stoop. We close our eyes. We rest our minds and let the music speak.*"

Willie Jerome is always on the roof, blowin' his cool jazz sounds throughout his urban neighborhood. His young sister Judy loves the "sizzlin' red hot beebop" that Jerome plays, but nobody else does. His mother, friends, and other neighbors say that Jerome has no talent and that his music is only noise. Finally, Judy, acting as an advocate for her brother, convinces Mama to really tune in and listen to Jerome. Mama does and appreciates his music for the first time. **Nonstandard English.**

You're Not My Best Friend Anymore [344]

Written by Charlotte Pomerantz
Illustrated by David Soman

Hardcover: Dial Books for Young Readers, Penguin
Published 1998

Ben, an African American boy, is best friends with his neighbor, Molly, a white girl. The two are inseparable, and do everything together, even sharing a common birthday party for their June birthdays. One day, just before their party, Ben and Molly have a fight. They don't even speak during the party, but their friendship pulls through because, not surprisingly, each has bought a present for the other. The story of this friendship is particularly special because neither their race nor their gender is ever an element of the story line.

Zamani Goes to Market [345]

Written by Muriel Feelings
Illustrated by Tom Feelings

Hardcover: Africa World
Published 1990

Young Zamani experiences one of the passages into adulthood when he is allowed, for the first time, to accompany his father and brother to market. Zamani's wide-eyed enthusiasm for every aspect of the excursion is pleasing. Moreover, Zamani selflessly takes his own money to buy a special gift for his mother. His kindness is a reflection of the way he was raised, a point that becomes obvious in the telling of this touching story.

Books for Middle Readers

CHILDREN IN THIS group (grades 4 through 8) have already mastered elementary skills, are proficient readers, and now focus on special-interest subjects. The books they read are often comprehensive, thoroughly exploring a subject in great detail. Many of the books that we recommend for this age group will give young readers much greater insights into earlier generations of our people. Several books of historical fiction, such as *Adventures of Midnight Son* [350], *I Thought My Soul Would Rise and Fly* [392], *Forty Acres and Maybe a Mule* [380], and *Letters from a Slave Girl* [409] share poignant insight into what it was like to be a slave or a newly emancipated one, and the socioeconomic and political climate of those times.

Other books, like *Black Hands, White Sails* [361], *Sink or Swim* [432], and *Till Victory Is Won* [444], detail the historically obscured endeavors of earlier generations of African Americans who transcended slavery and performed extraordinarily, in unexpected ways.

Still other books are simply interesting to peruse and valuable as references when young readers have the need to know. *The Biographical Dictionary of African Americans* [360] and *The New York Public Library Amazing African American History* [418] are two such

references. Both books are chock full of interesting tidbits for both young readers and their families.

Sometimes it is fun to read a book for the sheer pleasure of it. Following a good mystery or sharing the adventures of a favorite character can be very entertaining. Many of the titles we have selected will give children hours of reading enjoyment.

After all the required reading for school, young readers can enjoy books that take them away from reality and into a world of adventure and intrigue. Fortunately there are plenty of books that do just that. Young readers seem to enjoy serialized books that allow them to follow the same familiar characters through a number of episodes. There are several popular series that we highly recommend for this age group. Your daughters may enjoy Addy, of the American Girl series, featured in a six-book collection including *Addy Learns a Lesson* [348], or Keisha, of the Magic Attic series, who experiences fantasy adventures in *Keisha Discovers Harlem* [401] and five other books.

Your sons may like the fast-paced adventures found in the Patrick's Pal series, including *Large and In Charge!* [406], *Schoolin'* [431], and other books about the fictionalized youthful exploits of Patrick Ewing and his friends. Both boys and girls can relate to the adventures of the NEATE kids, who face a variety of adolescent situations in *Anthony's Big Surprise* [357] and *Elizabeth's Wish* [376].

Young readers also need exposure to books that help them develop the whole person. Among the books that can help nurture their social consciousness and sensitivities are *Dear Corinne, Tell Somebody! Love, Annie* [371], an important book about a child's sensitivity to her sexually abused friend; and *Bluish* [363], about a relationship among three girls—two healthy, the other a cancer patient. Each book has significant messages about human kindness and compassion.

We also recommend reflective books like *Gingersnaps* [385] and *Stretch Your Wings* [437], which give blossoming young minds food for thought and personal growth.

Abraham's Battle: A Novel of Gettysburg [346]   J/Banks

Written by Sara Harrell Banks

Hardcover: Atheneum
Published 1999

Abraham, an aging freed slave who lives and works in Gettysburg, Pennsylvania, in 1863, realizes that he must contribute to the Civil War effort that will ultimately abolish slavery. He becomes an ambulance driver for the Union Army, transporting the wounded from the historic Battle of Gettysburg. On one sojourn onto the battlefield, Abraham finds a mortally wounded Confederate soldier, Lamar, whom he had occasion to meet, man-to-man, days before when the young man was on a scouting mission. Here, lying on the battlefield, Lamar is neither black nor white, friend nor foe, but a human being who needs help. This book of historical fiction details the key events that led to the battle that helped determine the final outcome of the Civil War. **Nonstandard English.**

> "*A*nd while he didn't think anybody was much concerned about a solitary colored man bearing a wounded rebel. . . . he was scared to take the chance. . . . 'We gone' take this boy back to our side. They'll take care of him.' "

Across the Lines [347]   J/Reeder

Written by Carolyn Reeder

Hardcover: Atheneum
Softcover: Avon Camelot, Avon
Published 1997

Edward, a young slave master, and Simon, his young slave and playmate, are separated when their plantation home is overtaken by Union soldiers. Edward flees with his family to a Southern city, to a much different life than he had ever before experienced. Simon, at first happy to be liberated, is now on his own, working from hand to mouth to earn his keep, hoping that he will find somewhere to call home and someone to call friend. The lives of the two boys are still in deep contrast, as they live on different sides of the Civil War battle line. This eventful and captivating book is for more advanced young readers.

Addy Learns a Lesson: A School Story [348]

Written by Connie Porter
Illustrated by Melodye Rosales

Hardcover and softcover: Pleasant
Published 1993

Addy, a former slave, learns two important lessons in the second book of this American Girl series. After reaching her freedom in Philadelphia, Addy goes to school and enthusiastically learns to read and write. She takes her lessons very seriously, studying and practicing every chance she gets. At the same time Addy learns to value friendship after she shuns a true friend for the approval of a wealthier, more popular classmate. Other books in the Addy series are *Meet Addy* [v1-382]; *Addy's Surprise* [349]; *Happy Birthday, Addy!; Addy Saves the Day, Changes for Addy;* and *Welcome to Addy's World, 1864* [447]. **Nonstandard English.**

Addy's Surprise: A Christmas Story [349]

Written by Connie Porter
Illustrated by Melodye Rosales

Hardcover and softcover: Pleasant
Published 1993

Young Addy, a former slave girl, struggles with how to spend her hard-earned savings. She wants to buy a Christmas gift for her mother and a lamp for the family, both selfless gestures. But she knows that the money would be a valuable contribution to the charitable fund set up to help other blacks escape slavery. Addy takes the higher ground, and receives a kindness in return. Her mother's employer gives Addy her first special-occasion dress and the materials to make a gift for her mother. Other books in the Addy series are *Meet Addy* [v1-382]; *Addy Learns a Lesson* [348]; *Happy Birthday, Addy!; Addy Saves the Day; Changes for Addy;* and *Welcome to Addy's World, 1864* [447]. **Nonstandard English.**

Adventures of Midnight Son [350]

Written by Denise Lewis Patrick ☆ 133

Hardcover: Henry Holt
Published 1997

Midnight Son was a thirteen-year-old slave who escaped to Mexico where he found freedom and the adventures of a lifetime as a ranch hand. Midnight's early family life and daring escape are described in compelling detail in the first half of the book. In the second half, Midnight grows to manhood and is challenged to become one of the best cowboys in the region. He undertakes his new position on the ranch with vigor and encounters several dangerous but exciting challenges, such as driving his cattle herd through a twister. Underscoring the story is Midnight's struggle with his feelings about leaving his family behind in slavery, as he builds a new life among people who respect his humanity. *The Longest Ride* [412] is the sequel to this book.

African American Entrepreneurs [351]

Written by Jim Haskins

Hardcover: John Wiley
Published 1998

This well-formatted reference book profiles over thirty African Americans who, against the odds, lived up to the American dream by building and growing thriving entrepreneurial enterprises. Inspiring stories of men and women who succeeded in everything from cattle ranching to magazine publishing demonstrate what can happen when ingenuity and tenacity are paired with courage and hard work. Subjects from Marie-Thérèse Metoyer, an eighteenth-century woman who owned her own plantation, to Earl G. Graves, the founder of *Black Enterprise* magazine, are discussed in brief articles. Other books in the Black Stars series include *African American Military Heroes, African American Inventors, African American Women Writers, African American Healers, African American Musicians, African American Teachers,* and *African American Women Scientists and Inventors.*

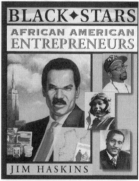

African-American Folktales for Young Readers: Including Favorite Stories from Popular African and African-American Storytellers [352]

Collected and edited by Richard and Judy Dockrey Young

Hardcover: August House
Published 1993

Young readers will enjoy over thirty very short folktales from the African and African American storytelling traditions. The stories are organized into seven category chapters, such as Young Heroes and Heroines, which has the story "Beautiful Brown Eyes," and Bigger Than Life, in which the story of John Henry appears. The stories, which can be read in a matter of minutes, will connect young readers to the characters and legacies passed down from generations of Africans and African Americans.

African American Quilting: The Warmth of Tradition [353]

Written by Sule Greg C. Wilson

Hardcover: Rosen
Published 1999

Quilting, a very old art form, is explored from the African American perspective in this informative book. Young readers will learn about the history of quilt making in Africa and around the world, the significance of quilts in African American culture, and the state of the art today. Most interesting is the discussion about quilts that were used as signal flags on the Underground Railroad. Other books in the Library of African American Arts and Culture series are *The African American Kitchen: Food for Body and Soul; Blues: Its Birth and Growth; Kwanzaa!: Africa Lives in a New World Festival* [405]; *Jazz Tap: From African Drums to American Feet; Jam!: The Story of Jazz Music;* and *Rap and Hip Hop: The Voice of a Generation.*

J/920/Pot ## African Americans Who Were First [354]

Written by Joan Potter and Constance Claytor

Hardcover: Cobblehill
Published 1997

More than sixty African American men and women who were first in their fields of endeavor—sports, medicine, entertainment, politics, the arts, and more—are featured in brief biographical sketches. The profiles include achievers past and present, some famous and some others who are little known.

African Beginnings [355]   *J/960/Has*

Written by James Haskins and Kathleen Benson
Illustrated by: Floyd Cooper

Hardcover: Lothrop, Lee & Shepard
Published 1998

This history book takes young readers back to the African continent, revealing it and its many cultures as far back as 3800 B.C. Short articles on the ancient cultures of Nubia, Egypt, Kush, Mere, and others demonstrate that the black people of Africa thrived in very advanced and sophisticated civilizations millennia before the Anglo-Saxon cultures that define the history that our children learn today. This outstanding book, the first in a series about the proud history and heritage of African Americans, is followed by *Bound for America: The Forced Migration of Africans to the New World* [365] and *Building a New Land: African Americans in Colonial America.*

THE CREATORS

Eleanora Tate

AUTHOR

"I'd like my readers to gain an appreciation of the many different personalities among African Americans and to recognize the great varieties of communities where we live."

OUR FAVORITES

Don't Split the Pole: Tales of Down-Home Folk Wisdom [373]

Front Porch Stories: At the One-Room School [383]

Just an Overnight Guest [vl-367]

J/398.2/Wil

And in the Beginning [356]

Written by Sheron Williams
Illustrated by Robert Roth

Hardcover: Atheneum
Published 1992

Grandmother Shammama tells an engaging story of creation to her two grandchildren. As she tells it, man began in Africa when Mahtmi, the Blessed One, created the earth, all kinds of creatures, and a single man named Kwanza. His body was made of the richest, darkest soil of Kilimanjaro, his hair and eyes from precious elements, and his teeth were the finest pearls from oysters. Later Mahtmi created other human beings and Kwanza began to feel less special. To show Kwanza how much he was loved, Mahtmi touched his hair and curled it tightly, which is why "to this very day every daughter and son of the generations of the original man has a crown of curled hair." ***Nonstandard English.***

Anthony's Big Surprise [357]

Written by Wade Hudson

Softcover: Just Us
Published 1998

Anthony is a member of NEATE, a wholesome group of kids named for the first letter in each member's name: Naimah, Elizabeth, Anthony, Tayesha, and Eddie. In the main story, Anthony comes face to face with his father, whom he has never met and whom he believed to be dead. Reeling from the reality, Anthony questions his single mother's explanation of past events and learns the truth. Other titles in the NEATE series are *NEATE to the Rescue* [v1-387] and *Elizabeth's Wish* [376].

At Her Majesty's Request: An African Princess in Victorian England [358]

J/Bio/Bonetta

Written by Walter Dean Myers ☆ 119

Hardcover: Scholastic
Published 1999

> " *While most of the English who lived in London had certainly seen black people, few had seen a young African girl who lived in such a manner as Sarah.*"

A young African girl facing imminent death as a human sacrifice in a brutal ritual in her village is saved by a kindly British naval officer. The officer negotiates with the tribal king for the girl's life and finally accepts her as a gift for Queen Victoria. In 1850, the girl, who became known as Sarah Forbes Bonetta, was brought to England, where she enjoyed the affection and protection of the queen. In the years that followed she experienced tragedy and triumph until her early death at about thirty-eight years of age. This true story is engrossing and dramatic.

Beyond Mayfield [359]

Written by Vaunda Micheaux Nelson

J Fiction Nelson

Softcover: G.P. Putnam's Sons
Published 1999

Young Meg lives in Mayfield Crossing, an unusually close community of caring neighbors, both black and white, living together in the 1960s. But Meg and her friends couldn't stay sheltered forever. When they transfer to the Parkview School in the next town, they are suddenly faced with stark realities. Meg is the only black child in her class and is quickly exposed to racism. The United States is in the midst of the Cold War with the Soviet Union, a constant source of fear and anxiety in Meg's life. And her best friend's older brother is killed during his brief experience as a Freedom Rider in the civil rights movement. Meg becomes aware, in a very short period of time, that life is much more than her comfortable home in Mayfield.

The Biographical Dictionary of African Americans [360]

Written by Rachel Kranz
Illustrated by Philip J. Koslow

RJ / 920 / Kra

Hardcover and softcover: Checkmark
Published 1992

A comprehensive collection of famous African Americans from all walks of life, both historical and contemporary, is listed alphabetically in this reference book. A brief article on each of almost 250 important activists, athletes, entertainers, artists, scientists, writers, politicians, and others gives young researchers ready access to the names and accomplishments of both famous and infamous black Americans. Several helpful indexes aid in the use of the book, including a list of entries by profession, a list of entries by birth year, and a timeline placing each person in his or her proper historical sequence, from Crispus Attucks in 1723 to Tiger Woods in the late twentieth century.

J 973.049 McK (handwritten)

Black Hands, White Sails: The Story of African-American Whalers [361]

Written by Patricia C. McKissack and Fredrick L. McKissack

Coretta Scott King Honor: Author

Hardcover: Scholastic
Published 1999

> *"The sea was an equalizer of men, therefore the captain chose his crew based on who could do the job best."*

Another little-known story from the chapters of African American history is told in this intriguing book about blacks in the whaling industry, 1730–1880. Blacks, many of whom were fleeing slavery, signed on to work on whaling vessels for the better life this line of work offered. African American whalers not only contributed to the whaling industry but also played critical roles in the Underground Railroad. A number of authentic black-and-white photographs, drawings, and documents help punctuate the story.

Black Hoops: The History of African Americans in Basketball [362]

Written by Fredrick McKissack, Jr.

Hardcover: Scholastic
Published 1999

This is a well-researched history of African Americans in basketball from the inception of the game to the present, when blacks dominate the popular sport. Included are many black-and-white photographs and stories about many of the greatest black players, such as Dr. J., Magic Johnson, Michael Jordan, and Shaquille O'Neal, and teams like the Harlem Rens and the Chicago Globetrotters (yes, Chicago). Young readers will learn about how the Civil Rights movement spilled over into basketball, forcing the integration of the game. There is even a chapter on black women in basketball, offering a complete view of the sport.

Bluish: A Novel [363]

Written by Virginia Hamilton

J Fiction Hamilton (handwritten)

Hardcover: Blue Sky, Scholastic
Published 1999

A young girl nicknamed Bluish, not because she was half black and half Jewish but because of her paling skin tone, is suffering from childhood leukemia. She attends school in a wheelchair, when she is well enough, but is uncomfortably ignored by her classmates until two of them, Dreenie and Tuli, reach out and befriend her. Soon the three are bonded in a lasting friendship. This comforting story is full of love, compassion, and understanding.

Bounce Back [364]

Written by Sheryl Swoopes with Greg Brown
Illustrated by Doug Keith

Hardcover: Taylor
Published 1996

Sheryl Swoopes offers an inspirational first-person account of her rise from playground athlete to a gold-medal winner on the 1996 U.S. Olympic women's basketball team. Sheryl's story chronicles her successes and accomplishments but also the failures, setbacks, and challenges that she overcame to achieve her goals. In a most poignant anecdote, a seven-year-old girl in a shopping mall revitalizes Sheryl's waning spirit with words of support, giving her the positive energy she needs to rededicate herself to her game.

Bound for America: The Forced Migration of Africans to the New World [365]

J/326/Has

Written by James Haskins and Kathleen Benson
Illustrated by Floyd Cooper

Hardcover: Lothrop, Lee and Shepard
Published 1999

This elegantly designed book contains pages of detailed descriptions of the captivity and transportation of black slaves from the African coast to the Americas. There are compelling accounts of every aspect of the middle passage, from the abductions of African tribesmen to slave-holding pens and the inhumane voyage conditions. While the material is shocking, the presentation of the historical facts along with numerous photographs and illustrations is well done. Several profound paintings depicting parts of the story, including the cover illustration of an iron-bound man, will move young history buffs. Other books in this series are *African Beginnings* [355] and *Building a New Land: African Americans in Colonial America*.

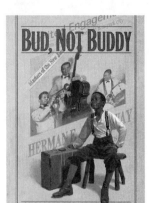

Bud, Not Buddy [366]

J Fiction Curtis

Written by Christopher Paul Curtis

Coretta Scott King Award: Author
Newbery Award

Hardcover: Delacorte
Published 1999

In the Depression era, a motherless ten-year-old boy named Bud is determined to find his father. The only clue he has, a flyer about Herman E. Calloway, bandleader of the Dusky Devastators of the Depression, is enough to start Bud on an unforgettable journey. Bud travels by hopping trains and survives by his wits, developed far beyond his years, in this fast-paced story.

The Canning Season [367]

Written by Margaret Carlson
Illustrated by Kimanne Smith

Hardcover: Carolrhoda
Published 1999

August 1959 is Peggie's coming-of-age season. While her grandmother, auntie, and mother are busy putting up canned goods, she is confronted with racism for the first time. Peggie's best friend, a white girl, declares that she can no longer spend the night because her parents are concerned that Peggie's black brothers may become attracted to her. Reeling from that news, Peggie retreats to home, where her mother comforts her by pouring her her first cup of coffee. Then Peggie is allowed to join the other women in the canning project, an adults-only activity, marking a rite of passage into womanhood.

The Children's Book of Kwanzaa: A Guide to Celebrating the Holiday [368]

J/394.261/Joh

Written by Dolores Johnson

Softcover: Atheneum, Simon & Schuster
Published 1996

An overview of African American history lays a foundation for young readers' understanding of how and why Kwanzaa was conceived. A thorough description of each of the seven principles includes practical examples of how young people and their families can apply them in their everyday lives. There are also detailed descriptions of how to celebrate the holiday, complete with craft activities, recipes, and a Kwanzaa planning calendar.

Glennette Tilley Turner

AUTHOR

"As a writer of biographies and fiction, I hope to be the teacher, parent, and mentor and to provide young readers examples of people who have overcome the odds of poverty, prejudice, sexism, and limited access to education and other resources. By extension I hope to inspire readers to believe, 'If those people made a way where there was none, I can too!'"

OUR FAVORITE

Take a Walk in Their Shoes [439]

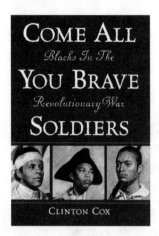

Come All You Brave Soldiers: Blacks in the Revolutionary War [369]

Written by Clinton Cox

Hardcover: Scholastic
Published 1999

Over five thousand black soldiers fought for America's independence during the Revolutionary War. The stories of these courageous but largely unsung patriots are told in this well-researched book. Accounts of such men as Peter Salem and Cuff Whitmore, who were there when the first shots were fired at Lexington and Concord; or Lemuel Haynes and Barzillai Lew, who fought with Ethan Allen and his Green Mountain Boys, will make young readers proud of the role that blacks played in the making of America.

Dance, Kayla! [370]

Written by Darwin McBeth Walton

Hardcover: Albert Whitman
Published 1998

Young Kayla lives happily with her Gran and Granpa on their country farm. The only thing missing from her life is her father, who left her to pursue his dancing career. Suddenly Kayla's life is turned upside down when Gran has a heart attack and dies during a violent thunderstorm. Kayla is sent to Chicago to live with her Aunt Martha and her family. She must adjust to her new family situation, a large city school, and urban life. The young girl throws herself headlong into the only other thing she loves—dancing—with the love and support of her new family.

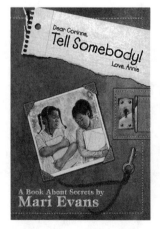

Dear Corinne, Tell Somebody! Love, Annie: A Book about Secrets [371]

Written by Mari Evans

Hardcover: Just Us
Published 1999

This poignant story is told in the form of twenty-seven letters from one pre-adolescent friend to another. Each letter from Annie is an appeal to her dear friend to share why she has become so remote and withdrawn. Through the successive letters, young readers will guess, as Annie did, that Corinne is the victim of sexual abuse at home, and that her shame and fear have isolated her from her friends. Annie eventually convinces Corinne to tell her secret to the school nurse, who helps stop the abuse and triggers the beginning of the healing process. This book can be an excellent tool for a caring adult to use to draw out a child in similar circumstances.

A Dime a Dozen [372] J/811/Gri

Written by Nikki Grimes
Illustrated by Angelo

Hardcover: Dial Books for Young Readers
Published 1998

These twenty-eight poems by Nikki Grimes are about growing up, facing the world, and preparing for the future. The title of the book comes from the discouraging phrase Ms. Grimes heard so often as a girl, "Writers are a dime a dozen." The title poem, the last selection in the book, is her response to that comment.

Don't Split the Pole: Tales of Down-Home Folk Wisdom [373]

Written by Eleanora E. Tate ☆ 165
Illustrated by Cornelius Van Wright and Ying-Hwa Hu ☆ 181

Hardcover and softcover: Yearling, Bantam Doubleday Dell Books for Young Readers
Published 1997

Seven short stories illustrate the points of seven well-known folksy sayings, like the story about Russell James, who goes hand-fishing with Uncle Bron. Bored with the day and tired of Uncle Bron's cautions, Russell jumps into the creek to catch a fish for himself. His hard-headed determination to do it his way lands Russell in a dangerous and then hilarious situation that brings home the proverb, "A hard head makes a soft behind." These stories are beautifully told with descriptive language and memorable characters.

A Drawing in the Sand: A Story of African American Art [374]

Written and Illustrated by Jerry Butler

Hardcover: Zino, Children's Books
Published 1998

African American artist Jerry Butler reflects on the inspirational encouragement and support of his family, friends, and neighbors in Magnolia, Mississippi, who encouraged him from an early age to develop his artistic talents. Interspersed between his accounts of his own journey into the world of art are the stories of sixteen other African American artists, ranging from the much-acclaimed Jacob Lawrence and Romare Bearden to contemporary artists like Faith Ringgold and Betye Saar. The descriptions of the artists' quest for their art are illustrated with examples of their finest work. This is a companion book to *Sweet Words So Brave: The Story of African American Literature* [v1-409].

Drylongso [375]

Written by Virginia Hamilton
Illustrated by Jerry Pinkney

Hardcover: Harcourt Brace Jovanovich
Published 1992

A great wall of dust sweeps across the land during the drought, blowing a tall "stick-fella" into the home of young Lindy and her family. The "stick fella," named Drylongso, brings seeds and hope to the struggling family who are desperate for rain for their crops. More importantly, Drylongso brings a dowser rod and helps the family find a deeply buried spring. The story is warm, the characters are compassionate, and the illustrations are expressive in this mature picture story.

Elizabeth's Wish [376]

Written by Debbi Chocolate

Softcover: Just Us
Published 1994

Elizabeth and her school friends—a group known as NEATE, an acronym derived from the first letter in each of their names: Naimah, Elizabeth, Anthony, Tayesha, and Eddie—are confronted with several opportunities and challenges. Elizabeth, a talented singer, decides to compete in a city-wide talent show, but has to overcome a severe case of laryngitis and a sprained ankle. Young Tayesha, a fair-skinned African American girl, faces down taunters who tease her for not being "black enough." Meanwhile, the entire group is involved in an enterprise to raise money to pay for a rap band for the DuSable Junior High School dance. Other books in the series include *NEATE to the Rescue* [v1-387] and *Anthony's Big Surprise* [357].

Ernestine & Amanda: Mysteries on Monroe Street [377]

Written by: Sandra Belton ☆ 25

Hardcover and softcover: Simon & Schuster
Published 1998

Though Ernestine and Amanda live in the same community, they are only connected by friends-in-common, the fact that their respective brother and sister are dating, and their mutual interest in the new dance studio on Monroe Street. Ernestine is the pianist for the fledgling dance school and Amanda the star dancer. On one occasion, when the two are lauded for their joint performance, for a brief moment they appreciate and respect each other more than ever before. The dance studio is plagued by a mysterious series of vandalisms at the same time that Ernestine struggles with a weight problem and Amanda faces her parents' divorce. The other books about the girls' ambivalent relationship are *Ernestine & Amanda* [v1-339]; *Ernestine & Amanda: Summer Camp, Ready or Not!*; and *Ernestine & Amanda: Members of the C.L.U.B.*

Fair Ball!: 14 Great Stars from Baseball's Negro Leagues [378]

Written and illustrated by Jonah Winter

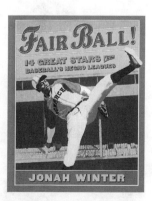

Hardcover: Scholastic
Published 1999

Fourteen unsung heroes of the game of baseball are at last recognized in this book about the little-known but talented members of the Negro Baseball Leagues. The players, such as Rube Foster and Bingo DeMoss, are presented in an oversized baseball-card format, with a colorful illustration of the athlete on one side of the page and vital statistics and a career profile on the other. Fans of the game will enjoy this book of almost-lost baseball greats.

First in the Field: Baseball Hero Jackie Robinson [379]

Written by Derek T. Dingle

J /B/ Robinson

Hardcover: Hyperion
Published 1998

This photo-filled biography of the acclaimed Jackie Robinson offers a thorough portrait of the man who broke the color barrier in major league baseball. The comprehensive story includes details about Jackie's family life, education, military life, and baseball career, both in the Negro Leagues and in the Major Leagues. A three-page addendum at the end of the book details other important milestones in black sports history from the beginning of record-keeping in 1845, when the New York Knickerbockers allowed blacks and integrated teams to play, to 1997, when Tiger Woods became the first African American to win the Masters Golf Tournament.

Forty Acres and Maybe a Mule [380]

Written by Harriette Gillem Robinet ☆ 142

J Robinet

Hardcover: Jean Karl, Atheneum
Published 1998

Twelve-year-old Pascal, his brother, and other newly emancipated slaves band together as a family in search of General Sherman's promise that there would be forty acres and maybe a mule for every ex-slave family in 1865, at the end of the Civil War. This credible work of historical fiction depicts the family's struggle to succeed on their small farm against all odds. In spite of their legal right to be free, the young family faces the treachery and violence of the white Southerners who stop at nothing to oppress them.

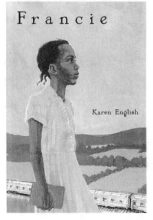

Francie [381]

Written by Karen English ☆ 57

J Fiction English

Coretta Scott King Honor: Author

Hardcover: Farrar, Straus and Giroux
Published 1999

Thirteen-year-old Francie struggles with her adolescent life as the daughter of an absentee father. Francie lives with her mother in rural Alabama and dreams of the day that her father, a Pullman porter in Chicago, will fulfill his promise to relocate the family in the North. In the meantime, Francie faces the extreme prejudice of the South, stands up to a bully, and manages a difficult situation with Jesse, a sixteen-year-old she is teaching to read.

From Slave Ship to Freedom Road [382]

Written by Julius Lester
Illustrated by Rod Brown

Hardcover: Dial, Penguin
Published 1998

This emotionally stirring book includes a series of paintings that depict slaves from their terrifying Middle Passage through the decades of their humiliating bondage and subjugation to their freedom fight and ultimate emancipation. The thought-provoking story challenges young readers to consider their feelings from the point of view of the slaves.

Front Porch Stories: At the One-Room School [383]

Written by Eleanora E. Tate ☆ 165
Illustrated by Eric Velasquez

Hardcover and softcover: Bantam Doubleday Dell
Published 1992

Daddy mesmerizes twelve-year-old Maggie and her cousin Ethel with stories from his childhood, when he attended a one-room school in Nutbrush, Missouri. Some of the eleven stories about Daddy and his friends and family are funny, others are scary, and some are even sad, but all are entertaining and just the right length for a quick bedtime read.

The Gift-Giver [384]

Written by Joyce Hansen

Softcover: Clarion, Houghton Mifflin
Published 1980

A sensitive portrait of life in an inner-city neighborhood is told through the eyes of ten-year-old Doris. Doris befriends Amir, a new boy in the neighborhood, who seems wise beyond his years. The two, and other neighborhood friends, share each other's pain when a local boy is felled by a playground shooting, when a friend's family is shattered when he and his brothers and sisters are sent to different foster homes, and when Doris's father loses his job. Despite the travails of the youths and their families, the story is hallmarked by the strong family values and virtues of these two children who face so much at such an early age.

"Who am I? What is my place in the scheme of things? We want our lives to have meaning and importance. Imagine seeking the meaning of your life if you had been a slave."

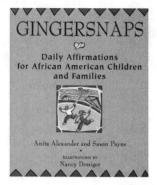

Gingersnaps: Daily Affirmations for African American Children and Families [385]

Written by Anita Alexander and Susan Payne
Illustrated by Nancy Doniger

Softcover: Jump at the Sun, Hyperion
Published 1998

This book contains 365 positive, self-reinforcing affirmations, one for every day of the year. A favorite affirmation from February's heritage theme, for example, is, "My heritage is as beautiful and as colorful as a hand-stitched quilt." This keepsake book would make a wonderful gift for a special child or would lend itself nicely to daily use in the classroom.

Going Back Home: An Artist Returns to the South [386]

Written by Toyomi Igus
Illustrated by Michele Wood

Hardcover: Children's Book Press
Published 1996

An artist's interest in her own roots is the subject of this collection of paintings. Ms. Wood journeyed to the South to collect images of the region and to research the place and times of her ancestors. Each painting contains small quiltlike panels in the background that represent pieces of her heritage. The text helps young readers see the art through the artist's eyes and interpret the images, which have significance for many African Americans.

Got Game? [387]

Written by Robb Armstrong
Illustrated by Bruce Smith

Softcover: HarperActive, HarperCollins
Published 1998

One of Patrick's best friends, Keith, is being disrespected by another friend and teammate, Zo. Ever since Zo's birthday he lords his age advantage and basketball skills over the younger Keith. Zo insists that Keith be the waterboy for the Bulldogs, their basketball team, rather than play, and he won't even give Keith the chance to show what he can do. Keith seizes his moment, however, and shows Zo and the rest of the team that he is worthy of their respect on the court. This book is one in the series based on the fictionalized young life of Patrick Ewing and other NBA greats. Other titles in the Patrick's Pals series include: *In Your Face* [394], *Large and In Charge!* [406], *Runnin' with the Big Dawgs, Schoolin'* [431], *Stuffin' It,* and *Trashmaster.*

Great African Americans In Business [388]   J/920/Red

Written by Karen Dudley and Pat Rediger

Softcover: Crabtree
Published 1996

Seven of the most noteworthy African Americans in the field of business, both historical and contemporary achievers, are included in this book. Each pro-file—of such people as Madame C. J. Walker and John H. Johnson—describes the subject's personality, gives an overview of his or her life story and signifi-cant career accomplishments, and is illustrated with several photographs. The Great African Americans In . . . series includes books on one hundred African Americans in the fields of arts, civil rights, entertainment, film, government, history, jazz, literature, music, Olympics, and sports.

Heaven [389]   YA/Johnson

Written by Angela Johnson   Coretta Scott King Award: Author

Hardcover: Simon & Schuster
Published 1998

Fourteen-year-old Marley is shattered by the revelation of a family secret. Her life in the town of Heaven is routine and predictable until the day she dis-covers that her Momma and Pops are really her uncle and aunt. Her real mother is dead and the man she has always known as her uncle is really her father. Every notion and emotion that Marley feels is sensitively explored through both her thoughts and her conversations with her friend Shoogy.

Hopscotch Love: A Family Treasury of Love Poems [390]

Written by Nikki Grimes
Illustrated by Melodye Benson Rosales

Hardcover: Lothrop, Lee & Shepard, William Morrow
Published 1999

Twenty-two poems from the hearts of the young are paired with superb illus-trations. The loving poems range in subject matter from sisterly love and mother love to new love and old love, reflecting the many dimensions of that special feeling.

paintings by michele wood
text by toyomi igus

I See the Rhythm [391]

Written by Michele Wood
Illustrated by Toyomi Igus

J/ 780.89/ Igu

Coretta Scott King Award: Illustrator

Hardcover: Children's Book Press
Published 1998

Five hundred years of African American music history are high-
lighted in this award-winning book. Provocative illustrations
capture the spirit of fourteen musical genres, including slave songs,
blues, ragtime, jazz, swing, rock 'n roll, funk, and rap. The essence
of each musical era is described in an expressive poem and accompanied by a timeline of the significant historical and musical events of
that period.

J Fiction
Dean

I Thought My Soul Would Rise and Fly:
The Diary of Patsy, a Freed Girl [392]

Written by Joyce Hansen

Coretta Scott King Honor: Author

Hardcover: Scholastic
Published 1997

Everyone assumes that young Patsy, a slave girl, is dim-witted, because her
speech is impaired and she is partially lame in one leg. But from her observant
diary entries, young readers will learn that Patsy is far from being dim. In fact,
as a house slave, she was clever enough to learn to read and write, a dangerous fact that she must conceal. The story of Patsy's life and that of others on
her South Carolina plantation are told through her diary, which spans the first
year of emancipation, 1865–1866. Her insightful entries expose many of the
human injustices that slaves faced both before and after their freedom, and
make young readers aware of the quandary that newly freed slaves faced in
their ambiguous freedom.

> *"I know that I am young, but I can read,
> write, cook, wash, and teach. I should be
> able to find work and care for myself."*

THE CREATORS

Cornelius Van Wright
ILLUSTRATOR

Ying-Hwa Hu
ILLUSTRATOR

"I am glad that my children and their generation can enjoy this golden age of multicultural books. I am honored that my wife and I can participate in the creation of some of these works. We hope that through our interpretations of manuscripts that children will be able to learn from, relate to, and remember the characters that they see in our works, even as I remember (and still have) those books I had as a child."

—CORNELIUS VAN WRIGHT

OUR FAVORITES

An Angel Just Like Me [122]

Don't Split the Pole: Tales of Down-Home Folk Wisdom [373]

Ginger Brown: The Nobody Boy [178]

Ginger Brown: Too Many Houses [179]

Jewels [215]

I, Too, Sing America: Three Centuries of African American Poetry [393]   J/811/Cl.

Written by Catherine Clinton
Illustrated by Stephen Alcorn

Hardcover: Houghton Mifflin
Published 1998

Thirty-six poems by great African American poets, from historical artists Lucy Terry and Langston Hughes to contemporary poets like Amiri Baraka and Nikki Giovanni, are included in this remarkable book. The gamut of African American experiences are topics of the selections. Brief biographical notes on the poets offer insight into their place in time and perspective. This impressive volume is illustrated with provocative, interpretive mixed-media paintings.

In Your Face [394]

Written by Robb Armstrong
Illustrated by Bruce Smith

Softcover: HarperActive, HarperCollins
Published 1998

Patrick Ewing and his basketball teammates, known as the Bulldogs, are challenged to a game of hoops by the Warriors, the meanest, toughest team in town. The game gets out of hand when tempers flare and the play gets more and more physical. When things are about to turn very ugly, the coach steps in to break up the game. Soon a fight challenge is issued by Carlos, captain of the Warriors. The Bulldogs depend on Patrick to stand up for their reputation and team pride. Face to face with Carlos, Patrick realizes that violence will only lead to more of the same. He makes the tough decision to end the nonsense by turning and walking away. This book features Patrick Ewing and fellow NBA players Dikembe Mutombo and Alonzo Mourning as adolescents in the fictionalized Patrick's Pals series. Other titles include: *Got Game?* [387], *Large and In Charge!* [406], *Runnin' with the Big Dawgs*, *Schoolin'* [431], *Stuffin' It*, and *Trashmaster*.

Jazmin's Notebook [395]

YA/Fiction/Grimes

Written by Nikki Grimes

Coretta Scott King Honor: Author

Hardcover: Dial
Published 1998

Jazmin is a fourteen-year-old streetwise kid living on a typical Harlem block in the 1960s. Young readers will see life through Jazmin's eyes as they read her daily journal entries. Each entry is a self-contained essay or poem about her sometimes difficult situations. But, all together, her daily expressions tell the story of the young girl's urban life. These vivid expressions from a bright young mind are well worth sharing.

Jazzimagination: A Journal to Read and Write [396]

Written by Sharon M. Draper ☆ 53

Hardcover: Scholastic
Published 1999

Thirteen-year-old Jazz Joy Jeffries is totally typical. Reading the entries in Jazz's daily journal, young readers who are going through puberty and other adolescent situations will understand that they are not alone in their feelings about their families, bodies, school, friends, and a number of other subjects. Jazz discusses her feelings frankly in this appealing book printed to simulate handwriting. There are plenty of extra pages at the end of each chapter to encourage young readers to respond to Jazz or to record their own feelings.

"Sometimes I get real moody, and I cry for no reason at all. Then Mama asks me what's wrong. I tell her nothing because there really is nothing wrong—nothing I can explain, anyway."

The Journal of Joshua Loper: A Black Cowboy, The Chisholm Trail, 1871 [397]

J Fiction Dear

Written by Walter Dean Myers ☆ 119

Hardcover: Scholastic
Published 1999

Sixteen-year-old Joshua Loper enters manhood the day he joins a cattle drive heading up the Chisholm Trail from Texas to Kansas. Joshua records his experiences in his daily journal from May through August, the duration of the drive. His reflections include personal accounts of the difficult journey, including dramatic stories about his challenging on-the-job training, stampeding cattle, and Indian encounters. Joshua's very personal diary, found after the real-life cowboy's death, in 1920, is a significant first-hand account of life as a black cowboy.

Jump Back, Honey: The Poems of Paul Laurence Dunbar [398]

J/811/Dun

Illustrated by Various Artists

Hardcover: Jump at the Sun, Hyperion Books for Children
Published 1999

Fourteen poems by the acclaimed poet Paul Laurence Dunbar are presented with stunning illustrations created by six well-known African American children's book artists: Ashley Bryan, Carole Byard, Jan Spivey Gilchrist, Brian Pinkney, Jerry Pinkney, and Faith Ringgold. The poems were expressly selected from Dunbar's body of work, because of their appeal to children. The now classic "Little Brown Baby" and the title poem, "Jump Back, Honey," are among the selections.

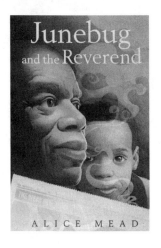

Junebug and the Reverend [399]

J Fiction Mead

Written by Alice Mead

Hardcover: Farrar, Straus and Giroux
Published 1998

Ten-year-old Junebug makes an honest attempt to adjust when the family moves to a new neighborhood because his mother has taken a job supervising a group home for the elderly. Junebug is challenged by a number of adolescent travails, like fitting in at the new school at the end of the school year, a confrontation with a bully, and hardest of all, accepting his mother's new boyfriend. The confused boy gets unexpected support and understanding from an unlikely friend, Reverend Ashford. The reverend, one of the home's elderly residents, gets as much as he gives from this touching relationship. The story is the sequel to *Junebug* [v1-365].

Keep on Singing: A Ballad of Marian Anderson [400]

Written by Myra Cohn Livingston
Illustrated by Samuel Byrd

Hardcover: Holiday House
Published 1994

In inspiring verse narrative, young readers are told of the talent and strength of character that propelled Marian Anderson from her humble beginnings in Philadelphia at the beginning of the twentieth century to become a triumphant, world-renowned singer. Marian's boundless talent and will to succeed enabled her to overcome both the poverty of her past and the racism she encountered along the way. Marian Anderson eventually sang on the steps of the Lincoln Memorial after being denied the opportunity to sing at Constitution Hall, and was the first African American woman to be invited to sing at the Metropolitan Opera in New York City.

Keisha Discovers Harlem [401]

Written by Zoe Lewis
Illustrated by Dan Burr and Rich Grote

Softcover: Magic Attic
Published 1998

JPB 50

Keisha takes a trip back in time to the 1920s and gets to experience the vibrancy of the Harlem Renaissance at first hand. This experience is just what she needs to prepare herself to write a term paper about an interesting period in history. Keisha is especially excited about her choice because it represents a special time in African American history when artists like Zora Neale Hurston, Langston Hughes, and Louis Armstrong thrived. Other books in the Magic Attic Club series include *Three Cheers for Keisha, Keisha the Fairy Snow Queen* [402], *Keisha to the Rescue, Keisha's Maze Mystery,* and *Keisha Leads the Way* [v1-372].

Keisha the Fairy Snow Queen [402]

Written by Teresa Reed
Illustrated by Eric Velasquez and Rich Grote

Softcover: Magic Attic
Published 1995

J PB 50

Young Keisha, a member of the Magic Attic Club, enters the attic and puts on a costume that magically transports her to another world. In the blink of an eye, Keisha finds herself the queen of the beautiful Crystal Kingdom. The kingdom will not survive unless Keisha can find the powerful energy crystal that warms the land. Keisha leads an exciting expedition to save her kingdom from extinction, delivering a dramatic reading experience for young readers. Other books in the Magic Attic Club series include *Three Cheers for Keisha, Keisha Discovers Harlem* [401], *Keisha to the Rescue, Keisha's Maze Mystery,* and *Keisha Leads the Way* [v1-372].

Kid Caramel, Private Investigator: The Werewolf of PS 40 [403]

Written by Dwayne J. Ferguson
Illustrated by Don Tate

Softcover: Just Us
Published 1998

Kid Caramel and his best friend Earnie are on their second intriguing case. When all of the neighborhood pets begin to disappear, Kid Caramel begins to ask some questions. But the answers suggest only one thing—that a werewolf is involved. Since Kid Caramel knows that there is no such thing as a werewolf, he begins to put two and two together until he uncovers the real culprit. Young readers will enjoy analyzing the clues to see if they can solve the mystery before Kid Caramel does. These young sleuths were introduced in *Kid Caramel, Private Investigator: Case of the Missing Ankh* [v1-373].

Kwanzaa: A Family Affair [404]

Written by Mildred Pitts Walter ☆ 188

Hardcover: Lothrop, Lee & Shepard
Published 1995

Everything a family needs to understand to celebrate Kwanzaa is in this family guide to the holiday. The early chapters share the story of Kwanzaa, including the history, principles, and traditional symbols and rituals of the season. Succeeding chapters offer detailed plans for celebrating the holiday, complete with recipes, activity ideas, and directions to make hand-crafted symbols and gifts. A glossary and pronunciation key help define new and unfamiliar terms.

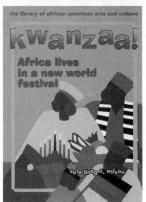

Kwanzaa!: Africa Lives in a New World Festival [405]

Written by Sule Greg C. Wilson

Hardcover: Rosen Publishing
Published 1999

This book about Kwanzaa does an excellent job of expressing the real objectives of the African American celebration. Through brief historical perspectives of the nations of Africa whose citizens came as slaves to America and a brief synopsis of African American history, young readers begin to appreciate the importance of connecting to and celebrating their heritage. A detailed description of the celebratory rites is also included. This book is for the true student who wishes to understand the holiday in both practical and historical terms. This book is part of the Library of African American Arts and Culture series, which also includes *African American Quilting: The Warmth of Tradition* [353]; *The African American Kitchen: Food for Body and Soul; Blues: Its Birth and Growth; Jazz Tap: From African Drums to American Feet; Jam!: The Story of Jazz Music;* and *Rap and Hip Hop: The Voice of a Generation.*

Large and In Charge! [406]

Written by Robb Armstrong
Illustrated by Bruce Smith

Hardcover: HarperEntertainment, HarperCollins
Published 1999

Patrick Ewing's teammate, Fat Craig Adams, loses confidence when DC, a kid from their rival team, begins to tease him about his weight. Suddenly, Craig wants to lose weight and becomes insecure on the basketball court. But when DC picks on Craig's younger, smaller teammate, Keith, Fat Craig reacts strongly and proves that he is "Phat" Craig on the court. This book is the seventh in the series based on the fictionalized young life of Patrick Ewing and other basketball greats. Other titles include *Got Game?* [387], *In Your Face* [394], *Runnin' with the Big Dawgs,* and *Schoolin'* [431].

The Last Safe House: A Story of the Underground Railroad [407]

Written by Barbara Greenwood
Illustrated by Heather Collins

Hardcover: Kids Can Press
Published 1998

Eleven-year-old runaway slave Eliza finds herself in the warmth and safety of the Reid home, an Underground Railroad safe house in St. Catharines, Canada. Eliza unfolds her harrowing story of escape to twelve-year-old Johanna Reid and her family, who listen sympathetically and remain determined to protect their secret guest. Even though she has crossed the border into Canada, she is still in jeopardy of being recaptured by mercenary slave catchers. Young readers will be chilled by some of the stories that Eliza tells, but will gain a broad understanding of the Underground Railroad operation and the treacherous route that escaping slaves took to freedom. Interspersed with the story are a series of short articles about aspects of the Underground Railroad, slavery, and important people and events of the time.

THE CREATORS

Mildred Pitts Walter

Author

"I hope that my writing will be made available to all children. When African American boys and girls read my books, I hope that they will see themselves and hear voices that ring true. I hope they identify with the characters, and find pleasure in being part of the black experience."

Our Favorites

Kwanzaa: A Family Affair [404]

My Mama Needs Me [81]

Suitcase [438]

Two and Too Much [329]

Ty's One-Man Band [331]

Let My People Go: Bible Stories Told by a Freeman of Color [408]

Written by Patricia and Fredrick McKissack
Illustrated by James E. Ransome

Hardcover: Atheneum Books for Young Readers, Simon & Schuster
Published 1998

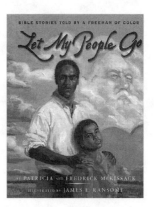

Inspired by memories of their African American Sunday-school teachers and driven by their understanding of the depth of African American spirituality, the McKissacks have prepared a keepsake book for our children. Twelve Bible stories are told by Price Coleman, a former slave, to his young daughter, Charlotte Jefferies Coleman, in South Carolina in the early 1800s. Traditional Bible stories like that of the Creation, Cain and Abel, and Noah and the ark take on new meaning when colorfully shared by Coleman. Notes by the author, the illustrator, and even by Charlotte herself lend a meaningful backdrop to this special book.

Letters from a Slave Girl: The Story of Harriet Jacobs [409]

YA/Lyons

Written by Mary E. Lyons

Hardcover: Charles Scribner's Sons
Published 1992

Based on Harriet Jacobs's 1861 autobiography, this book offers a compelling account of slave life and escape to the North by a woman who spent the first twenty-one years of her life as a slave. The author has converted Harriet's autobiography into a series of letters that chronicle her fears, struggles, and hopes for a new and better life. The first-person accounts of her experiences make Harriet's story very tangible and real for young readers and will offer a riveting reading experience. ***Nonstandard English.***

J Cooper

Life Riddles [410]

Written by Melrose Cooper

Hardcover: Henry Holt
Published 1993

Twelve-year-old Janelle and her family cope with her parents' separation and reunion, unemployment, and near poverty, which are all fodder for her fledgling writing career. Janelle is a talented young writer who is determined to learn and practice her craft. Through all of their difficult times, her family is loving and supportive of Janelle and encourages her to pursue her dreams. Janelle writes from the heart about her own experiences and gets early reinforcement that she is on the right track.

Listen Children: An Anthology of Black Literature [411]

Edited by Dorothy S. Strickland
Interior Illustrations by Leo Dillon and Diane Dillon ☆ 47

Softcover: Yearling, Bantam Doubleday Dell
Published 1982

These twenty-two stories, poems, speeches, and recollections by renowned African American writers and poets—from Eloise Greenfield and James Haskins to Martin Luther King Jr. and Maya Angelou—were specifically selected for young readers. The selections, divided into four sections—Feeling the Joy of Being Me; Feelings about My Roots; Feeling the Pain and Pride of Struggle; and Feelings about Who I Am and What I Want to Be—were chosen to help create an understanding of self and to pave a path to self-determination for young people.

> "*Midnight had heard so many stories from other cowboys at the Crazy Eight and in the towns they'd passed through about the 'bloodthirsty Injuns' and 'murdering red men.' Yet the one Indian he'd really known was a hard-working man like any other.*"

The Longest Ride [412]

Written by Denise Lewis Patrick ☆ 133

J Fiction Patrick

Hardcover: Henry Holt
Published 1999

Fifteen-year-old Midnight Son sets out on a quest from Colorado to Louisiana to find his family at the end of the Civil War. Midnight passes through an Indian village during his journey and is compelled to help two new friends, brother and sister Eagle Eye and Winter Mary, whose people are under attack by the United States Calvary. Midnight is brave and responsible beyond his years in this dramatic, action-packed story, the sequel to *Adventures of Midnight Son* [350].

Madam C. J. Walker: Entrepreneur [413]

Written by A'Lelia Perry Bundles

Hardcover and softcover: Chelsea House
Published 1991

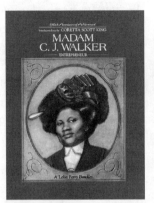

Madame C. J. Walker is just one of the note-worthy African American women from past and present who are profiled in the Black Americans of Achievement series. In this book, Sarah Breedlove, the daughter of former slaves, transforms her life by developing and selling a line of popular hair preparation products, becoming America's first black female millionaire in the early 1900s. By then she was known by her married name, Madame C. J. Walker, and her company and products carried her name. Her life story, including accounts of her political activism and social consciousness, is thoroughly presented for young readers. Other black female achievers in the Black Americans of Achievement series include Josephine Baker, Mary McLeod Bethune, Whoopi Goldberg, Barbara Jordan, Toni Morrison, Rosa Parks, Diana Ross, Sojourner Truth, Harriet Tubman, Tina Turner, Alice Walker, Vanessa Williams, and Oprah Winfrey.

Melitte [414]

Written by Fatima Shaik

Hardcover: Dial
Published 1997

This is a richly told story, seen through the eyes of Melitte, a young slave girl who lives a difficult life with her French master and mistress on a small farm in the bayou country of Louisiana in 1772. Melitte is treated cruelly by the couple, who do not acknowledge that she is her master's illegitimate daughter. Melitte bonds lovingly with Marie, the couple's younger daughter, who is actually her half-sister. Melitte accompanies her young mistress on a trip to New Orleans and is exposed, for the first time, to the concept of freedom. From then on she dreams only of her own emancipation. Melitte's innermost feelings of love, hate, resentment, fear, and hope are well developed in this mature story.

> "*She heard the dead quiet of bodies exhausted from working beyond human limits. She heard the soft sounds of weeping from empty stomachs and no relief. She heard the loud arguments over one crust of bread. . . . They were part of the language of slavery.*"

191

J Fiction Holt

Mister and Me [415]

Written by Kimberly Willis Holt
Illustrated by Leonard Jenkins

Hardcover: G. P. Putnam's Sons
Published 1998

Young Jolene is more than upset when Leroy comes into her widowed mother's life. Jolene, her mother, and her grandfather had been a happy little family until now. But Leroy wants to marry Momma. To show her disdain for the intruder, Jolene refuses to acknowledge him by name, calling him only Mister. Then she strikes out in the cruelest way to try to dissuade him from joining the family. Mister demonstrates that he is a big man with a very big heart. In time his kindness and patience endear him to Jolene, resulting in a touching conclusion to the sweet story.

Moaning Bones: African-American Ghost Stories [416]

J 398.25 Has

Written by Jim Haskins
Illustrated by Felicia Marshall

Hardcover: Lothrop, Lee & Shepard
Published 1998

Seventeen haunting short stories from the African American oral tradition have been collected and presented in this book for middle readers. Each story (most are only two or three pages long) conjures up images of ghosts and spirits who are sometimes frightening or evil, but just as often funny. The funniest, "Big Fraid and L'il Fraid," is about a boy who is asked if he is afraid to walk alone in the dark woods at night. The boy misunderstands the question and seeks a "fraid" during his late night walks, never realizing the danger.

My Home Is over Jordan [417]

Written by Sandra Forrester

Hardcover: Lodestar, Penguin
Published 1997

Maddie Henry is a brave young woman who journeys with her family from their temporary home in the Sea Islands of Georgia, where they took refuge during the Civil War, to South Carolina in search of a home to call their own. The family of ex-slaves meets another black family that leads them to a small town in South Carolina. They buy land and begin a new life that is filled with joys and opportunities but still plagued by racial injustice and bitterness. Maddie dreams of ultimately leaving the South and going to college in the North, but her goals change as she comes to terms with her new life. This book is the sequel to *Sound the Jubilee*.

The New York Public Library Amazing African American History: A Book of Answers for Kids [418]

Written by Diane Patrick

Softcover: John Wiley
Published 1998

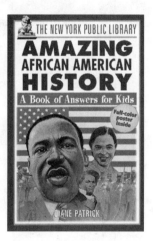

Hundreds of questions about the African American experience have been collected and answered in this interesting reference book. Nine chapters cover aspects of black history from Africa and colonial America through the Harlem Renaissance, the Civil Rights Movement, and the New Renaissance. Through the question-and-answer format, young readers will understand an issue and the natural series of questions that follow. In the section on FDR's New Deal, for example, are questions such as "How did the New Deal programs affect African Americans in the arts?," and "Did the New Deal programs help solve the economic problems of African Americans?" Sidebars and a large selection of photographs add to the knowledge-building resource.

Nobody's Family Is Going to Change [419]

Written by Louise Fitzhugh

Softcover: Sunburst, Farrar, Straus and Giroux
Published 1974

Eleven-year-old Emma dreams of becoming an attorney, an idea that neither her mother nor her father embraces. Her mother thinks that she should grow up, marry, and raise a family, while her father, a practicing attorney, thinks that women lawyers are a joke. The dream of Emma's younger brother, Willie, who wants to be a dancer, is equally unacceptable to their conservative parents. Despite all attempts to earn her parents' respect and support, Emma realizes that they are incapable of change and that she will have to strive toward her dream despite their attitudes.

Carole Boston Weatherford

AUTHOR

"For today's children, African American books are a part of growing up. My own children have benefited from the bounty of African American books in the marketplace. Books with black children characters affirm children's self-worth and lift the ceiling off their dreams by introducing them to fictional and real-life role models who achieved despite adversity."

OUR FAVORITES

Juneteenth Jamboree [vl-213]

Me and My Family Tree [vl-71]

Mighty Menfolk [vl-72]

Sink or Swim: African-American Lifesavers of the Outer Banks [432]

Once on This River [420]

Written by Sharon Dennis Wyeth ☆ 201

Softcover: Knopf
Published 1998

Eleven-year-old Monday and her mother set sail on a voyage from Madagascar to America in 1760. Their mission, to rescue Monday's uncle from slavery, is a dangerous one, since they could be illegally forced into slavery themselves. On the voyage Monday witnesses other Africans being transported as slaves from the African continent. Her horror at their condition makes it even more important to save her uncle. This intense story is presented in vivid detail.

Osceola: Memories of a Sharecropper's Daughter [421]

Collected and edited by Alan Govenar
Illustrated by Shane W. Evans

Hardcover: Jump at the Sun, Hyperion
Published 2000

Osceola Mays, born a sharecropper's daughter in 1909, recalls poignant memories of her life in a series of conversations and interviews with the writer that spanned a fifteen-year period. Osceola's recollections, told in short two- or three-page vignettes, include stories about the day she was baptised, what it was like to grow up in a one-bedroom house with no running water or electricity, and her fear of white people, which caused her to hide whenever the postman delivered the mail.

The Other Side: Shorter Poems [422]

Written by Angela Johnson   **Coretta Scott King Honor: Author**

Hardcover: Orchard
Published 1998

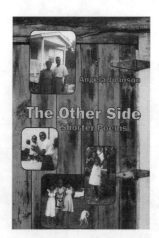

Thirty-three poems come from the heart, in this book about a girl growing up in Shorter, Alabama. The contents are full of deep thought and emotion about the girl's (the author's) actual experiences growing up. In one particularly telling poem, entitled "Crazy," she reflects on the state of mind one must have to want to live in Shorter, Alabama.

Phoebe the Spy [423]

Written by Judith Berry Griffin
Illustrated by Margot Tomes

Softcover: Scholastic
Published 1977

Thirteen-year-old Phoebe accepts a terrifying assignment when her father asks her to go undercover as a housekeeper for General George Washington in this true story. Phoebe's father, a free black man, is a patriot supportive of America's quest for independence from England during the American Revolution. He fears that an assassination attempt will be made on General Washington's life by someone loyal to the king of England. Phoebe's mission is to spy on General Washington's guests and associates to identify the traitor. Young Phoebe was truly an unsung American heroine, because it was through her heroic actions that the assassination attempt was foiled. This book was originally titled *Phoebe and the General*.

Pink and Say [424]

Written and illustrated by Patricia Polacco

Hardcover: Philomel
Published 1994

This heart-stinging true story has been passed down through the generations of the family of Sheldon Curtis (Say), a white Union soldier in the Civil War, and is offered in tribute to the black soldier, Pinkus Aylee (Pink), who befriended him. Pink found the wounded Say in a pasture and carried him to the home of his own mother for nursing and recovery. The two men, as Union soldiers, and the black woman, living alone in Confederate territory, defied the odds in this dramatic story. Their kindness cost Pink and his mother their lives but brought them Say's undying gratitude.

Reflections of a Black Cowboy: Pioneers [425]

Written by Robert H. Miller
Illustrated by Floyd Cooper

Hardcover: Silver Burdett
Published 1991

The stories of six African American pioneers are expressively told, adding them to the pages of American history. Young readers will read, perhaps for the first time, about York, an invaluable guide and interpreter on the Lewis and Clark Expedition; Biddy Mason, a slave woman who walked from

Mississippi to California with her West-bound master and then sued him for her freedom once they reached their destination; and others. Each story is brought to life with great panache and a few well-placed black-and-white illustrations. The Reflections of a Black Cowboy series also includes titles on the Buffalo Soldiers [v1-468], cowboys, and mountainmen.

The Righteous Revenge of Artemis Bonner [426]

Written by Walter Dean Myers ☆ 119

Softcover: HarperTrophy, HarperCollins
Published 1992

Artemis Bonner tells his side of the story in this spirited novel about a young man who travels to the Old West to hunt down the "murderous scalawag" Catfish Grimes, who killed his uncle. Artemis teams up with a young Cherokee boy named Frolic, and they chase the no-good Catfish and his girl-friend, Lucy Featherdip, across the West. Along the way, the two teams try to find the hidden treasure that Uncle Ugly buried before he died. Artemis and Frolic encounter the evil Catfish more than once, but they can't bring him to justice until the big gunfight scene at the end—and even then it is not over. The thoroughly entertaining story is humorously told by the proper young Artemis in a colorful language all his own.

> *"I heard that Catfish Grimes was not an easy sort to deal with, nor would the Featherdip woman be a pushover. But they would learn that Artemis Bonner knew more than what lay between the pages of his Hymnal and would not tolerate being taken lightly."*

Rimshots: Basketball Pix, Rolls, and Rhythms [427]

Written by Charles R. Smith, Jr.

Hardcover: Dutton, Penguin Putnam
Softcover: Puffin
Published 1999

Fourteen in-your-face selections about the game of basketball are guaranteed to get your young slam-dunker off the court and into a book, even if only for a few minutes. The selections—some poems, some stories, some personal reflections—are presented with bold graphic type and action photographs of the game.

> *"Wipe the sweat off the face with the left hand first. That's for Mom. Wipe the sweat off with the right hand. That's for Dad. Spin the ball in a quick vertical motion. Dribble, Dribble, Dribble, Deep breath. Eye on the rim. Shoot."*

Run Away Home [428]

Written by Patricia C. McKissack

J/Mckissack

Softcover: Scholastic
Published 1997

Young Sarah sees a young Apache boy, named Sky, escape from a train bound for a new Indian reservation in Florida. She also knows that Sky has taken secret refuge in her family's barn. Sarah and her family, led by her proud ex-slave father, are struggling to make a living on their small Alabama farm in 1888. Their hopes are dashed when their crops fail and there seems to be no way to save the farm from their white neighbors, who are anxious to take over the land and force the proud family into sharecropping. Sky, who now lives with the family, becomes an unexpected asset in their fight to save the farm. **Nonstandard English.**

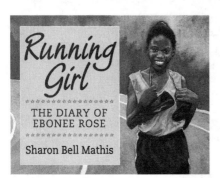

Running Girl: The Diary of Ebonee Rose [429]

Written by Sharon Bell Mathis ☆ 108

Hardcover: Browndeer, Harcourt Brace
Published 1997

As eleven-year-old Ebonee Rose prepares for the All-City track meet, she fills the pages of her diary with her most heartfelt thoughts. Each entry reveals some of Ebonee's fears and anxieties, as well as inspirations that she got from female track stars like Jackie Joyner-Kersee, Wilma Rudolph, and Flo Jo (Florence Griffith-Joyner). Poetic journal entries, quotations from famous female track athletes, and photographs of some of the female greats embellish the story and are reinforcing to young readers interested in this sport.

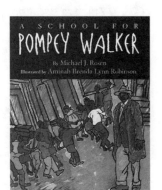

A School for Pompey Walker [430]

J/Fiction/Rosen

Written by Michael J. Rosen
Illustrated by Aminah Brenda Lynn Robinson

Hardcover: Harcourt Brace
Published 1995

A ninety-year-old man, Pompey, captivates a group of schoolchildren by discussing his experiences as a tortured slave many decades before. He shares a riveting story about his early days as an abused stable boy who yearned to go to school. One day his master's son-in-law, Jeremiah, who hated slavery, buys Pompey and immediately offers him his freedom. Pompey convinces Jeremiah to help him reach the North, where his freedom will be assured.

Along the way, the two create a plan to make money for the journey. Over and over again, Jeremiah sells Pompey back into slavery and then helps him escape again. They share the money made with the dangerous con and put it to good use later, when Pompey fulfills his dream of establishing a school for black children.

Schoolin' [431]

Written by Robb Armstrong
Illustrated by Bruce Smith

Softcover: HarperCollins
Published: 1999

Young Patrick Ewing learns how one little lie can spin out of control. It all starts innocently enough when Patrick is chosen to play on the father-son basketball team for the school's Family Day. But Patrick, still mourning the death of his mother, decides not to ask his father to come. He knows that Dad has an important presentation at work that day, and the thought of Family Day without his mother is still too painful. One little white lie Patrick tells to avoid the whole problem leads to another and another, until he looses control of the situation. When he is finally forced to reveal the whole story to Dad, he is comforted by the love and support of his dedicated father and clearly understands the consequences of lying. This book is one in the series based on the fictionalized young life of Patrick Ewing and other basketball greats. Other titles include: *Got Game* [387], *In Your Face* [394], *Large and In Charge* [406], and *Runnin' with the Big Dawgs*.

Sink or Swim: African-American Lifesavers of the Outer Banks [432]

Written by Carole Boston Weatherford ☆ 194

Hardcover and softcover: Coastal Carolina
Published 1999

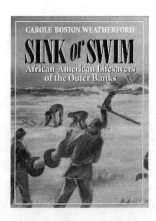

Another little-known chapter in African American history is thoroughly told in this book about the all-black crew of the U.S. Lifesaving Service (forerunner to the U.S. Coast Guard), which operated from 1880 to 1947, from Pea Island off the North Carolina coast. This crew, led by Richard Etheridge, was never recognized for their hundreds of heroic life-saving missions in the hurricane-prone Outer Banks until 1996, when President Clinton honored the brave seamen posthumously with the Coast Guard's esteemed Gold Lifesaving Medal.

Sky Kings: Black Pioneers of Professional Basketball [433]

Written by Bijan C. Bayne

Softcover: Franklin Watts, Grolier
Published 1997

The game of basketball, invented in 1890 by James Naismith, has become at least as popular as baseball, if not more so. Yet young fans may not know of the history of the sport nor of the black pioneers who opened the game for other African Americans. Young readers will learn about the trials and tribulations of early black players like those on the Harlem Renaissance, the team that won the 1938–39 world championship; and of Chuck Cooper, Earl Lloyd, and Nat Clifton, who were the first to break through the color lines to integrate professional basketball. The book covers select pioneers and their achievements through the 1960s, when African Americans began to dominate the sport.

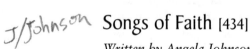

Songs of Faith [434]

Written by Angela Johnson

Hardcover: Orchard
Published 1998

No one really understands how difficult it is for thirteen-year-old Doreen to adjust to her parents' divorce and her new life in a small town in Ohio. Doreen misses her father, who lives in another city, and her mother, who is absorbed in working toward a college degree. Matters are made worse when her best friend moves away and her brother, Robert, shuts her out. Doreen feels all alone until her mother gives her a reason to have faith.

The Spray-Paint Mystery [435]

Written by Angela Shelf Medearis

Softcover: Little Apple, Scholastic
Published 1996

Young Cameron and his best friend, Tarann, are on the trail of the someone who painted graffiti on a school wall. Cameron has honed his detective skills and powers of observation to narrow the suspects down to three possibilities. Now he and Tarann embark on a plan to figure out the puzzling case. Young readers will enjoy trying to second-guess the two young sleuths and figure out the case before the surprising end.

THE CREATORS

Sharon Dennis Wyeth

AUTHOR

"Today's books give kids their rightful place in the culture of imagination and artistry, which is the world of literature! Who wants to fully embrace a world that leaves us out?"

OUR FAVORITES

Always My Dad [118]

Ginger Brown: The Nobody Boy [178]

Once on This River [420]

Something Beautiful [302]

Vampire Bugs: Stories Conjured from the Past [446]

Storyteller's Beads [436] J / Fiction / Kurtz

Written by Jane Kurtz

Hardcover: Gulliver, Harcourt Brace
Published 1998

Two girls, Sahay and Rachel, are bonded together during their brave journey from their Ethiopian homeland to the Sudan, where they hope to find peace and food. The story takes place during the Ethiopian famine of the 1980s, a time when millions were dying of starvation and internal warfare. The two girls—one Jewish, one Christian—ultimately find that they have more in common than not, once they overlook their different ethnic upbringings and inbred prejudices against each other. The story, rich with details about the customs, superstitions, and traditions of two distinctly different Ethiopian groups, is a good read for young readers of historical fiction.

Stretch Your Wings: Famous Black Quotations for Teens [437]

Selected and edited by Janet Bell and Lucille Usher Freeman

Softcover: Little, Brown
Published 1999

❝*T*hank goodness I had two parents who loved me enough to stay on my case.❞
—Shaquille O'Neal

Quotes from more than 150 African Americans, past and contemporary, from all walks of life, are organized into fourteen topical sections for teen readers. The collection includes thoughts that are at times provocative, inspirational, humorous, sad, and revealing.

Suitcase [438] J Fiction Walker

Written by Mildred Pitts Walter ☆ 188
Illustrated by Teresa Flavin

Hardcover: Lothrop, Lee & Shepard, William Morrow
Published 1999

Eleven-year-old Alexander, also known as "Suitcase" because of his big feet, is over six feet tall and seems like a natural for the basketball court. But Alexander doesn't like basketball at all and would prefer to become an artist. Young Alexander is torn between trying to please his father, who wants him to play ball, and following his own heart. Eventually, Alexander does get the opportunity to demonstrate his artistic ability and makes his father proud of him for his own special gifts.

Take a Walk in Their Shoes [439] J/920.009/Tur

Written by Glennette Tilley Turner ☆ 171
Illustrated by Elton C. Fax

Hardcover: Cobblehill
Published 1989

Brief biographical portraits of fourteen historical figures from Martin Luther King Jr. and Rosa Parks to Daniel "Chappie" James and Ida B. Wells are followed by a short scripted skit for young readers to act out. The learning experience will be reinforced when they assume the roles of these important people and "walk in their shoes."

Talking with Tebé: Clementine Hunter, Memory Artist [440]

Edited by Mary E. Lyons

Hardcover: Houghton Mifflin
Published 1998

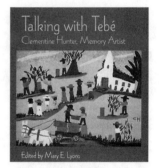

The life and times of plantation worker and self-taught folk artist Clementine Hunter are captured in ten short chapters. Samples of her acclaimed work on a variety of subjects from "Girlhood" and "Success" to "Housework" and "My People" are displayed with some of the artist's own words, which were gleaned from newspaper articles and taped interviews. Hunter's body of work, done during her seventy-five years as a laborer on a Louisiana plantation, depicts all aspects of black plantation life.

Teresa Weatherspoon's Basketball for Girls [441]

Written by Teresa Weatherspoon with Tara Sullivan and Kelly Whiteside

Softcover: John Wiley
Published 1999

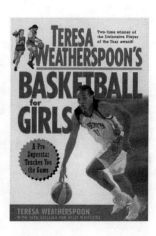

Young basketball enthusiasts will learn the game from Teresa Weatherspoon, the Olympian and WNBA New York Liberty player who was twice named Defensive Player of the Year. Teresa offers detailed drills and strategies to improve all essential game skills, including passing, dribbling, defending, and shooting. Complete game rules are also given. Teresa's insights into the attributes of successful players supplement the technical skills that are offered in this photo-packed guide to the game.

Through My Eyes [442]   J/Bio/ Bridges

Written by Ruby Bridges
Articles and interviews compiled by Margo Lundell

Hardcover: Scholastic
Published 1999

Ruby Bridges, the six-year-old black girl who integrated the William Franz public school in Baton Rouge, Louisiana, in 1960 under the protection of federal marshals, tells her own story in this poignant book. Ruby looks back on her early life, the events leading up to her historic walk into that school, and the aftermath of the event. She also describes the special relationship that she had, as the only student in the class, with her teacher, Barbara Henry. The story is reinforced by a series of articles and interviews that took place during that time and a large collection of photographs.

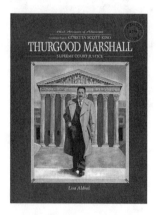

Thurgood Marshall: Supreme Court Justice [443]

Written by Lisa Aldred   J/B/ Marshall

Hardcover and softcover: Chelsea
Published 1990

Thurgood Marshall—lawyer, judge, and civil rights leader—is just one of over sixty noteworthy African American men who are profiled in the Black Americans of Achievement series. This book tracks Marshall's life from his birth in Baltimore through his esteemed position as a justice of the nation's highest court. Other black male achievers profiled in the series include Alex Haley, Denzel Washington, Josh Gibson, and Romare Bearden.

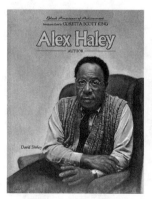

Till Victory Is Won: Black Soldiers in the Civil War [444]

Written by Zak Mettger

Softcover: Puffin, Penguin
Published 1994

A comprehensive history of African Americans' role in the Civil War is described in six fact-filled chapters. The book offers insights into the political climate, the motivation of the Union, and the motivation of blacks themselves during this turbulent time in our history. It also recounts the significant contributions made by blacks and their influence on the outcome of the war. The book is full of illustrations, including some antique photographs from the time.

To Hell with Dying [445]

Written by Alice Walker
Illustrated by Catherine Deeter

Hardcover: Harcourt Brace Jovanovich
Published 1988

A compassionate young girl and her family befriend a neighbor, Mr. Sweet, a diabetic and an alcoholic who has endeared himself to the family, who regard him as one of their own. On any number of occasions, Mr. Sweet has been near death, but the family has always come to his bedside and cajoled him back to life. It was somehow assumed that they could always revive the dying Mr. Sweet, until many years later, when the young girl, now a woman, loses the friend she has held so dear.

Vampire Bugs: Stories Conjured from the Past [446]

Written by Sharon Dennis Wyeth ☆ 201   *J/ Wyeth*
Illustrated by Curtis E. James

Softcover: Bantam Doubleday Dell Books for Young Readers
Published 1995

This collection of dark stories is inspired by the folktales, legends, and history of the Georgia Sea Islands. The six scary stories feature voodoo queens, conjurers, and other characters from the spirit world who perform magical transformations and mysterious acts. The fascinating stories can entertain the strong of heart, but young readers should be wary not to get carried away!

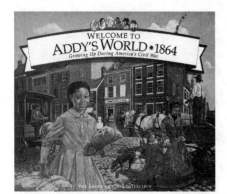

Welcome to Addy's World, 1864: Growing Up During America's Civil War [447]

Written by Susan Sinnott
Illustrated by Dahl Taylor

Hardcover: Pleasant
Published 1999

Addy Walker is the featured character in the American Girl series about an ex-slave girl who makes a new life as a free person in Philadelphia. Young Addy's world is seen in this picture-rich reference book. Life in both the North and South during the American Civil War is illustrated with real photographs, diary entries, letters, stories, and photographs from the time. Stories about the fictional Addy include: *Meet Addy* [v1-382]; *Addy Learns a Lesson* [348]; *Addy's Surprise* [349]; *Happy Birthday, Addy; Addy Saves the Day;* and *Changes for Addy.*

Witnesses to Freedom: Young People Who Fought for Civil Rights [448]

Written by Belinda Rochelle

Softcover: Puffin, Penguin
Published 1997

It is commonly understood that no single person or event was responsible for the success of the civil rights movement of the 1950s and 1960s. But very few realize the contributions of children to the movement. This book explores the stories of the young people who took stands, along with adults, to make a difference. Stories of the brave youngsters involved in the Little Rock school desegregation, freedom rides, sit-ins, and other nonviolent demonstrations are illustrated with plentiful black-and-white pictures. Personal profiles of some of the young individuals involved are also included.

Ziggy and the Black Dinosaurs: Lost in the Tunnel of Time [449]

Written by Sharon M. Draper ☆ 53
Illustrated by Michael Bryant

Softcover: Just Us
Published 1996

Ziggy and his friends are intrigued by a lecture about the secret hiding places in their town that used to be a part of the Underground Railroad. The adventurous boys go exploring and discover a trap door that leads to a tunnel under their school that they believe is the threshold to the hidden rooms. The door slams shut and the four are hopelessly trapped and then lost in the dark maze. After several frightening hours and the wild imaginings of the young boys, they are dramatically rescued. Other books in this series include *Ziggy and the Black Dinosaurs* [v1-420] and *Ziggy and the Black Dinosaurs: Shadows of Caesar's Creek* [450].

Ziggy and the Black Dinosaurs: Shadows of Caesar's Creek [450]

Written by Sharon M. Draper ☆ 53
Illustrated by James E. Ransome

Softcover: Just Us
Published 1997

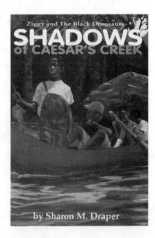

Ziggy and his friends, members of the Black Dinosaurs Club, go on an exciting camping trip to Caesar's Creek State Park. Intrigued by the stories of the area, which was once inhabited by Native Americans, the mischievous boys sneak out late at night when they are supposed to be asleep in their tent. The four become hopelessly lost in the woods, and then victims of their own imaginations. Other books in this series include *Ziggy and the Black Dinosaurs* and *Ziggy and the Black Dinosaurs: Lost in the Tunnel of Time* [449].

APPENDIX A

BOOKS FOR PARENTS AND FAMILIES

As a natural extension of our work with African American children's books, we often find books that, although not specifically for children, are wonderful resources for African American parents and families. We would like to share a few of them with you.

The African American Baby Name Book: A Treasury of Over 10,000 Unique, Traditional, and Creative Names for the New Millennium by Teresa Norman (Berkley Books, 1998). Boys' names from Aaron to Zuri and girls' names from Aaliyah to Zuwena are included in this inspirational naming guide. In addition to the traditional names, expectant parents can research a host of contemporary ethnic or religious Muslim and African names, complete with information on each name's origin, meaning, and alternative spellings.

The Beauty of Creation: Inspiration for Pregnancy & Childbirth by Elisa Roberson, Lorinda Griffin, Michelle Hendricks, and Zaakira Muhammad (NanKira Books, 1998). Four African American mothers have collaborated with medical experts—a perinatologist and an obstetrician—on this informative book for the expectant mother. The book is full of essential information about the entire child-bearing process from the beginning of the pregnancy to the delivery of a healthy baby. There are also meaningful sections on complications and high-risk pregnancies to prepare every mother-to-be.

Black Authors and Illustrators of Books for Children and Young Adults: A Biographical Dictionary by Barbara Thrash Murphy (Garland Publishing, 1999). This book offers the other side of our guides to great African American children's books. In this comprehensive reference book, readers can learn about the many talented authors and illustrators who create the books for and about African American children. A brief biographical sketch, photographs, and artistic credits for each author and illustrator are included, and there are several informative appendixes.

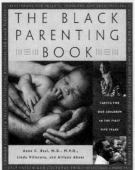

The Black Parenting Book: Caring for Our Children in the First Five Years by Anne C. Beal, M.D., M.P.H., Linda Villarosa, and Allison Abner (Broadway Books, 1999). You may have heard that new babies do not come with instructions. But all that has changed. This comprehensive guide to parenting is an excellent resource for parents raising young children. It contains practical advice and information on subjects ranging from taking care of a new baby and feeding young children to subjects particularly germane to African American parents like fostering spirituality and self-esteem in the black child.

A Circle of Love: A Record Book of Our Family by Monica Stewart (Havoc Publishing, 1999). Create a keepsake book of family memories in this well-designed journal. There are pages and places to record treasured information about family members from great-grands to parents, births, special family occasions, favorite family recipes, photographs, and more.

The Complete African-American Baby Checklist: A Total Organizing System by Elyse Zorin Karlin and Daisy Spier with Diane Williams (Avon Books, 1999). This book will help expectant parents prepare for their new baby from conception to the early care and keeping. Loads of tips and pointers about the practical matters are followed by checklists to help parents manage new additions to the family. While this material is suitable for any parent, there are also relevant inclusions just for African Americans, like information about sickle-cell anemia and lists of black publications and organizations.

Footsteps: African American History (A Cobblestone Publication). *Footsteps,* a magazine published five times annually, focuses on a variety of interesting African American historical topics for young readers and their families. For example, the January/February 1999 issue contained articles and special features on different aspects of blacks' roles in the Civil War, including the Glory Soldiers—the 54th Massachusetts Volunteer Infantry. Each edition also features kid-friendly activities, such as recipes and crafts that reinforce the theme. A regular subscription to this magazine will help families build a fine reference file of African American history.

Grandparents as Parents: A Survival Guide for Raising a Second Family by Sylvie deToledo and Deborah Edler Brown (The Guildford Press, 1995). While not specifically addressed to African Americans, this guide is an excellent resource for the growing population of grandparents who are assuming the child-rearing responsibilities for their grandchildren. There are thorough discussions about the children, the changing roles and relationships, the law, and support resources available to help manage this new family profile.

In the Black: The African-American Parent's Guide to Raising Financially Responsible Children by Fran Harris (Fireside Books, Simon & Schuster, 1997). This paperback financial primer should be in the hands of all African American parents to help them guide their children through the complex process of learning how to manage money responsibly. The two-hundred-page guide is full of useful ideas and tips, practical exercises, and anecdotes to help establish an early understanding of personal finance.

Mama's Little Baby: The Black Woman's Guide to Pregnancy, Childbirth, and Baby's First Year by Dennis Brown, M.D., and Pamela A. Toussaint (A Plume Book, 1997). This is more than just a book about the medical and physiological details of pregnancy and childbirth. It is also chock full of historical, spiritual and cultural information uniquely relevant for African American women. Two special features— Mother to Mother, anecdotal reflections from mothers, and Historically Speaking, glimpses into past cultural practices—add an interesting dimension to this thorough book on the subject.

Proud Heritage: 11,001 Names for Your African American Baby by Eliza Dinwiddie-Boyd (Avon Books, 1994). With the selection of over 11,000 names found in this book you will be assured that your child can be blessed with a traditional or distinctive name taken from either the Euro-American culture or from African roots. The listings include information on the origin and the meaning of each moniker to help you find a special name for your new baby.

Smart Parenting for African Americans: Helping Your Kids Thrive in a Difficult World by Jeffry Gardere, Ph.D. (Carol Publishing Group, 1999). In addition to general parenting information that would be useful to any parent, this book contains an abundance of information that is more specifically (maybe even sadly) addressed for parents of African American kids who face different threats. Special considerations such as understanding the hip-hop culture, gang life, and police interactions are frankly discussed, with insights and practical coping ideas. The book is very soundly written, exploring contemporary parenting problems and solutions.

The Ties That Bind: Timeless Values for African American Families by Joyce A. Ladner, Ph.D. (John Wiley & Sons, 1998). Offering thought-provoking insight into the traditional black value system, and principles for living that can continue to guide black families in comtemporary life, this book contains potent thoughts about the power of self-identity, the power of the extended family, the power of the community, and the power of the past to influence the future. Most importantly, parents can learn methods for keeping these values alive in their own families through the home, church, school, and community.

APPENDIX B

BOOK AWARDS

THE CORETTA SCOTT KING AWARDS

The Coretta Scott King Award was first conceived in 1969 at an American Library Association Conference. School librarians Mabel McKissick and Glyndon Greer and publisher John Carroll were lamenting the fact that in the more than sixty years of the Newbery and Caldecott Medals so few minority authors or illustrators had been recognized. The three award founders developed their idea and drew on other librarians to support their plan. Their next step was to determine a name for the award program. They decided to commemorate the life and work of Martin Luther King Jr. and to honor his wife, Coretta Scott King, for her "courage and determination in continuing the work for peace and brotherhood."

The first award presentation was made in 1970, although the award program was not officially adopted by the American Library Association until 1982. The Coretta Scott King Award is now a highly recognized and coveted professional honor. The criteria for selection include that "recipients are African American authors and illustrators whose distinguished books promote an understanding and appreciation of the culture and contributions of all people to the realization of the 'American dream.'"

Coretta Scott King Author Awards

2001 AWARD: *Miracle Boys,* Jacqueline Woodson
  HONOR: *Let It Shine,* Andrea Pinkney
2000 AWARD: *Bud, Not Buddy,* Christopher Paul Curtis [366]
  HONOR: *Francie,* Karen English [381]
     *Black Hands, White Sails: The Story of African-American
      Whalers,* Patricia C. and Fredrick L. McKissack [361]
     Monster, Walter Dean Myers
1999 AWARD: *Heaven,* Angela Johnson [389]
  HONOR: *Jazmin's Notebook,* Nikki Grimes [395]
     *Breaking Ground, Breaking Silence: The Story of New York's African
      Burial Ground,* Joyce Hansen and Gary McGowen
     The Other Side: Shorter Poems, Angela Johnson [422]

1998 AWARD: *Forged by Fire*, Sharon M. Draper [vI-44I]

    HONOR: *I Thought My Soul Would Rise and Fly: The Diary of Patsy, a Freed Girl*, Joyce Hansen [392]

        Bayard Rustin: Behind the Scenes of the Civil Rights Movement, James Haskins

1997 AWARD: *Slam!*, Walter Dean Myers [vI-476]

    HONOR: *Rebels Against Slavery: American Slave Revolts*, Patricia C. and Fredrick McKissack [vI-467].

1996 AWARD: *Her Stories: African American Folktales, Fairy Tales and True Tales*, Virginia Hamilton [vI-359]

    HONOR: *The Watsons Go to Birmingham—1963*, Christopher Paul Curtis [vI-490]

        Like Sisters on the Homefront, Rita Williams-Garcia

        From the Notebooks of Melanin Sun, Jacqueline Woodson

1995 AWARD: *Christmas in the Big House, Christmas in the Quarters*, Patricia and Fredrick L. McKissack [vI-328]

    HONOR: *I Hadn't Meant to Tell You This*, Jacqueline Woodson [vI-448]

        The Captive, Joyce Hansen [vI-326]

        Black Diamond: The Story of the Negro Baseball League, Patricia C. and Fredrick L. McKissack Jr. [vI-426]

1994 AWARD: *Toning the Sweep*, Angela Johnson [vI-487]

    HONOR: *Brown Honey in Broomwheat Tea*, Joyce Carol Thomas [vI-137]

        Malcolm X: By Any Means Necessary, Walter Dean Myers

1993 AWARD: *The Dark-Thirty: Southern Tales of the Supernatural*, Patricia C. McKissack [vI-434]

    HONOR: *Mississippi Challenge*, Mildred Pitts Walter [vI-458]

        Sojourner Truth: Ain't I a Woman? Patricia C. and Fredrick L. McKissack [vI-477]

        Somewhere in the Darkness, Walter Dean Myers [vI-478]

1992 AWARD: *Now Is Your Time! The African American Struggle for Freedom*, Walter Dean Myers

    HONOR: *Night on Neighborhood Street*, Eloise Greenfield [vI-242]

1991 AWARD: *The Road to Memphis*, Mildred D. Taylor

    HONOR: *Black Dance in America: A History Through Its People*, James Haskins

        When I Am Old With You, Angela Johnson [vI-II3]

1990 AWARD: *A Long Hard Journey: The Story of the Pullman Porter*, Patricia C. and Fredrick L. McKissack

    HONOR: *Nathaniel Talking*, Eloise Greenfield [vI-238]

        The Bells of Christmas, Virginia Hamilton [130]

        Martin Luther King, Jr., and the Freedom Movement, Lillie Patterson

1989 AWARD: *Fallen Angels*, Walter Dean Myers
    HONOR: *A Thief in the Village and Other Stories*, James Berry
       Anthony Burns: The Defeat and Triumph of a Fugitive Slave,
         Virginia Hamilton
1988 AWARD: *The Friendship*, Mildred D. Taylor
    HONOR: *An Enchanted Hair Tale*, Alexis DeVeaux [vl-l65]
       The Tales of Uncle Remus: The Adventures of Brer Rabbit, Julius
         Lester
1987 AWARD: *Justin and the Best Biscuits in the World*, Mildred Pitts Walter [vl-370]
    HONOR: *Lion and the Ostrich Chicks and Other African Folk Tales*,
         Ashley Bryan
       Which Way Freedom?, Joyce Hansen [vl-493]
1986 AWARD: *The People Could Fly: American Black Folktales*, Virginia Hamilton
         [vl-393]
    HONOR: *Junius Over Far*, Virginia Hamilton
       Trouble's Child, Mildred Pitts Walter
1985 AWARD: *Motown and Didi: A Love Story*, Walter Dean Myers [vl-460]
    HONOR: *Circle of Gold*, Candy Dawson Boyd [vl-329]
       A Little Love, Virginia Hamilton
1984 AWARD: *Everett Anderson's Goodbye*, Lucille Clifton [vl-167]
    CITATION: *The Words of Martin Luther King, Jr.*, Coretta Scott King
    HONOR: *The Magical Adventures of Pretty Pearl*, Virginia Hamilton
       Lena Horne, James Haskins
       Bright Shadow, Joyce Carol Thomas
       Because We Are, Mildred Pitts Walter
1983 AWARD: *Sweet Whispers, Brother Rush*, Virginia Hamilton [vl-483]
    HONOR: *This Strange New Feeling*, Julius Lester [vl-484]
1982 AWARD: *Let the Circle Be Unbroken*, Mildred D. Taylor
    HONOR: *Rainbow Jordan*, Alice Childress
       Lou in the Limelight, Kristin Hunter
       Mary: An Autobiography, Mary E. Mebane
1981 AWARD: *This Life*, Sidney Poitier
    HONOR: *Don't Explain: A Song of Billie Holiday*, Alexis DeVeaux
1980 AWARD: *The Young Landlords*, Walter Dean Myers [vl-499]
    HONOR: *Movin' Up: Pop Gordy Tells His Story*, Berry Gordy Sr.
       Childtimes: A Three-Generation Memoir, Eloise Greenfield
         and Lessie Jones Little
       Andrew Young: Young Man with a Mission, James Haskins
       James Van Der Zee: The Picture Takin' Man, James Haskins
       Let the Lion Eat Straw, Ellease Southerland

1979 AWARD: *Escape to Freedom: A Play about Young Frederick Douglass,*
Ossie Davis [vi-340]

HONOR: *Skates of Uncle Richard,* Carol Fenner

Justice and Her Brothers, Virginia Hamilton

Benjamin Banneker: Genius of Early America, Lillie Patterson

I Have a Sister: My Sister Is Deaf, Jeanne Whitehouse Peterson

1978 AWARD: *Africa Dream,* Eloise Greenfield

HONOR: *The Days When the Animals Talked: Black Folk Tales and How
They Came to Be,* William J. Faulkner

Marvin and Tige, Frankcina Glass

Mary McLeod Bethune, Eloise Greenfield

Barbara Jordan, James Haskins

Coretta Scott King, Lillie Patterson

*Portia: The Life of Portia Washington Pittman, the Daughter of
Booker T. Washington,* Ruth Ann Stewart

1977 AWARD: *The Story of Stevie Wonder,* James Haskins

HONOR: *Everett Anderson's Friend,* Lucille Clifton [31]

Roll of Thunder, Hear My Cry, Mildred D. Taylor [vi-469]

Quiz Book on Black America, Clarence N. Blake and Donald F.
Martin

1976 AWARD: *Duey's Tale,* Pearl Bailey

HONOR: *Julius K. Nyerere: Teacher of Africa,* Shirley Graham

Paul Robeson, Eloise Greenfield

Fast Sam, Cool Clyde, and Stuff, Walter Dean Myers [vi-439]

Song of the Trees, Mildred D. Taylor [vi-479]

1975 AWARD: *The Legend of Africania,* Dorothy Robinson

1974 AWARD: *Ray Charles,* Sharon Bell Mathis

HONOR: *A Hero Ain't Nothin' but a Sandwich,* Alice Childress

Don't You Remember?, Lucille Clifton

Ms. Africa: Profiles of Modern African Women, Louise Crane

Guests in the Promised Land, Kristin Hunter

Mukasa, John Nagenda

1973 AWARD: *I Never Had It Made: The Autobiography of Jackie Robinson,*
Alfred Duckett

1972 AWARD: *17 Black Artists,* Elton Fax

1971 AWARD: *Black Troubadour: Langston Hughes,* Charlemae Rollins

HONOR: *I Know Why the Caged Bird Sings,* Maya Angelou

Unbought and Unbossed, Shirley Chisholm

I Am a Black Woman, Mari Evans

Every Man Heart Lay Down, Lorenz Graham

The Voice of the Children, June, Jordan, and Terri Bush
Black Means . . . , Gladys Groom and Barney Grossman
Ebony Book of Black Achievement, Margaret Peters
Mary Jo's Grandmother, Janice May Udry

1970 AWARD: *Dr. Martin Luther King, Jr., Man of Peace,* Lillie Patterson

Coretta Scott King Illustrator Awards

2001 AWARD: *Uptown,* Bryan Collier
HONOR: *Freedom River,* Bryan Collier
Only Passing Through: The Story of Sojourner Truth, R. Gregory Christie
Virgie Goes to School with Us Boys, E. B. Lewis [334]

2000 AWARD: *In the Time of the Drums,* Brian Pinkney [208]
HONOR: *My Rows and Piles of Coins,* E. B. Lewis [263]
Black Cat, Christopher Myers

1999 AWARD: *I See the Rhythm,* Toyomi Igus [391]
HONOR: *I Have Heard of a Land,* Floyd Cooper [51]
The Bat Boy and His Violin, E. B. Lewis [128]
Duke Ellington: The Piano Prince and His Orchestra, Brian Pinkney [165]

1998 AWARD: *In Daddy's Arms I Am Tall: African Americans Celebrating Fathers,* Javaka Steptoe [205]
HONOR: *Ashley Bryan's ABC of African American Poetry,* Ashley Bryan [vl-7]
The Hunterman and the Crocodile: A West African Folktale, Baba Wagué Diakité
Harlem, Christopher Myers [vl-357]

1997 AWARD: *Minty: A Story of Young Harriet Tubman,* Jerry Pinkney [vl-230]
HONOR: *The Palm of My Heart: Poetry by African American Children,* Gregory Christie [vl-392]
Running the Road to ABC, Reynolds Ruffins [vl-271]
Neeny Coming, Neeny Going, Synthia Saint James [vl-240]

1996 AWARD: *The Middle Passage: White Ships, Black Cargo,* Tom Feelings [vl-457]
HONOR: *Her Stories: African America Folktales, Fairy Tales and True Tales,* Leo and Diane Dillon [vl-359]
The Faithful Friend, Brian Pinkney [vl-169]

1995 AWARD: *The Creation,* James Ransome [vl-152]
HONOR: *The Singing Man: Adapted from a West African Folktale,* Terea Shaffer [vl-277]
Meet Danitra Brown, Floyd Cooper [vl-383]

1994 AWARD: *Soul Looks Back in Wonder,* Tom Feelings [vI-403]
    HONOR: *Brown Honey in Broomwheat Tea,* Floyd Cooper [vI-137]
            Uncle Jed's Barber Shop, James Ransome [vI-294]
1993 AWARD: *The Origin of Life on Earth: An African Creation Myth,*
            Kathleen Atkins Wilson [274]
    HONOR: *Little Eight John,* Wil Clay [237]
            Sukey and the Mermaid, Brian Pinkney [vI-282]
            Working Cotton, Carole Byard [vI-312]
1992 AWARD: *Tar Beach,* Faith Ringgold [vI-287]
    HONOR: *All Night, All Day: A Child's First Book of African-American*
            Spirituals, Ashley Bryan [vI-118]
            Night on Neighborhood Street, Jan Spivey Gilchrist [vI-242]
1991 AWARD: *Aïda: A Picture Book for All Ages,* Leo and Diane Dillon [vI-318]
1990 AWARD: *Nathaniel Talking,* Jan Spivey Gilchrist [vI-238]
    HONOR: *The Talking Eggs,* Jerry Pinkney [vI-286]
1989 AWARD: *Mirandy and Brother Wind,* Jerry Pinkney [vI-231]
    HONOR: *Under the Sunday Tree,* Mr. Amos Ferguson
            Storm in the Night, Pat Cummings [vI-279]
1988 AWARD: *Mufaro's Beautiful Daughters: An African Tale,* John Steptoe [vI-233]
    HONOR: *What a Morning! The Christmas Story in Black Spirituals,* Ashley
            Bryan
1987 AWARD: *Half a Moon and One Whole Star,* Jerry Pinkney [vI-44]
    HONOR: *Lion and the Ostrich Chicks and Other African Folk Tales,*
            Ashley Bryan
            C.L.O.U.D.S., Pat Cummings
1986 AWARD: *The Patchwork Quilt,* Jerry Pinkney [vI-256]
    HONOR: *The People Could Fly: American Black Folktales,* Leo and Diane
            Dillon [vI-393]
1985 AWARD: None
1984 AWARD: *My Mama Needs Me,* Pat Cummings [81]
1983 AWARD: *Black Child,* Peter Magubane
    HONOR: *All the Colors of the Race,* John Steptoe [vI-319]
            I'm Going to Sing: Black American Spirituals, Ashley Bryan
            Just Us Women, Pat Cummings [vI-214]
1982 AWARD: *Mother Crocodile: An Uncle Amadon Tale from Senegal,*
            John Steptoe
    HONOR: *Daydreamers,* Tom Feelings [vI-334]
1981 AWARD: *Beat the Story Drum, Pum-Pum,* Ashley Bryan
    HONOR: *Grandmama's Joy,* Carole Byard [vI-42]
            Count on Your Fingers African Style, Jerry Pinkney

1980 AWARD: *Cornrows*, Carole Byard [vl-151]
1979 AWARD: *Something on My Mind*, Tom Feelings
1978 AWARD: *Africa Dream*, Carole Byard
1974 AWARD: *Ray Charles*, George Ford
1970 AWARD: None

THE NEWBERY AWARDS

The Newbery Medal is one of the highest and best known literary awards in the United States. The first Newbery Medal, named after distinguished English bookseller John Newbery, was awarded in 1922. Every year since then, the American Library Association selects the author of the most outstanding children's book published in the United States during the preceding year to receive the coveted medal. The ALA also selects other authors whose notable works are distinguished as Newbery Honor Books.

In the seventy-nine-year history of these awards, only six African American or African-themed children's books have won the prestigious medal, and only twelve have been named as honor books.

Newbery Award Books with African American or African Themes

Medal Winners

2000	*Bud, Not Buddy*, Christopher Paul Curtis [366]
1977	*Roll of Thunder, Hear My Cry*, Mildred D. Taylor [vl-469]
1975	*M.C. Higgins the Great*, Virginia Hamilton
1974	*The Slave Dancer*, Paula Fox
1970	*Sounder*, William H. Armstrong
1951	*Amos Fortune: Free Man*, Elizabeth Yates [vl-320]

Honor Books

1997	*A Girl Named Disaster*, Nancy Farmer
1996	*Yolanda's Genius*, Carol Fenner [vl-498]
	The Watsons Go to Birmingham—1963, Christopher Paul Curtis [vl-490]
1993	*The Dark-Thirty: Tales of the Supernatural*, Patricia C. McKissack [vl-434]
	Somewhere in the Darkness, Walter Dean Myers [vl-478]
1989	*Scorpions*, Walter Dean Myers
1983	*Sweet Whispers, Brother Rush*, Virginia Hamilton [vl-483]
1976	*The Hundred Penny Box*, Sharon Bell Mathis [vl-361]
1975	*Phillip Hall Likes Me, I Reckon Maybe*, Bette Greene [vl-464]
1972	*The Planet of Junior Brown*, Virginia Hamilton

1969   *To Be a Slave,* Julius Lester [vl-486]

1949   *Story of the Negro,* Arna Bontemps

The Caldecott Awards

Since its creation in 1937, the Caldecott Medal has been awarded annually by the American Library Association to the artist of the most distinguished American picture book for children. This prestigious medal, named after the nineteenth-century English illustrator Randolph J. Caldecott, was originated as an equivalent to the Newbery Medal, to honor the works of illustrating artists. While only one artist each year receives the Caldecott Medal, other outstanding artists receive the Caldecott Honor distinction for their excellent works.

Only three African American or African-themed children's books have been recognized as Caldecott Medal winners and seventeen have been named as Caldecott Honor books since the inception of the program.

Caldecott Award Books with African American or African Themes

Medal Winners

1977   *Ashanti to Zulu: African Traditions,* Leo and Diane Dillon [vl-6]

1976   *Why Mosquitoes Buzz in People's Ears,* Leo and Diane Dillon

1963   *The Snowy Day,* Ezra Jack Keats [vl-98]

Honor Books

1999   *Duke Ellington: The Piano Prince and His Orchestra,* Brian Pinkney [165]

1998   *Harlem,* Christopher Myers [vl-357]

1997   *The Paperboy,* Dav Pilkey [vl-254]

1996   *The Faithful Friend,* Brian Pinkey [vl-169]

1995   *John Henry,* Jerry Pinkney [vl-209]

1993   *Working Cotton,* Carole Byard [vl-312]

1992   *Tar Beach,* Faith Ringgold [vl-287]

1990   *The Talking Eggs,* Jerry Pinkney [vl-286]

1989   *Mirandy and Brother Wind,* Jerry Pinkney [vl-231]

1988   *Mufaro's Beautiful Daughters: An African Tale,* John Steptoe [vl-233]

1987   *The Village of Round and Square Houses,* Ann Grifalconi [vl-295]

1984   *Ten, Nine, Eight,* Molly Bang [vl-103]

1980   *Ben's Trumpet,* Rachel Isadora

1975   *Jambo Means Hello: Swahili Alphabet Book,* Tom Feelings [61]

1973   *Anansi the Spider,* Gerald McDermott

1972   *Moja Means One: Swahili Counting Book,* Tom Feelings [vl-73]

1970   *Goggles,* Ezra Jack Keats

READING RAINBOW SELECTIONS

The *Reading Rainbow* public television program was created in 1983 with the primary goal of encouraging children to read for pleasure. The program selects books for children five to eight years old based on their literary merit, visual impact, artistic achievement, adaptability to the television format, and ability to interest children. *Reading Rainbow* programs are theme-oriented and highlight a Feature Book that is the focal point for each episode. Additional Review Books are selected to support the program theme. Each program is carefully produced, employing the talents of well-cast celebrity narrators to help give voice to the stories.

Reading Rainbow selections include a significant number of outstanding African American and African-themed children's books. In the list below, Feature Books appear in **bold** type.

Reading Rainbow Selections with African American or African Themes

All the Colors of the Race, Arnold Adoff [vl-319]

Alvin Ailey, Andrea Davis Pinkney [vl-120]

Always My Dad, Sharon Dennis Wyeth [118]

Amazing Grace, Mary Hoffman [vl-121]

Ben's Trumpet, Rachel Isadora

Boundless Grace, Mary Hoffman [138]

Bringing the Rain to Kapiti Plain, Verna Aardema [9]

The Car Washing Street, Denise Lewis Patrick

Charlie Parker Played Be Bop, Chris Raschka [18]

Daddy Is a Monster Sometimes, John Steptoe

Dancing with the Indians, Angela Shelf Medearis [vl-154]

Daydreamers, Eloise Greenfield [vl-334]

An Enchanted Hair Tale, Alexis DeVeaux [vl-165]

Everett Anderson's Goodbye, Lucille Clifton [vl-167]

Follow the Drinking Gourd, Jeanette Winter [vl-176]

Galimoto, Karen Lynn Williams [vl-182]

Grandmama's Joy, Eloise Greenfield [vl-42]

Great Women in the Struggle, Toyomi Igus

Half a Moon and One Whole Star, Crescent Dragonwagon [vl-44]

Honey, I Love: And Other Love Poems, Eloise Greenfield [vl-360]

How Many Stars in the Sky?, Lenny Hort [195]

Jafta, Hugh Lewin [55]

Jafta and the Wedding, Hugh Lewin

Jafta's Father, Hugh Lewin [56]

Jafta's Mother, Hugh Lewin [57]

Jafta—The Town, Hugh Lewin

Jamaica's Find, Juanita Havill [vl-58]

Jambo Means Hello: Swahili Alphabet Book, Muriel Feelings [61]

Just Us Women, Jeannette Caines [vl-214]

Kwanzaa, Deborah Newton Chocolate [228]

Maebelle's Suitcase, Tricia Tusa [68]

Max Found Two Sticks, Brian Pinkney [vl-228]

Me and Nessie, Eloise Greenfield

Mufaro's Beautiful Daughters: An African Tale, John Steptoe [vl-233]

My Little Island, Frané Lessac [vl-235]

Night on Neighborhood Street, Eloise Greenfield [vl-242]

The Patchwork Quilt, Valerie Flournoy [vl-256]

Pet Show!, Ezra Jack Keats

Peter's Chair, Ezra Jack Keats [88]

A Picture Book of Harriet Tubman, David A. Adler

Shake It to the One That You Love Best, Cheryl Warren Mattox [295]

The Snowy Day, Ezra Jack Keats [vl-98]

Sweet Clara and the Freedom Quilt, Deborah Hopkinson [vl-284]

The Talking Eggs, Robert D. San Souci [vl-286]

Tar Beach, Faith Ringgold [vl-287]

This Is the Key to the Kingdom, Diane Worfolk [vl-104]

The Train to Lulu's, Elizabeth Fitzgerald Howard [vl-291]

Ty's One-Man Band, Mildred Pitts Walter [331]

Uncle Jed's Barber Shop, Margaret King Mitchell [vl-294]

Wagon Wheels, Barbara Brenner [vl-298]

Why Mosquitoes Buzz in People's Ears, Verna Aardema

Willie Jerome, Alice Faye Duncan [343]

Zora Hurston and the Chinaberry Tree, William Miller [vl-315]

APPENDIX C

READING INTEREST WEB SITES

AUTHOR WEB SITES

For those of you who may wish to learn more about some of the authors and illustrators or books that they write, we recommend beginning your search in these informative Web sites, many of which are also linked to other helpful sites.

Dillon, Leo and Diane
www.best.com/~libros/dillon

Hamilton, Virginia
www.virginiahamilton.com

Hudson, Wade and Cheryl
www.justusbooks.com/founders.html

Lewis, E. B.
www.eblewis.com

Nolen, Jerdine
www.jerdinenolen.com

Ringgold, Faith
www.artincontext.org/artist/ringgold

Rosales, Melodye
www.rosalesnet.com/mystery.html

Saint James, Synthia
www.synthiasaintjames.com

Smalls, Irene
www.melanet.com/johnkankus

Thomas, Joyce Carol
www.joycecarolthomas.com

GENERAL WEB SITES

Learning about the Author and Illustrator
www.scils.rutgers.edu/special/kay/author.html

Dr. Kay E. Vandergrift of Rutgers University maintains this informative Web site, which features information about a number of authors and illustrators of African American children's books, including:

Verna Aardema	Deborah Hopkinson	Angela Shelf Medearis
Ashley Bryan	Zora Neale Hurston	Walter Dean Myers
Floyd Cooper	Joanne Hyppolite	Gloria Pinkney
Pat Cummings	Ezra Jack Keats	Jerry Pinkney
Leo and Diane Dillon	Jane Kurtz	Mildred Taylor
Tom Feelings	Julius Lester	Joyce Carol Thomas
Rosa Guy	Mary Lyons	Rita Williams-Garcia
Nikki Giovanni	Suse Macdonald	Jacqueline Woodson
Virginia Hamilton	Fredrick and Patricia McKissack	Sharon Dennis Wyeth

Visual Interpretive Analysis of Children's Picture Book Illustrations
  www.scils.rutgers.edu/special/kay/analyses.html

This page, also by Dr. Vandergrift of Rutgers University, answers the question, "What does this illustration communicate to viewers?" for many books, including the following African American children's books:

Amistad Rising [119]
Dinner at Aunt Connie's House [vl-160]
Dream Keeper and Other Poems
Gregory Cool [vl-189]
Mirandy and Brother Wind [vl-231]
Nappy Hair [vl-237]
Sweet Clara and the Freedom Quilt [vl-284]
What a Truly Cool World

Children's Literature   www.childrenslit.com

This site, maintained by Lesley College, has a Meet the Authors and Illustrators section that includes book reviews and interviews with many creators, including:

Evelyn Coleman	Jerry Pinkney
Jim Haskins	James Ransome
Julius Lester	Courtni Wright
Patricia McKissack	

The Virginia Hamilton Conference Information Web site,
  www.kent.edu/virginiahamiltonconf/index.html, includes information on:

Tom Feelings	James Ransome
Jan Spivey Gilchrist	Joyce Carol Thomas
Eloise Greenfield	Jacqueline Woodson
Walter Dean Myers	

223

INDEX OF TITLES

Italic type indicates a book that is mentioned only within the main entry or entries listed.

INDEX OF AUTHORS

INDEX OF ILLUSTRATORS

Alcorn, Stephen [393]
Allen, Thomas B. [312]
Andrews, Benny [300]
Angelo [372]
Auzary-Luton, Sylvie [1]
Ayliffe, Alex [54]

Baker, Garin [145]
Bennett, Nneka [20, 114, 177, 219, 301]
Bent, Jennifer [14]
Binch, Caroline [134, 138]
Blair, Culverson [1]
Bognomo, Joël Eboueme [241]
Bootman, Colin [206, 257]
Brierley, Louise [148]
Broeck, Fabrico Vanden [332]
Brown, Dan [281]
Brown, Ken [70]
Brown, Marc [338]
Brown, Rod [382]
Brown, Sterling [101]
Bryan, Ashley [16, 121, 194, 268, 307, 328]
Bryant, Michael [449]
Buchanan, Yvonne [174, 176, 182]
Burr, Dan [401]
Burrowes, Adjoa [83]
Butler, Jerry [374]
Byard, Carole [197]
Byrd, Samuel [235, 400]

Catalanotto, Peter [239]
Cedric, Lucas [337]
Cepeda, Joe [227]
Chen, Yong [253]
Chesworth, Michael [291]
Christie, Gregory [290]
Clay, Wil [237, 318]
Clouse, Nancy L. [282]
Collier, Bryan [107]
Collins, Heather [407]

Colón, Raúl [118, 126, 147]
Condy, Roy [152]
Cook, Scott [265, 266]
Cooper, Floyd [51, 159, 170, 185, 252, 271, 278, 326, 355, 365, 425]
Corcoran, Mark [70]
Cote, Nancy [36, 276]
Couch, Greg [172]
Courtney-Clarke, Margaret [82]
Cravath, Lynne [322]
Crews, Donald [132]
Crews, Nina [111, 113]
Cummings, Pat [13, 77, 81, 89, 329]

Daly, Niki [19, 90, 117, 140, 175, 213, 273, 277]
Davis, Lambert [130]
Deeter, Catherine [445]
Diakité, Baba Wagué [189]
Diaz, David [220]
Dillon, Diane [411]
Dillon, Leo [411]
Doniger, Nancy [385]

Evans, Shane W. [296, 421]

Falwell, Cathryn [22]
Fax, Elton C. [439]
Feelings, Tom [61, 345]
Fiore, Peter M. [162]
Flavin, Teresa [270, 297, 438]
Ford, George [43, 112]
Fox, Neal [47, 67]
Fuchs, Bernie [146, 286]

Garland, Sarah [133]
Garnett, Ron [157, 173]
Geter, Tyrone [209, 314, 343]
Gilchrist, Jan Spivey [8, 52, 76, 78, 98, 109, 124, 151, 166, 233, 240, 298]
Gold, Gary [264]

Golembe, Carla [340]
Greedseid, Diane [335]
Grifalconi, Ann [31, 32, 33, 108, 207]
Griffith, Gershom [218]
Grote, Rich [401, 402]

Hackney, Richard [75]
Hale, Christy [30]
Halverson, Lydia [230]
Hamilton, Thomas [106]
Handelman, Dorothy [40]
Harper, Betty [168]
Harter, Debbie [7]
Hays, Michael [129, 226, 321]
Hehenberger, Shelly [210]
Hewitt, Kathryn [37]
Hoff, Syd [163]
Hogan, Victor [150]
Holbert, Raymond [127]
Holliday, Keaf [188]
Honeywood, Varnette P. [131, 160, 246, 255, 258, 272, 295, 317, 325]
Hu, Ying-Hwa [122, 178, 179, 215, 373]

Igus, Toyomi [391]
Isadora, Rachel [15, 105]

James, Curtis E. [446]
Jean-Bart, Leslie [310]
Jeffers, Susan [2]
Jenkins, Leonard [203, 316, 415]
Johnson, Cathy [70, 92, 181]
Johnson, Dolores [186, 262]
Johnson, Larry [184]
Johnson, Stephen T. [192]
Joysmith, Brenda [295]

Katz, Karen [23]
Keats, Ezra Jack [88]

Baby–Preschool [1–115]   K–Grade 3 [116–345]   Grades 4–8 [346–450]

INDEX OF TOPICS

Baby–Preschool [1–115]   K–Grade 3 [116–345]   Grades 4–8 [346–450]

To Be a Drum [323]
Too Much Talk [324]
Turtle Knows Your Name [328]
Vacation in the Village: A Story from West Africa [333]
What's So Funny, Ketu? [338]
Why the Sky Is Far Away: A Nigerian Folktale [340]
Zamani Goes to Market [345]

animals. *see* pets

art/craft

All Around the Town: The Photographs of Richard Samuel Roberts [116]
Aneesa Lee and the Weaver's Gift [121]
A Drawing in the Sand: A Story of African American Art [374]
Going Back Home: An Artist Returns to the South [386]
Madelia [240]
Painted Dreams [275]
Pink Paper Swans [282]
Rainbow Joe and Me [287]
Talking with Tebé: Clementine Hunter, Memory Artist [440]

baby (new)

A Baby Just Like Me [4]
Billy and Belle [133]
Daniel's Dog [27]
Everett Anderson's Year [33]
My Mama Needs Me [81]
One Round Moon and a Star for Me [273]
Peter's Chair [88]
Silver Rain Brown [297]
Wilhe'mina Miles: After the Stork Night [342]
You Are My Perfect Baby [114]

baby's day

Baby Animals [2]
Baby Dance [3]
My Five Senses [80]
My Mama Needs Me [81]
Ring! Bang! Boom! [91]

babysitters

Bye, Mis' Lela [144]
Dear Willie Rudd, [162]
Shoes Like Miss Alice's [99]

baseball. *see* sports

basketball. *see* sports

beach

Beach Babble [6]
The Boy on the Beach [140]
Flip-Flops [35]

bedtime

Baby Animals [2]
Good Night Baby [43]
Joshua's Night Whispers [63]
A South African Night [105]

bible stories. *see* religion

biography

African American Entrepreneurs [351]
African Americans Who Were First [354]
The Biographical Dictionary of African Americans [360]
Black Cowboy, Wild Horses: A True Story [136]
The Bus Ride [143]
Duke Ellington: The Piano Prince and His Orchestra [165]
Explore Black History with Wee Pals [169]
Five Brave Explorers [173]
Fly, Bessie, Fly [174]
Great African Americans in Business [388]
I Have a Dream: Dr. Martin Luther King, Jr. [198]
If a Bus Could Talk: The Story of Rosa Parks [202]
If I Only Had a Horn: Young Louis Armstrong [203]
Keep on Singing: A Ballad of Marian Anderson [400]
Leagues Apart: The Men and Times of the Negro Baseball Leagues [232]
Letters from a Slave Girl: The Story of Harriet Jacobs [409]
Madam C. J. Walker: Entrepreneur [413]
Malcolm X [243]
Meet Martin Luther King, Jr.: A Man of Peace with a Dream for All People [247]
Osceola: Memories of a Sharecropper's Daughter [421]
A Picture Book of George Washington Carver [281]
Ragtime Tumpie [286]
The Story of Jean Baptiste DuSable [306]
Take a Walk in Their Shoes [439]
Through My Eyes [442]
Thurgood Marshall: Supreme Court Justice [443]

birthday

Birthday [135]
Courtney's Birthday Party [157]
Flower Garden [36]
Glo Goes Shopping [181]
Jackson Jones and the Puddle of Thorns [212]

Caribbean

The Calypso Alphabet [14]
Caribbean Dream [15]
Cendrillon: A Caribbean Cinderella [149]
Cocoa Ice [153]
The Crab Man [158]
I Have a News: Rhymes from the Caribbean [50]
Island in the Sun [54]
Jump Up Time: A Trinidad Carnival Story [221]
Mama Rocks, Papa Sings [244]
Painted Dreams [275]
Tiny and Bigman [322]
Under the Breadfruit Tree: Island Poems [332]

church. *see* religion

city life

The Boy Who Didn't Believe in Spring [141]
Carolina Shout! [146]
Enid and the Dangerous Discovery [168]
Faraway Drums [170]
The Gift-Giver [384]
Girls Together [180]
Granddaddy's Street Songs [185]
Irene and the Big, Fine Nickel [209]
Jazmin's Notebook [395]
The Jazz of Our Street [214]
Jonkonnu: A Story from the Sketchbook of Winslow Homer [217]
My Steps [83]
Red Light, Green Light, Mama and Me [90]
Something Beautiful [302]
Somewhere in Africa [303]
A Street Called Home [309]

Christmas. see holidays

civil rights

The Bus Ride [143]
Granddaddy's Gift [184]
I Have a Dream: Dr. Martin Luther King, Jr. [198]
If a Bus Could Talk: The Story of Rosa Parks [202]
Let Freedom Ring: A Ballad of Martin Luther King, Jr. [235]
Witnesses to Freedom: Young People Who Fought for Civil Rights [448]

Civil War

Abraham's Battle: A Novel of Gettysburg [346]
Across the Lines [347]
Pink and Say [424]
Welcome to Addy's World, 1864: Growing Up During America's Civil War [447]

conjure. see magic

cousins. see siblings

cowboys. see pioneers

crafts. see art

dance

Ballerina Girl [5]
Brothers of the Knight [142]
Dance [25]
Dance, Kayla! [370]
How Many Stars in the Sky? [195]
I Have Another Language: The Language Is Dance [199]
Mimi's Tutu [76]
Papa Lucky's Shadow [277]

death

Bye, Mis' Lela [144]
Dance, Kayla! [370]
Miz Berlin Walks [252]
Sophie [104]
To Hell with Dying [445]

family life/situations

Always My Dad [118]
Angel to Angel: A Mother's Gift of Love [123]
Baby Dance [3]
Back Home [125]
Because You're Lucky [129]
The Bells of Christmas [130]
Boundless Grace [138]
The Canning Season [367]
Celebration! [147]
Charlie's House [19]
Daddy Calls Me Man [24]
Dance, Kayla! [370]
Everett Anderson's Nine Month Long [32]
Father's Day Blues: What Do You Do about Father's Day When All You Have Are Mothers? [171]
Francie [381]
The Genie in the Jar [39]
Gettin' Through Thursday [177]
Ginger Brown: Too Many Houses [179]
Grandma's Hands [186]
Heaven [389]

How Many Stars in the Sky? [195]
I Have Another Language: The Language Is Dance [199]
In Daddy's Arms I Am Tall: African Americans Celebrating Fathers [205]
In My Momma's Kitchen [206]
Jafta's Father [56]
Jafta's Mother [57]
Jewels [215]
Just Right Stew [222]
Keepers [224]
Kevin and His Dad [226]
The Longest Wait [239]
Mimi's Tutu [76]
Mister and Me [415]
Momma, Where Are You From? [254]
My Mama Needs Me [81]
My Mama Sings [260]
My Man Blue [261]
Nobody's Family Is Going to Change [419]
Octopus Hug [85]
One Round Moon and a Star for Me [273]
Poppa's Itchy Christmas [283]
Read for Me, Mama [289]
Sam [93]
Stevie [304]
Tanya's Reunion [320]
Tiny's Hat [108]
Trina's Family Reunion [327]
We Had a Picnic This Sunday Past [335]
The Wedding [336]
What's in Aunt Mary's Room? [337]
Wilhe'mina Miles: After the Stork Night [342]

fantasy

Bear on a Bike [7]
Daniel's Dog [27]
Kofi and the Butterflies [65]
Maebelle's Suitcase [68]
A Million Fish . . . More or Less [248]
Raising Dragons [288]
Swinging on a Rainbow [106]
When I'm Alone [110]
You Are Here [113]

Gullah Islands

Cumbayah [159]
Imani and the Flying Africans [204]
In the Time of the Drums [208]
Little Muddy Waters: A Gullah Folk
   Tale [238]
A Net to Catch Time [265]
Shaina's Garden [97]

hair

Happy to Be Nappy [48]
Haircuts at Sleepy Sam's [188]
I Love My Hair! [200]
Palm Trees [276]

history/heritage

African American Quilting: The
   Warmth of Tradition [353]
African Beginnings [355]
Amistad Rising: A Story of Freedom
   [119]
A Band of Angels: A Story Inspired by
   the Jubilee Singers [126]
Black Hands, White Sails: The Story
   of African-American Whalers
   [361]
Bound for America: The Forced
   Migration of Africans to the New
   World [365]
Come All You Brave Soldiers: Blacks
   in the Revolutionary War [369]
A Drawing in the Sand: A Story of
   African American Art [374]
Explore Black History with Wee Pals
   [169]
I Am African American [196]
The New York Public Library Amazing
   African American History: A Book
   of Answers for Kids [418]
Phoebe the Spy [423]
Sink or Swim: African-American
   Lifesavers of the Outer Banks
   [432]
Through My Eyes [442]
Till Victory Is Won: Black Soldiers in
   the Civil War [444]
To Be a Drum [323]
Tree of Hope [326]

holidays

Christmas

An Angel Just Like Me [122]
The Bells of Christmas [130]
Carol of the Brown King: Nativity
   Poems [16]
Christmas for 10 [22]
Elijah's Angel: A Story for Chanukah
   and Christmas [167]
Poppa's Itchy Christmas [283]

Easter

Easter Parade [166]
Miz Fannie Mae's Fine New Easter
   Hat [253]

Fourth of July

Celebration! [147]

Jonkonnu

Jonkonnu: A Story from the
   Sketchbook of Winslow Homer
   [217]

Kwanzaa

The Children's Book of Kwanzaa: A
   Guide to Celebrating the Holiday
   [368]
K Is for Kwanzaa: A Kwanzaa
   Alphabet Book [223]
Kwanzaa [228]
Kwanzaa [229]
Kwanzaa [230]
Kwanzaa: A Family Affair [404]
Kwanzaa!: Africa Lives in a New
   World Festival [405]
Seven Days of Kwanzaa: A Holiday
   Step Book [95]

Valentine's Day

Don't Be My Valentine: A Classroom
   Mystery [163]
Secret Valentine [94]
Super-Fine Valentine [317]

illness

Bluish: A Novel [363]

Juneteenth. *see* holidays

Kwanzaa. *see* holidays

legends. *see* folktales

literacy

Read for Me, Mama [289]
Richard Wright and the Library Card
   [290]

literature

Listen Children: An Anthology of
   Black Literature [411]

magic (conjure)

All the Magic in the World [117]
The Conjure Woman [156]
Moaning Bones: African-American
   Ghost Stories [416]
The Secret of the Stones [293]
Vampire Bugs: Stories Conjured from
   the Past [446]
Wiley and the Hairy Man [341]

music/musicians

A Band of Angels: A Story Inspired by
   the Jubilee Singers [126]
The Bat Boy and His Violin [128]
Charlie Parker Played Be Bop [18]
Cumbayah [159]
Duke Ellington: The Piano Prince and
   His Orchestra [165]
I Make Music [52]
I See the Rhythm [391]
If I Only Had a Horn: Young Louis
   Armstrong [203]
Island in the Sun [54]
The Jazz of Our Street [214]
The Music in Derrick's Heart [257]
My Mama Sings [260]
The Old Cotton Blues [270]
1, 2, 3, Music! [86]
The Piano Man [279]
Ragtime Tumpie [286]
Shake It to the One That You Love
   the Best: Play Songs and Lullabies
   from Black Musical Traditions
   [295]

Summertime: From Porgy and Bess [313]
Tiny's Hat [108]
Ty's One-Man Band [331]
Willie Jerome [343]

mystery

Case of the Missing Cookies [17]
Don't Be My Valentine: A Classroom Mystery [163]
Ernestine & Amanda: Mysteries on Monroe Street [377]
Kid Caramel, Private Investigator: The Werewolf of PS 40 [403]
The Spray-Paint Mystery [435]
What's in Aunt Mary's Room? [337]

nursery rhymes

Bringing the Rain to Kapiti Plain [9]
The Many Colors of Mother Goose [70]
Singing Black: Alternative Nursery Rhymes for Children [100]

pets/animals

Baby Animals [2]
Big Friend, Little Friend [8]
Digby [29]
Get the Ball, Slim [40]
The Girl Who Wore Snakes [41]
Honey Hunters [49]
Jafta [55]
Julius [64]
Lake of the Big Snake: An African Rain Forest Adventure [231]
Kofi and the Butterflies [65]
Max [71]
Pickin' Peas [89]
Raising Dragons [288]
Willie's Wonderful Pet [112]

pioneers and cowboys

Adventures of Midnight Son [350]
Black Cowboy, Wild Horses: A True Story [136]
I Have Heard of a Land [51]

The Journal of Joshua Loper: A Black Cowboy, The Chisholm Trail, 1871 [397]
The Longest Ride [412]
My Heroes, My People: African Americans and Native Americans in the West [259]
Reflections of a Black Cowboy: Pioneers [425]
The Righteous Revenge of Artemis Bonner [426]

playtime

Beach Babble [6]
The Best Way to Play [131]
Fingers, Nose, and Toes [34]
Flip-Flops [35]
From My Window [37]
It's Raining Laughter [211]
Jamaica Tag-Along [59]
Matthew and Tilly [245]
Miss Tizzy [250]
Octopus Hug [85]
Sharing Danny's Dad [98]

preschool skills

alphabet

C Is for City [13]
The Calypso Alphabet [14]
Jambo Means Hello: Swahili Alphabet Book [61]
K Is for Kwanzaa: A Kwanzaa Alphabet Book [223]

colors

Chidi Only Likes Blue: An African Book of Colors [21]

counting

Christmas for 10 [22]
Joe Can Count [62]

shapes

Afro-Bets Book of Shapes [1]

words

Furaha Means Happy!: A Book of Swahili Words [38]
Halala Means Welcome!: A Book of Zulu Words [46]

poetry (rhymes)

Aneesa Lee and the Weaver's Gift [121]
Angels [124]
Can I Pray with My Eyes Open? [145]
Caribbean Dream [15]
Carol of the Brown King: Nativity Poems [16]
Cherish Me [20]
Daddy Calls Me Man [24]
A Dime a Dozen [372]
Everett Anderson's Friend [31]
Everett Anderson's Nine Month Long [32]
Everett Anderson's Year [33]
Flower Garden [36]
The Genie in the Jar [39]
Good Rhymes, Good Times [183]
Greetings, Sun [45]
Hopscotch Love: A Family Treasury of Love Poems [390]
I Have a News: Rhymes from the Caribbean [50]
I Want to Be [201]
I, Too, Sing America: Three Centuries of African American Poetry [393]
In Daddy's Arms I Am Tall: African Americans Celebrating Fathers [205]
Isn't My Name Magical?: Sister and Brother Poems [210]
Jump Back, Honey: The Poems of Paul Laurence Dunbar [398]
Jump Rope Magic [220]
Kevin and His Dad [226]
Lemonade Sun: And Other Summer Poems [233]
Let Freedom Ring: A Ballad of Martin Luther King, Jr. [235]
Mama Rocks, Papa Sings [244]
My Aunt Came Back [77]
My Man Blue [261]
The Other Side: Shorter Poems [422]
Picking Peas for a Penny [280]
Some of the Days of Everett Anderson [102]
Swinging on a Rainbow [106]
Under the Breadfruit Tree: Island Poems [332]
When I'm Alone [110]
You Are My Perfect Baby [114]

Virgie Goes to School with Us Boys [334]

What's In Aunt Mary's Room? [337]

When Will Sarah Come? [111]

You Are Here [113]

sports

baseball

The Bat Boy and His Violin [128]

Fair Ball!: 14 Great Stars from Baseball's Negro Leagues [378]

First in the Field: Baseball Hero Jackie Robinson [379]

Leagues Apart: The Men and Times of the Negro Baseball Leagues [232]

basketball

Black Hoops: The History of African Americans in Basketball [362]

Bounce Back [364]

Got Game? [387]

Hoops [192]

In Your Face [394]

Large and In Charge! [406]

NBA Game Day: From Morning Until Night Behind the Scenes in the NBA [264]

Schoolin' [431]

Strong to the Hoop [310]

other

Jump Rope Magic [220]

Night Golf [267]

Running Girl: The Diary of Ebonee Rose [429]

slavery

emancipation

Addy Learns a Lesson: A School Story [348]

Addy's Surprise: A Christmas Story [349]

Forty Acres and Maybe a Mule [380]

I Thought My Soul Would Rise and Fly: The Diary of Patsy, a Freed Girl [392]

Imani and the Flying Africans [204]

In the Time of the Drums [208]

My Home Is over Jordan [417]

Run Away Home [428]

A School for Pompey Walker [430]

Virgie Goes to School with Us Boys [334]

Welcome to Addy's World, 1864: Growing Up During America's Civil War [447]

slave life

Amistad Rising: A Story of Freedom [119]

From Slave Ship to Freedom Road [382]

Letters from a Slave Girl: The Story of Harriet Jacobs [409]

Melitte [414]

Once on This River [420]

Sky Sash So Blue [300]

A Strawbeater's Thanksgiving [308]

Underground Railroad

Follow the Drinking Gourd: A Story of the Underground Railroad [176]

Journey to Freedom: A Story of the Underground Railroad [218]

The Last Safe House: A Story of the Underground Railroad [407]

toddler skills and development

Dexter Gets Dressed! [28]

Max [71]

Max Loves Sunflowers [72]

Max's Letter [73]

Max's Money [74]

These Hands [107]

toys

Elizabeti's Doll [30]

My Doll, Keshia [78]

Nettie Jo's Friends [266]

virtue

Billy the Great [134]

Christopher, Please Clean Up Your Room! [152]

Don't Be My Valentine: A Classroom Mystery [163]

Enid and the Dangerous Discovery [168]

Gingersnaps: Daily Affirmations for African American Children and Families [385]

The Hired Hand: An African American Folktale [190]

The Honest-to-Goodness Truth [191]

Jamaica and the Substitute Teacher [58]

Jamaica Tag-Along [59]

Jamaica's Blue Marker [60]

Little Eight John [237]

The Meanest Thing to Say [246]

Messy Bessey's Closet [75]

Money Troubles [255]

My Big Lie [258]

Peter's Chair [88]

Quotes for Kids: Words for Kids to Live By [285]

Stretch Your Wings: Famous Black Quotations for Teens [437]

Summer Wheels [312]

weather. *see* seasons

weddings

Sky Sash So Blue [300]

The Wedding [336]

PERMISSIONS AND CREDITS

The following illustrations are reprinted with permission:

Page 19: Cover illustration by Culverson Blair. From *Afro-Bets Book of Shapes* by Margery Brown. Copyright © 1991. Reprinted by permission of Just Us Books. Cover illustration from *Afro-Bets 1 2 3 Book* by Cheryl Hudson. Copyright © 2000. Reprinted by permission of Just Us Books. Cover illustration from *Afro-Bets A B C Book* by Cheryl Hudson. Copyright © 2000. Reprinted by permission of Just Us Books.

Page 24: Cover illustration by Ashley Bryan from *Carol of the Brown King: Nativity Poems by Langston Hughes* by Langston Hughes. Illustration copyright © 1998 by Ashley Bryan. Courtesy of Atheneum Books for Young Readers, an imprint of Simon & Schuster Children's Publishing. From *Charlie Parker Played Be Bop* (jacket cover) by Chris Raschka. Copyright © 1992 by Christopher Raschka. Reprinted by permission of the publisher, Orchard Books, New York.

Page 27: From *Christmas for 10* (jacket cover) by Cathryn Falwell. Copyright © 1998. Reprinted by permission of Clarion Books/Houghton Mifflin Company. From *The Colors of Us* (jacket cover) by Karen Katz. Text and illustrations copyright, © 1999 by Karen Katz. Reprinted by permission of Henry Holt & Co., LLC.

Page 28: Cover photograph by Susan Kuklin from *Dance* by Bill T. Jones and Susan Kuklin. Copyright © 1998. Reprinted by permission of Jump at the Sun, Hyperion.

Page 29: Cover illustration by Christy Hale from *Elizabeti's Doll* by Stephanie Stuve-Bodeen. Illustration copyright © 1998 by Christy Hale. Permission granted by Lee & Low Books, Inc., 95 Madison Avenue, New York, NY 10016.

Page 30: From *Everett Anderson's Nine Month Long* (jacket cover) by Lucille Clifton, illustrated by Ann Grifalconi. Text copyright © 1978 by Lucille Clifton. Illustrations copyright © 1978 by Ann Grifalconi. Reprinted by permission of Henry Holt & Co., LLC. From *Everett Anderson's Year* (jacket cover) by Lucille Clifton, illustrated by Ann Grifalconi. Text copyright © 1974 by Lucille Clifton. Illustrations copyright © 1974 by Ann Grifalconi. Reprinted by permission of Henry Holt & Co., LLC.

Page 31: Cover photograph by John Pinderhughes from *Fingers, Nose, and Toes*. Illustrations copyright © 1997 by John Pinderhughes. Reprinted by permission of

Essence Books. Cover illustration by Kathryn Hewitt from *Flower Garden* by Eve Bunting. Jacket illustration copyright © 1994 by Kathryn Hewitt. Reproduced by permission of Harcourt, Inc.

Page 34: Cover illustration from *Give Me Grace: A Child's Daybook of Prayers* by Cynthia Rylant. Copyright © 1999. Courtesy of Simon & Schuster Books for Young Readers, an imprint of Simon & Schuster Children's Publishing.

Page 36: Cover illustration from *Halala Means Welcome!: A Book of Zulu Words* by Ken Wilson-Max. Copyright © 1998. Reprinted by permission of Jump at the Sun, Hyperion. Cover illustration by Chris Raschka from *Happy to Be Nappy* by bell hooks. Copyright © 1999 by Chris Raschka. Reprinted by permission of Jump at the Sun, a division of Hyperion.

Page 40: From *Jafta's Mother* (jacket cover) by Hugh Lewin. Illustrations by Lisa Kopper. Copyright © 1983 by Carol Rhoda Books, Inc. Used by permission of the publisher. All rights reserved.

Page 41: Cover illustration by Anne Sibley O'Brien from *Jamaica and the Substitute Teacher* by Juanita Havill. Copyright © 1999. Reprinted by permission of Jump at the Sun, a division of Hyperion.

Page 45: Cover illustration from *Max Loves Sunflowers* by Ken Wilson-Max. Copyright © 1998. Reprinted by permission of Hyperion.

Page 46: Cover illustration from *Max's Money* by Ken Wilson-Max. Copyright © 1999. Reprinted by permission of Jump at the Sun, Hyperion.

Page 48: Illustration by Jan Spivey Gilchrist from *Mimi's Tutu* (jacket cover) by Tynia Thomassie. Illustration copyright © 1996 by Jan Spivey Gilchrist. Reprinted by permission of Scholastic Inc.

Page 49: Cover photograph by John Pinderhughes from *My First Words*. Illustrations copyright © 1997 by John Pinderhughes. Reprinted by permission of Essence Books. Cover photograph by John Pinderhughes from *My Five Senses*. Copyright © 1997. Reprinted by permission of Essence Books.

Page 50: Book cover from *No Mirrors in My Nana's House* by Ysaye Barnwell, jacket illustration copyright © 1998 by Synthia Saint James, reproduced by permission of Harcourt Inc.

Page 51: From *1, 2, 3, Music!* (jacket cover) by Sylvie Auzary-Luton. Copyright ©

1997 by Kaleidoscope. First American edition 1999 by Orchard Books. First published in France in 1997 by Kaleidoscope under the title *Un, Deux, Trois, Musique!* Reprinted by permission of Orchard Books, New York.

Page 54: Cover photograph by John Pinderhughes from *Ring! Bang! Boom!*. Illustrations copyright © 1997 by John Pinderhughes. Reprinted by permission of Essence Books. Cover illustration by Cathy Johnson from *Robo's Favorite Places* by Wade Hudson. Copyright © 1999. Reprinted by permission of Just Us Books.

Page 55: Cover illustration by Donna Perrone from *Shadow Dance* by Tololwa M. Mollel. Copyright © 1998. Reprinted by permission of Clarion Books/Houghton Mifflin Company.

Page 56: From *Shoes Like Miss Alice's* (jacket cover) by Angela Johnson, illustrated by Ken Page. Text © 1995 by Angela Johnson. Illustrated © 1995 by Ken Page. Reprinted by permission of the publisher, Orchard Books, New York.

Page 58: Cover illustration by Ramon Price from *Singing Black* by Mari Evans. Illustrations copyright © by Ramon Price. Reprinted by permission of Just Us Books.

Page 60: Cover illustration by Bryan Collier from *These Hands* by Hope Lynne Price. Copyright © 1999. Reprinted by permission of Jump at the Sun, a division of Hyperion Books for Children.

Page 61: Cover illustration by Nina Crews from *When Will Sarah Come?* by Elizabeth Fitzgerald. Copyright © 1999. Reprinted by permission of Grenwillow Books, a division of William Morrow & Company, Inc. Illustration by George Ford from *Willie's Wonderful Pet* (jacket cover) by Mel Cebulash. Illustration copyright © 1993 by George Ford. Reprinted by permission of Scholastic Inc.

Page 62: Cover photograph from *You Are Here* by Nina Crews. Copyright © 1998. Reprinted by permission of Greenwillow, a division of William Morrow & Company, Inc.

Page 66: Cover illustration by Paul Lee from *Amistad Rising: A Story of Freedom* by Veronica Chambers. Jacket illustration copyright © 1998 by Paul Lee. Reproduced by permission of Harcourt, Inc. Cover illustration by Ashley Bryan from *Aneesa Lee and the Weaver's Gift* by Nikki Grimes. Copyright © 1999. Reprinted by permission of Lothrop, Lee & Shepard, a division of William Morrow & Company, Inc.

Page 67: Cover illustration by Jan Spivey Gilchrist from *Angels* by Eloise Greenfield.

Benson Rosales. Reprinted by permission. Cartwheel Books is a registered trademark of Scholastic Inc.

Page 115: From *The Longest Wait* (jacket cover) by Marie Bradby, illustrated by Peter Catalanotto. Text © 1998 by Marie Bradby. Illustrations © 1998 by Peter Catalanotto. Reprinted by permission of the publisher, Orchard Books, New York.

Page 116: Cover illustration by E. B. Lewis from *The Magic Tree: A Folktale from Nigeria* by T. Obinkaram Echewa. Copyright © 1999. Reprinted by permission of William Morrow & Company, Inc.

Page 120: Cover illustration by Catherine Stock from *Miss Viola and Uncle Ed Lee* by Alice Faye Duncan. Copyright © 1997. Courtesy of Atheneum Books for Young Readers, an imprint of Simon & Schuster Children's Publishing.

Page 121: Cover illustration by Yong Chen from *Miz Fannie Mae's Fine New Easter Hat* by Melissa Milich. Copyright © 1997. Reprinted by permission of Little, Brown.

Page 127: Cover illustration from *The Night Has Ears: African Proverbs* by Ashley Bryan. Copyright © 1999 by Ashley Bryan. Courtesy of Atheneum Books for Young Readers, an imprint of Simon & Schuster Children's Publishing.

Page 129: Illustration by Varnette P. Honeywood from *One Dark and Scary Night* (jacket cover) by Bill Cosby Little Bill Books for Beginning Readers published by Cartwheel Books, a division of Scholastic Inc. Copyright © 1999 by Bill Cosby. Reprinted by permission. Cartwheel Books is a registered trademark of Scholastic Inc.

Page 130: Cover illustration by Catherine Stock from *Painted Dreams* by Karen Lynn Williams. Copyright © 1998. Reprinted by permission of Lothrop, Lee & Shepard, a division of William Morrow & Company, Inc.

Page 132: Cover illustration by Dan Brown from *A Picture Book of George Washington Carver* by David A. Adler. Copyright © 1999. Reprinted by permission of Holiday House. Cover illustration by Nancy L. Clouse from *Pink Paper Swans* by Virginia Kroll. Copyright © 1994. Reprinted by permission of William B. Eerdmans.

Page 134: Cover illustrations by Howard Simpson from *Quotes for Kids* by Katrina Hudson. Reprinted by permission of Just Us Books. Copyright © 1999.

Page 135: Cover illustration from *Rainbow Joe and Me* by Maria Diaz Strom. Copyright © 1999 by Maria Diaz Strom. Permission granted by Lee & Low Books, Inc., 95 Madison Avenue New York, NY 10016.

Page 136: Cover illustration by Elise Primavera from *Raising Dragons* by Jerdine Nolen. Jacket illustration copyright © 1998 by Elise Primavera. Reproduced by permission of Harcourt, Inc. Cover illustration by Gregory

Christie from *Richard Wright and the Library Card* by William Miller. Illustration copyright © 1997 by Gregory Christie. Permission granted by Lee & Low Books, Inc., 95 Madison Avenue, New York, NY 10016.

Page 138: Illustration by Shane W. Evans from *Shaq and the Beanstalk* (jacket cover) by Shaquille O'Neal. Published by Cartwheel Books, a division of Scholastic Inc. Illustration copyright © 1999 by Shane W. Evans. Reprinted by permission. Cartwheel Books is a registered trademark of Scholastic Inc.

Page 139: Cover illustration by Teresa Flavin from *Silver Rain Brown* by M. C. Helldorfer. Copyright © 1999. Reprinted by permission of Houghton Mifflin Company.

Page 146: From *Sunday Week* by Dinah Johnson. Text copyright © 1999 by Dinah Johnson. Illustrations copyright © 1999 by Tyrone Geter. Reprinted by permission of Henry Holt & Co., LLC.

Page 147: Illustration by Varnette P. Honeywood from *Super-Fine Valentine* (jacket cover) by Bill Cosby Little Bill Books for Beginning Readers published by Cartwheel Books, a division of Scholastic Inc. Copyright © 1998 by Bill Cosby. Reprinted by permission. Cartwheel is a registered trademark of Scholastic Inc.

Page 148: Cover illustration by Terry Widener from *Tambourine Moon* by Joy Jones. Copyright © 1999. Courtesy of Simon & Schuster Books for Young Readers, an imprint of Simon & Schuster Children's Publishing.

Page 155: Cover illustration by Diane Greedseid from *We Had a Picnic This Sunday Past* by Jacqueline Woodson. Illustration copyright © 1997. Reprinted by permission of Hyperion. From *The Wedding* (jacket cover) by Angela Johnson, illustrated by David Soman. Text © 1999 by Angela Johnson. Illustration © 1999 by David Soman. Reprinted by permission of the publisher, Orchard Books, New York.

Page 157: Jacket design by Harvey Stevenson from *Wilhe'mina Miles: After the Stork Night* by Dorothy Carter. Jacket art copyright © 1999 Harvey Stevenson. Reprinted by permission of Farrar, Straus and Giroux, LLC.

Page 163: Cover illustration from *African American Entrepreneurs* by Jim Haskins. Copyright © 1998. Reprinted by permission of John Wiley & Sons, Inc. Cover illustration from *African American Military Heroes* by Jim Haskins. Copyright © 1998. Reprinted by permission of John Wiley & Sons, Inc.

Page 164: Cover illustration from *African American Quilting: The Warmth of Tradition* by Sule Greg C. Wilson. Copyright © 1999. Reprinted by permission of Rosen Publishing Group. Cover illustration by Floyd Cooper from *African Beginnings* by James Haskins and Kathleen Benson. Copyright © 1998. Reprinted by permission of Lothrop, Lee &

Shepard, William Morrow & Company, Inc.

Page 168: Illustration by Leo & Diane Dillon from *Bluish* (jacket cover) by Virginia Hamilton. Published by The Blue Sky Press, an imprint of Scholastic Inc. Illustration copyright © 1999 by Leo & Diane Dillon. Reprinted by permission.

Page 169: Cover illustration by Floyd Cooper from *Bound for America: The Forced Migration of Africans to the New World* by James Haskins and Kathleen Benson. Copyright © 1999. Reprinted by permission of Lothrop, Lee & Shepard, William Morrow & Company, Inc.

Page 170: Cover illustration from *Bud, Not Buddy* by Christopher Paul Curtis. Copyright © 1999. Reprinted by permission of Delacorte Press Books for Young Readers, a division of Random House, Inc. Cover illustration from *The Children's Book of Kwanzaa: A Guide to Celebrating the Holiday* by Dolores Johnson. Copyright © 1996 by Dolores Johnson. Courtesy of Atheneum Books for Young Readers, an imprint of Simon & Schuster Children's Publishing.

Page 172: Illustration by John Thompson from *Come All You Brave Soldiers: Blacks in the Revolutionary War* (jacket cover) by Clinton Cox. Published by Scholastic Press, a division of Scholastic Inc. Jacket illustration copyright © 1998 by John Thompson. Reprinted by permission. Cover illustration from *Dear Corinne, Tell Somebody! Love, Annie* by Mari Evans. Copyright © 1999. Reprinted by permission of Just Us Books.

Page 174: Cover illustration from *A Drawing in the Sand: A Story of African American Art* by Jerry Butler. Copyright © 1998 Zino Press Children's Books.

Page 175: Cover illustration from *Ernestine & Amanda: Mysteries on Monroe Street* by Sandra Belton. Copyright © 1998. Courtesy of Simon & Schuster Books for Young Readers, an imprint of Simon & Schuster Children's Publishing. From *Fair Ball!* (jacket cover) by Jonah Winter. Published by Scholastic Press, a division of Scholastic Inc. Copyright © 1999 by Jonah Winter. Reprinted by permission.

Page 176: Cover illustration from *First in the Field: Baseball Hero Jackie Robinson* by Derek T. Dingle. Copyright © 1998. Reprinted by permission of Hyperion. Cover illustration from *Forty Acres and Maybe a Mule* by Harriette Gillem Robinet. Copyright © 1996. Courtesy of Atheneum Books for Young Readers, an imprint of Simon & Schuster Children's Publishing. Jacket design by Tim Hall from *Francie* by Karen English. Jacket art copyright © 1999 by Tim Hall. Reprinted by permission of Farrar, Straus and Giroux, LLC.

Page 178: Cover illustration by Nancy Doniger from *Gingersnaps: Daily Affirmations for African American Children and Families* by Anita Alexander and Susan Payne. Copyright

© 1998. Reprinted by permission of Hyperion Press.

Page 179: Cover illustration from *Heaven* by Angela Johnson. Copyright © 1998. Courtesy of Simon & Schuster Books for Young Readers, an imprint of Simon & Schuster Children's Publishing. Cover illustration by Melodye Benson Rosales from *Hopscotch Love: A Family Treasury of Love Poems* by Nikki Grimes. Copyright © 1999. Reprinted by permission of Lothrop, Lee & Shepard, William Morrow & Company, Inc.

Page 180: Cover illustration by Michelle Wood from *I See the Rhythm* by Toyomi Igus. Reprinted with permission of the publisher, Children's Book Press, San Francisco, CA. Paintings copyright © 1998 by Michelle Wood, text copyright © 1998 by Toyomi Igus.

Page 182: Cover illustration by Stephen Alcorn from *I, Too, Sing America: Three Centuries of African American Poetry* by Catherine Clinton. Copyright © 1998. Reprinted with permission of Houghton Mifflin Company.

Page 184: Cover illustration from *Jump Back, Honey* by Paul Laurence Dunbar. Copyright © 1999. Reprinted by permission of Jump at the Sun, a division of Hyperion. Cover illustration from *Junebug and the Reverend* by Alice Mead. Copyright © 1998. Reprinted by permission of Farrar, Straus & Giroux.

Page 186: Cover illustration from *Kwanzaa: A Family Affair* by Mildred Pitts Walter. Copyright © 1995. Reprinted by permission of Lothrop, Lee & Shepard, William Morrow & Company, Inc. Cover illustration from *Kwanzaa!: Africa Lives in a New World Festival* by Sule Greg C. Wilson. Copyright © 1999. Reprinted by permission of Rosen Publishing Group.

Page 189: Cover illustration by James E. Ransome from *Let My People Go: Bible Stories Told by a Freeman of Color* by Patricia and Fredrick McKissack. Copyright © 1997. Courtesy of Atheneum Books for Young Readers, an imprint of Simon & Schuster Children's Publishing. Cover illustration from *Letters from a Slave Girl: The Story of Harriet Jacobs* by Mary E. Lyons. Copyright © 1992. Courtesy of Atheneum Books for Young Readers, an imprint of Simon & Schuster Children's Publishing.

Page 191: Cover illustration from *Madam C. J. Walker* (Black Americans of Achievement series) by A'Lelia Perry Bundles. Copyright © 1991. Courtesy Chelsea House Publishers.

Cover illustrations from *Mary McLeod Bethune* (Black Americans of Achievement series) by Malu Halasa. Copyright © 1989. Courtesy of Chelsea House Publishers. Cover illustration from *Alice Walker* (Black Americans of Achievement series) by Tony Gentry. Copyright © 1992. Courtesy of Chelsea House Publishers. Cover illustration from *Oprah Winfrey* (Black Americans of Achievement series) by Lois Nicholson. Copyright © 1994. Courtesy Chelsea House Publishers.

Page 193: Cover illustration from *The New York Public Library Amazing African American History: A Book of Answers for Kids* by Diane Patrick. Copyright © 1998. Reprinted by permission of John Wiley & Sons, Inc. Jacket design from *Nobody's Family Is Going to Change* by Louise Fitzhugh. Copyright © 1974. Reprinted by permission of Farrar, Straus and Giroux, LLC.

Page 195: From *The Other Side: Shorter Poems* (jacket cover) by Angela Johnson. Jacket photographs: Background photograph copyright © 1998 by Michele Jan Baylis. Family photographs from Angela Johnson. Reprinted by permission of the publisher, Orchard Books, New York.

Page 198: Cover illustration by E. B. Lewis from *Running Girl: The Diary of Ebonee Rose* by Sharon Bell Mathis. Jacket illustration copyright © 1997 by Sharon Bell Mathis. Reproduced by permission of Harcourt, Inc. Book cover from *A School for Pompey Walker* by Michael J. Rosen, jacket illustration copyright © 1995 by Aminah Brenda Lynn Robinson, reproduced by permission of Harcourt Brace, Inc.

Page 199: Cover illustration from *Sink or Swim: African-American Lifesavers of the Outer Banks*. Jacket illustration copyright © 1999. Reprinted by permission of Coastal Carolina Press.

Page 202: Cover illustration by Teresa Flavin from *Suitcase* by Mildred Pitts Walter. Copyright © 1999. Reprinted by permission of Lothrop, Lee & Shepard, William Morrow & Company, Inc.

Page 203: Cover illustration from *Talking with Tebé* edited by Mary E. Lyons. Copyright © 1998. Reprinted by permission of Houghton Mifflin Company. Cover photograph from *Teresa Weatherspoon's Basketball for Girls* by Teresa Weatherspoon with Tara Sullivan and Kelly Whiteside. Copyright © 1998. Reprinted by permission of John Wiley & Sons, Inc.

Page 204: Cover illustration from *Thurgood Marshall* (Black Americans of Achievement series) by Lisa Aldred. Copyright © 1990 by Chelsea House Publishers. Reprinted with permission. Cover illustration from *Alex Haley* (Black Americans of Achievement series) by David Shirley. Copyright © 1993. Courtesy of Chelsea House Publishers. Cover illustration from *Denzel Washington* (Black Americans of Achievement series) by Anne Hill. Copyright © 1990. Courtesy of Chelsea House Publishers. Cover illustration from *Josh Gibson* (Black Americans of Achievement series) by John B. Holway. Copyright © 1995. Courtesy of Chelsea House Publishers. Cover illustration from *Romare Bearden* (Black Americans of Achievement series) by Kevin Brown. Copyright © 1995. Courtesy of Chelsea House Publishers.

Page 206: Cover illustration from *Welcome to Addy's World, 1864* by Susan Sinnott/Pleasant Company. Jacket illustration copyright © 1999 by Pleasant Company. All rights reserved. Used by permission.

Page 207: Cover illustration from *Ziggy and the Black Dinosaurs: Lost in the Tunnel of Time* by Sharon Draper. Copyright © 1996. Reprinted by permission of Just Us Books. Cover illustration from *Ziggy and the Black Dinosaurs: Shadow of Caesar's Creek* by Sharon Draper. Copyright © 1997. Reprinted by permission of Just Us Books.

Page 209 Cover illustration from *The Beauty of Creation* by E. Roberson, L. Griffin, M. Hendricks, and Z. Muhammed. Copyright © 1998 by Nankira Books, an imprint of Kujichagulia Press, Inc.

Page 201: Cover illustration from *The Black Parenting Book: Caring for Our Children in the First Five Years* by Anne C. Beal, M.D., M.P.H., Linda Villarosa, and Allison Abner. Copyright © 1999. Reprinted by permission of Broadway Books.

Page 211: Cover illustration from *The Ties That Bind* by Joyce A. Ladner, Ph.D. Copyright © 1998. Reprinted by permission of John Wiley & Sons, Inc.

Photo credits:

Page 32, Andrea Curtis; page 108, Marcia C. Bell; page 165, Zack Hamlett III; page 171, Lynard M. Jones.

ABOUT THE AUTHORS

Donna Rand

Ms. Rand joined Black Books Galore! in 1992 as the next step in her search for great books to read to her baby daughter and ten-year-old son. An executive who quit her job to raise her children, she brought to her new mission the formidable professional skills she honed as MCI Telecommunications' former director of service marketing and as a longtime marketing manager at Xerox Corporation.

Ms. Rand lives in Stamford, Connecticut, with her husband and two school-age children.

Toni Trent Parker

Ms. Parker graduated of Oberlin College and did graduate work in Black Studies at the University of California, Berkeley. Ms. Parker's professional credentials include service as a program officer for the Phelps-Stokes Fund.

A founding member of the Black Family Cultural Exchange, Ms. Parker lives in Stamford, Connecticut, with her husband and three daughters. She is active in a variety of civic organizations.